MEETING JESUS TODAY

Smyth & Helwys Publishing, Inc.
6316 Peake Road
Macon, Georgia 31210-3960
1-800-747-3016
©2013 by Jeanie Miley
All rights reserved.
Printed in the United States of America.

The paper used in this publication meets the minimum requirements of
American National Standard for Information Sciences—
Permanence of Paper for Printed Library Materials.
ANSI Z39.48–1984. (alk. paper)

Library of Congress Cataloging-in-Publication Data

Miley, Jeanie.
Meeting Jesus today : for the cautious, the curious, and the committed / by Jeanie Miley.
pages cm
Includes bibliographical references and index.
ISBN 978-1-57312-677-9 (pbk. : alk. paper)
1. Jesus Christ--Person and offices. I. Title.
BT203.M53 2013
232--dc23

2013016350

Cover image
One of the earliest known icons, this type, known as Christ the Pantocrator reveals the gaze of a strong
Jesus who meets the human gaze in a straight-forward, calm, and open way. One eye seems to hold judgment
while the other holds mercy. One hand holds the Bible, and the other is raised in blessing. (Photo courtesy
of Ross Heinsohn.)

Author's note
Unless otherwise noted, Scripture citations are taken from the New International Version (NIV).

Meeting Jesus *Today*

For the Cautious, the Curious, and the Committed

Jeanie Miley

Also by Jeanie Miley

Dedicated to
to all who question
to all who ask, seek, and knock
to all who wonder
to those who understand that all who wander are not lost
to all who ask, "Who is this Jesus person?"
to all who struggle to believe
to the cautious, the curious, and the committed

I am all of that.
I am a sojourner.
I am a fellow pilgrim on the seeking path.

Acknowledgments

I am forever indebted to my parents for introducing me to the life of Jesus and showing me what it meant to be a follower of Jesus.

I am so grateful to the many people in the classes I have taught through the years. The willingness of others to engage in dialogue about the Jesus story has expanded my consciousness and deepened my faith.

I am especially grateful to the brave people of River Oaks Baptist Church in Houston, Texas, who were willing to participate with me in the first year-long Bible study titled "Meeting Jesus Today: For the Cautious, the Curious, and the Committed." It was that study that inspired this book.

For those who have introduced me to a broader world-view about the life of Jesus, for those who have lived out the principles of Jesus in everyday life, and for those whose spirit matches what I believe is "the Jesus spirit," I am so grateful.

For Keith Hosey, who introduced me to the idea of imagining Jesus with me in everyday life, I am forever indebted.

Even, too, I am grateful for the people who have irritated me about Jesus, for I have learned from them, as well. Sometimes, I have observed, I know more about what I do believe when I see what I don't believe.

I am grateful for the composers, artists, sculptors, and writers who have expanded my understanding of the life of Jesus through their various works of art.

To my editor, Leslie Andres, and to my publisher and the staff at Smyth & Helwys, I say "thank you" for letting me take creative risks in both this book and *ChristHeart*, so that I could understand more fully who Jesus was and who the Living Christ is now.

To my husband, Martus Miley, I am most grateful, for I have learned from his teaching and preaching the importance of good theology and sound biblical scholarship. It was his syllabus and teaching notes from his years of teaching at the university level that gave me the foundation of a lifetime of study of the life of Jesus.

Contents

Who Is This Jesus Person?

A friend tells about attending the formal and lengthy Christmas Eve service at St. Martin's Episcopal Church in Houston, Texas, with her parents, husband, and two young sons. My friend's father was a devout and devoted churchman, and he assumed that his daughter was raising his grandchildren within the warmth and nurture of the church. Attending this Christmas Eve service together—the three generations lined up on the same pew—was a big deal for the grandfather.

Midway through the service, the younger son couldn't contain himself any longer. "Who is this *Jesus person* they keep talking about?" he said loudly and impatiently.

Indeed, who is this Jesus person?

The child's innocent and weary outburst is funny, but isn't it also a "little child shall lead them" moment, a moment when the unbridled honesty of a child cuts through any pretense we adults try to hide?

Pondering that funny moment, a moment decorated with candles and permeated with incense, I take that question and ask it over and over.

"Who is this Jesus person they keep talking about?"

Caution, Curiosity, and Commitment

From the time I was a child, I heard the stories of my father's dramatic conversion experience that detailed how he resisted anything that had to do with church or church people, religion or "being saved," until one night at a revival service in Tucumcari, New Mexico, something happened to him that was so big and transformative that he was brought to his knees and his life was changed. As a child, I heard the stories and sang the songs about how "Jesus saves," and what I learned in my home and in my church was that "accepting Jesus as your personal Savior" and "inviting Jesus into your heart" would blot away your sins, keep you out of hell, and get you into heaven for eternity.

How sad it would have been if my natural curiosity and a degree of rebellion hadn't pushed me to discover for myself who this Jesus person really is.

I'll admit that I had to overcome some of my cherished prejudices and biases to get past childish images and ideas of what it meant to be a Christian, but the truth is that accepting Jesus as my Savior was just a beginning. Learning how to follow him and coming to my own adult faith has required caution, curiosity, and commitment.

Are you cautious about Jesus?

For many years, if someone had asked me if I were cautious about Jesus, I would have said, "Well, yes, aren't you?" Then, feeling guilty, I probably would have said, "It's . . . complicated," and let my voice trail into silence. After all, Jesus is the one who might lead you to Africa to be a missionary, or he might want you to be serious and pious and miss out on the fun of life.

Jesus does make me nervous, and sometimes really nervous, but so do the people who claim to be his followers. The more easily or casually someone talks about Jesus, the more nervous I get.

"I like your Christ," said Mahatma Gandhi. "I do not like your Christians. Your Christians are so unlike your Christ."

I like Gandhi, but I don't like his quote. It makes me tremble. In fact, his opinion coupled with my own experience with Christ and Christians make me nervous to write a book about Jesus. My nervousness, however, hasn't seemed to stop me from wanting to know him.

I'll admit it. I am cautious, especially when it comes to Jesus. I have had a long relationship with Jesus, although it might be more accurate to say that my relationship with Jesus has evolved over time. I have wondered and worried if that relationship has been with Jesus himself, with my ideas about Jesus, or with others' ideas about Jesus that I either accepted as truth or rebelled against.

Have I thought that I had a relationship with Jesus, when in reality my primary connection was with my church? Did I ever think that observing and keeping the rites, rules, and rituals, having right doctrine, or going through the motions of doing the right thing (as defined by certain authority figures) was the same as having a personal, vital, dynamic love relationship with the Living Christ?

Have I thought that I had a relationship with Jesus, when in reality my primary connection was with my church?

"You overthink things," I've been told, but I'm not sure that I do when it comes to something as important as *a relationship with the Living Christ.* Besides, there's a lot of weirdness about Jesus in the culture, don't you think? Is the weirdness about Jesus himself, or is it about how Jesus is interpreted and represented?

The voice on the phone was friendly, so I had no reason to anticipate the curve in the road of the conversation.

"We're looking forward to your coming to speak to our spring luncheon, Jeanie," the woman said, and I responded to her southern charm in kind. She told me about the decorations for the luncheon, the format, and how many guests had already paid for their place at the tables in a large church in my city.

"There's just one thing," the woman added. "We don't want you to talk about Jesus."

I hadn't seen it coming. My topic was appropriate for a spring luncheon of women in that church—light enough to be in the swing of spring decorations but substantive enough to give the women something to think about post-Easter.

"We just want to make sure," the woman continued. "You know, we'll have some visitors there. We didn't know if you might try to, well, you know—evangelize us."

As a speaker and retreat leader, I run into this kind of moment now and then, and I can understand how people in that particular church, in that particular denomination, might be nervous about whether I might try to push Jesus on them.

I am embarrassed, frankly, by some of the "Jesus talk" in the church and in the culture, and the truth is that I have never been comfortable with that approach. Witnessing, evangelizing, and sharing the gospel have always made me uncomfortable, especially when

• it appears that I think I'm right and everyone else is wrong;
• it appears that I think I have the answers and others don't;
• it appears that I am going to try to get someone to follow a formulaic process in order to be "saved";
• the sacred is used to manipulate, coerce, shame, or guilt people into making a decision in order to help an evangelist increase his or her number of converts.

It's no small thing to try to be a Christ follower. It's costly and hard, and even he said that you don't want to "put your hand to the plough and look back" (Luke 9:62).

But two things made me especially sad about that conversation with the luncheon hostess. I was sad that she was nervous enough about me that she felt she had to call to ensure I wouldn't do to her group what she didn't want done, and I was sad that we've come to the point in our culture where faithful followers of Christ are embarrassed by the trivializing of the holy.

I'm sad, as well, that "being a Christian" has become so secularized and politicized that many believers are calling themselves something other than "Christian." In a time when the term "Christian" is defined and described by politicians, radio hosts, and wannabe celebrities, I shudder at how everything I cherish and treasure is tainted with the shabbiness of public discourse.

So if you are cautious about a "Jesus" book, I understand. It's appropriate to be cautious, I think, about the mysterious and holy, for wherever there is the possibility of great mystery, there is also the possibility of perversion, quackery, and even sacrilege.

It's also smart, I think, to be cautious about Jesus himself. It's no small thing to try to be a Christ follower. It's costly and hard, and even he said that you don't want to "put your hand to the plough and look back" (Luke 9:62). In other words, Jesus seemed to be saying, "You need to be careful following me."

Indeed, following Jesus is dangerous. History is cluttered with people, from the time of Jesus' life on earth until now, who have lost their lives because they dared to follow the man from Nazareth. You can't follow him sincerely and consistently and not be changed because Jesus is all about healing, transforming, liberating, and empowering people who follow him. He's all about redemption and rebirth and reformation, and the truth is that it's no small thing to be born again.

I tremble at flippant responses to the Living Christ. I resist being casual about taking on the Jesus Way, and though I don't need to defend Jesus, I am careful with him. I handle with tender, loving, cautious care the fragile love life between the Living Christ and any other human being. Faith is holy ground, and the only appropriate response to it is reverence and awe.

I have finally come to believe that it may be good if the church could bless people's caution. Perhaps it is appropriate to say that, in some places, we need to exert a healthy dose of caution that is closely akin to discernment. When asked today if you are a Christian, it is appropriate to say, "By whose definition?"

The more I think about it, the more I respect the caution of my luncheon hostess.

Are you curious about Jesus?

It's a good question, isn't it? It's a question I ask myself when I'm standing in front of people, teaching or speaking about that Jesus person. It's a question I ask myself in the middle of the night when I'm wrestling with one of life's hard moments and wondering how and if that Jesus person makes a difference.

My curiosity about Jesus was born and nurtured in my family of origin, though sometimes my curiosity had a bit of a rebellious streak to it. There were times I witnessed what felt to me like excesses of emotion or distortions of facts, but there were other times when I was drawn to faith by people who seemed to have an unusual peace and a radical joy about them. Early, I began to observe and wonder about this Jesus person.

What is it about that Jesus person that makes people willing to "accept him into their hearts" and go to the far corners of the earth to tell other people about him?

What is it about Jesus that has inspired some of the greatest music, art, architecture and sculpture in human history? Why do hundreds of people gather year after year to listen to Handel's *Messiah*?

What was it that was so compelling about Jesus that my dad, who had resisted Christianity and church involvement with a fierce stubbornness, changed so dramatically within a year of his conversion? He left his growing career, took his wife and young daughters to another state, and went to an unbelievable extreme to put himself through college and seminary. He then gave himself to the active pastorate for over forty years.

What was it that made him fall so in love with Jesus that he said at the end of his life, "There were many things I would have enjoyed doing, but if I had it to do over again, I would do what I've done—preach the gospel of Jesus."

I remember well the night when I accepted Christ into my heart, and I remember the day when my father baptized me.

"I baptize you my daughter," he said as he lowered me into the baptismal waters at First Baptist Church, Lamesa, Texas, "and raise you my sister in Christ."

At age nine, I wasn't sure what that meant, but I do know this: at that time, I gave as much as I knew of myself to as much as I knew of Jesus, a Jesus I knew through the Bible stories I heard in Sunday school and my father's preaching.

Thanks be to God I didn't stay stuck in that nine-year-old understanding of who this Jesus person is.

My serious quest into the life of Jesus, which led me to my life-long fascination about the life and teachings of Jesus and an adult relationship with the Living Christ, began one Sunday morning when I was in front of a room full of single adults, pretending I knew what I was talking about as I taught a Sunday school lesson.

I was brought up to work in the church. Everybody in my family preached or taught Sunday school, so it was as natural to me to take on the role of teacher in an adult class as it was for me to prepare Thanksgiving dinner by my mother's recipes.

On that Sunday morning, I noticed a huge gap among the students in their knowledge of who Jesus was and what Jesus taught. Suddenly, I heard myself saying, "What if we take the next year and study the life of Jesus chronologically?"

I heard a resounding agreement to my suggestion. And then I got scared, for I was face to face with enormous gaps in my knowledge of Jesus.

I was a curriculum writer for Bible studies in my denomination at the time, but it hit me that I had taken on a big challenge that would test my nerve and my courage. Thankfully, my husband supplied me with his course syllabus and outline from the college course he had taught, "The Life and Teachings of Jesus Christ," and I began to gather commentaries and other resources, laying out a schedule that started with the birth of Jesus, a story I knew fairly well, and ended with his ascension.

I was afraid each week, thinking about the task ahead of me. "Who do you think you are that you can do this?" I asked myself. It's a question I've asked myself a lot through the years.

Week after week, motivated by the rapidly approaching Sunday morning and the commitment I had made to class, I pushed through my insecurities, gathered my resources around me, and began pulling together the next Sunday's lesson. I noticed an interesting phenomenon.

Sitting at my desk, the more I worked, the more empowered I felt. The more I poured over the commentaries and the Scriptures, the more liberated I felt; I was liberated from my fears and insecurities and able to present each week's lesson in a way that connected its truth to the lives of the students in my class, and, interestingly, to my own life.

In that year of asking, seeking, and knocking on the doors of the Jesus story, I began my own adult relationship with the Living Christ. Week by week, I left my dependence on the faith of my father and my mother and moved into the deeper waters of my own faith. I always got up from my desk with something that felt like new life; every Sunday, the exchange between the students and my life expanded my mind and heart.

I wondered how this process of discovery was transforming the way I felt about church and the Bible, religion and spirituality, and even life itself?

Are you committed to Jesus?

Recently, direction in my relationship with the Living Christ came to me through the back door, catching me off guard, irritating me a bit, and then, finally, inspiring me to write this book. It is to these unlikely, surprising catalysts that I also say, "thank you."

Three things happened in the span of a few weeks that shocked me into a new level of commitment to what I have come to call "this Jesus Way," echoing a phrase used by Eugene Peterson.

One Sunday I ate lunch with acquaintances and my husband at a restaurant near River Oaks Baptist Church, our church in Houston. The conversation was pleasant, if slightly superficial, but suddenly a question lobbed in my direction turned the mood a few degrees south.

"Why don't you make _____ the central focus of your teaching and writing?" the person demanded.

Fill in the blank with any of the current social issues or hot topics talked about in public discourse as if it were the most important social issue of all time and as if it were the first time anyone had ever considered that particular issue.

You know the issues: the presidency, abortion, homosexuality, prayer in public schools, creationism and other topics taught in science classes, etc.

"You have a blog and you have your books. You speak to people all the time, so you have this influence. *Why don't you make _____ your central message?*"

Besides the fact that I was offended by the tone of the questioner, I was shocked at the narrow focus of his interest. I was also stunned that he would assume I agreed with his position without ever asking me what I thought or believed. More than anything, though, the question kicked up something deep within my heart and soul, and I said quietly and firmly, "That isn't the central focus of what I teach. Jesus is."

I told about how agitated and irritated my dad would become when, in his day, there were those who wanted to do the same thing. More than once I heard my dad say, sometimes in despair and sometimes in utter frustration, "When people in the church take Christ out of the center of their theology, they will always wrangle (his word) over peripheral issues."

When you start wrangling over those peripheral issues, you forget about the central mission of the church, the Body of Christ on earth. When you lose the sense of that central figure of our faith, you lose the Spirit of what it means to be the church. When you lose the Spirit at the center of the church, it's easy to drift into thinking you are yet another nonprofit organization or even a political action force.

When you take Christ out of the center of your theology and your thinking and your focus, you may put good things in his place, such as missions and ministries, but without Christ as the motivating force, the animating energy, the Dunamis (the Greek word for "power"), those missions and ministries eventually run out of gas.

When you take Christ out of the center of the church, people forget what it means to be a Christ follower. And when people forget what it means to be a Christ follower, they lose interest in the church or pervert it for their own social, political, or power needs.

The second incident happened on a flight from the East Coast to Houston.

"What do you do?" the man in the next seat asked as we waited for takeoff.

I explained about the retreat I had just led, and, interrupting me, he said, "Oh, You're a Christian. I'm a Christian. I follow the Ten Commandments."

I sucked in my breath, bowed my head, and closed my eyes in lament for what we have lost. Did the man really think that following the Ten Commandments was the mark of a Christian? Did he not realize the difference in the Old Testament and the New, law and grace?

Did he also think that voting for Candidate A (or B or C) revealed his credentials as a card-carrying Christian? Was he one of those people who believed that being a Christian meant you could cherry-pick the sins listed in the Bible that would send you to hell but still do the other ones that didn't seem as bad?

As we made our way across the country, I began to question how we had lost a sense of what it means to be a Christian, "follow Christ," and how some of us in my part of Christ's church have become reticent to talk about Jesus.

Frankly, I had to admit to myself that I never want to be one of "them"—the Jesus freaks, the women who wear T-shirts that declare that they are "Jesus chicks," the people who talk "Jesus talk," flippantly throwing his name around or shouting out "Praise Jesus" in public places as easily as some folks declare, "Well, I'll be darned!"

I knew what I didn't want to be, what offended me, and what repelled me, but how could I witness to my deep faith in the Living Christ and my ongoing desire to be a Christ follower in ways that had integrity for me and did not offend others?

The Origin of Meeting Jesus Today

The third experience caught me off guard, too.

On a warm, sunny Thursday afternoon, I sat in a spiritual direction session with Nancy, a directee* who grew up in a church with beautiful liturgy. Going into detail about a funeral she had attended at a large Baptist church in Houston, she described the evangelistic sermon she heard at the funeral.

The sermon included insights about the afterlife and what we Baptists talk about as issues of "soul security" for those who have accepted Jesus as their personal Savior. Suddenly, Nancy paused in her narrative and said, "Aren't you a Baptist? Why haven't you ever told me this? I want what he was talking about!"

Stunned, I managed to tell her why I hadn't given her what is often called "the plan of salvation" in our session of spiritual direction. As I heard myself talking, I could sense the questions she would later articulate.

"You come from a liturgical tradition," I said, "and I respect that."

She sat there silently, her eyes almost broadcasting her thoughts: "Yeah? And so why haven't you told me what I heard at that funeral?"

"Spiritual direction is not about simply following a formula or responding appropriately to a question," I continued, and her eyes bored into mine.

My answer about giving her the plan of salvation was complicated, just as Jesus is complicated.

"Frankly," I finally told her, "I don't fit in the mold of the evangelists who think that salvation is just about saying yes to Jesus and then going about your way." I could see in her eyes that these words connected with her. "I'm careful about those things because I don't want to be identified with the street-corner or television evangelists.

*A spiritual director is a person who listens attentively to a person's story and attempts to discern with the person (called a directee) what the Spirit of God is attempting to do in that person's life and the direction God is leading that person. Another definition for a spiritual director is that that person loves the directee in God's stead and loves that person toward God. The author has written more about this process in her books Joint Venture: Practical Spirituality for Everyday Pilgrims and Dance Lessons: Moving to the Beat of God's Heart.

I'm interested in your whole life being transformed because of a vital, personal, love relationship with the Living Christ."

Then I attempted to explain that I was "coming alongside her" in spiritual direction, becoming a companion in her spiritual quest as we attempted to discern together where the Spirit of Christ might be working in her life. I explained that my approach was to respect her tradition and not assume that she had to follow my path, my tradition, or anyone's formula in order to follow Jesus and be "saved."

Salvation is more than staying out of hell and getting into heaven. The word "salvation" comes from the same word as wholeness or health, and the process of being saved is just that—a *process*. When people invite you to say yes to Jesus, you need to know what that means. "Following Jesus," a term evangelicals throw around with alarming ease, is a rigorous challenge, a worthy calling, and an adventure that calls for courage and a willingness to be transformed.

The Apostle Paul understood that the work of salvation is a joint venture in which the Holy Spirit/the Living Christ works in mysterious ways in the inner life, transforming a person from within. "Work out your own salvation," he counsels in Philippians 2:12, and then he adds "with fear and trembling," indicating his firsthand knowledge of the challenges of following Jesus, knowing Jesus, and *being saved*!

I related the phone conversation with the person who was worried about my coming on too strong about Jesus at the women's luncheon as part of my defense. The truth, though, is that nothing I said changed Nancy's point of view. Nothing I said satisfied her deep hunger for God. I knew that, and I was determined to find an answer to her question.

Of course I wanted her to "know Jesus" and "be saved," but the definitions of those terms is much deeper than my childhood understanding of them, and I didn't want her to think that simply following four "laws," however spiritual they might be, was her guarantee of "salvation."

I knew I was nailed, however. In my own eyes and opinion, I had been exposed as someone who is part of a group that teaches and proclaims "the path to salvation" with great confidence, but who had not developed an adequate and authentic way to communicate that to people.

As I went to bed that night, I still had Nancy's questions on my mind. In the middle of the night, the outline for a course I wanted to teach in my church woke me up, startling me out of a deep sleep and pushing me to my study. Quickly, before the inspiration left me, I found a legal pad and began writing down what would become the outline of this course, which I called "Meeting Jesus Today," that I taught at my church recently. That course ultimately became this book.

From day when I declared that I would teach the life and teachings of Jesus to that first adult Bible study class until now, I have been captivated both intellectually and emotionally by the life and teachings of Jesus, and through these years I have both written and taught about his life and teachings from many different perspectives.

The human Jesus transformed, liberated, and empowered person after person, changing their lives forever. And that is still happening to me as I write and teach about the Living Christ and attempt to follow him.

It's so simple, this complicated Way of following Jesus.

It's simple, but it's not easy.

It's not easy, but it's a hard path worth following and a challenge worth pursuing, especially if you let go of how you think the Way is going to be or how you want it to be and let the Spirit of the Living Christ lead you, one step at a time, one day at a time. That's not easy, either.

It's doable, following Jesus, but only if you do it and not just talk about it.

"I have come," Jesus stated in John 10:10, "that you might have life in all its abundance." I have experienced that abundance of grace and mercy, joy and peace, and the fullness of life that comes from falling in love with the life and teachings of Jesus.

With whatever capacities I have, I understand better what Paul meant when he wrote, "Christ in you, the hope of glory" (Col 1:27).

In moments of great sorrow, I have come to understand the "peace that passes all understanding" (Phil 4:7) that comes to someone in a vital, personal, dynamic love relationship with the Living Christ.

I have also come face to face with the huge challenge of *following Jesus.* Indeed, I understand that the Living Christ comes again and again to us, through the Mystery of the Holy Spirit. I affirm that whether you are curious or cautious or committed, the Living Christ can meet you right where you are.

Before you Begin

This book is intended to be used as a workbook. It is designed to move you from the Scriptures and the content here to recording your journey with the Living Christ, either in the spaces after the questions, in the margins, or in a separate notebook.

You can simply read the book, of course, but if you write your responses to the questions, you may find that the process weaves the life and teachings of Jesus more deeply into your mind and heart. Using one of my favorite terms, this book employs "a dance"—a dynamic and moving process between you and the material and between you and the Living God, whose name is Love.

I like to call this process of interacting with the biblical record and your personal thoughts, experiences, feelings, and yearnings *soulwork*, and I believe that this process is one of the ways in which the Living Christ/the Holy Spirit works to do what Jesus did: healing, transforming, liberating, and empowering you as you give yourself to the process.

The book is composed of seven sections. In each section, I offer commentary from my personal research and from my life experiences. Then I suggest questions for reflection on the Scriptures under the headings *Exploring the Scriptures* and *What About You?* You will also find *For Your Eyes Only* questions that are intended to move the ideas in each section to a deeper level where you live in Christ and he lives in you.

Feel free to add another dimension to this workbook by using it in a Bible study or discussion group. Through speaking your own thoughts and hearing the thoughts of others, you may experience greater clarity about who this Jesus person really is. At times, you may hear something from another perspective that rattles your brain. That can be disturbing or even upsetting, but even that is *soulwork*.

Often, we learn by hearing what we've never heard or by hearing the opposite of what we've always believed. By hearing and wrestling with what we don't believe, we can either open our minds and hearts to new understanding, or we can discover that we know what we do believe more fully.

As you study the life of Jesus, read the various Scriptures in different translations. You might want to purchase what is called a Harmony of the Gospels, which positions the sections, stories, and teachings of the four Gospels in columns so that you can see how each Gospel writer rendered the events in Jesus' life. You can also see which parts were included in which of the four Gospels, and which ones were not included.

If you are serious about going deeper into the biblical material, choose a good commentary to give you insight and information into the original language of the New Testament, the historical setting of the events, the original meaning of the text, and an interpretation of the text.

The application of the truths in the Gospels and in the Jesus story will be left up to you!

As you begin this exploration of the life and teachings of Jesus, take time to respond to the following "Twenty Questions for Personal Reflection." These will help you assess your experience of knowing Jesus and your attitudes about him. You might want to go through the questions quickly at first, jotting down your first responses in the space provided or in a separate notebook.

After each section of this book, return to these questions and reflect on them, asking yourself if your perceptions or beliefs about who Jesus is have changed.

Write down any shifts in your understanding.

In your journal, keep a section of your own written questions: questions you might have about Jesus, questions this study provokes, or questions you want to ask in prayer. It might even be interesting to keep an account of the questions that pop into your mind unbidden, questions that perhaps Jesus would ask you.

Twenty Questions for Personal Reflection

1. What is your first memory of Jesus?

2. Who first taught you about Jesus?

3. What were you taught about "having a personal relationship with Jesus"?

4. What was the purpose, according to your childhood understanding, of having a personal relationship with Jesus?

5. When you were a child, what did "being saved" mean to you?

6. Were you ever afraid when you heard stories about heaven and hell?

7. When you became an adolescent, what was your connection with Jesus?

8. Were you ever embarrassed by "Jesus freaks"?

9. When was the first time you heard Jesus' name used as a curse word?

10. Did you like going to church when you were an adolescent? Why or why not?

11. Were you ever shamed or scared into "being a good Christian"?

12. According to your adolescent understanding, what did it mean to "be a good Christian"?

13. What is the difference between being a church member and being a disciple of Christ?

14. Can you be a church member without being a follower of Christ?

15. If you could meet Jesus face to face today, what do you think you would do or say? How would you feel?

16. What is your current understanding of what it means to be a "Christian"?

17. Does your current relationship with Christ give you joy and peace?

18. Is your relationship with the Living Christ more like a friendship, or is it more like being a slave? What would you like it to be?

19. If you could change one thing about your relationship with the Living Christ, what would it be?

20. Do you believe that it is possible to have a vital, dynamic, personal love relationship with the Living Christ?

Part One
Meeting Jesus Today

Introduction

We like Baby Jesus, don't we?

There's something endearing about the infant born in a manger and wrapped in swaddling clothes on a dark, wintry night in a country far, far away. As a culture, we like the Christmas story and the celebrations, and then, when the holiday is over, it's convenient to pack up the Nativity sets and put them out of sight until the next year.

Baby Jesus is manageable, isn't he? And sweet.

We like the Easter Jesus, too, and especially the Risen Christ. The drama captivates us, reassuring us that Jesus came to save us from our sins. Remembering that, we can feel confident that if we should die tonight, we would join the resurrected Jesus in heaven.

The Christmas Jesus and the Easter Jesus sell, and businesses make a lot of money tapping into what was originally intended to be a sacred and religious commemoration of two important events in the Christian year.

There is so much more to know about Jesus, however, and the parts between his birth and his death, burial, and resurrection give the meaning to both the beginning and the end of his life. It is the way Jesus interacted with people in those brief years of teaching and ministry, the things he said and taught, and the way he healed, transformed, liberated, and empowered others that are so powerful.

The Rabbi Jesus invited people first into a relationship with him, making himself open, transparent, and vulnerable to his friends and followers. Apparently, he wanted to be known, and indeed, he himself defined eternal life as *knowing him* (John 17:3). That knowledge is not about knowing mere facts about him; it's the knowledge and intimacy that come with being with him, close-up and personal, and learning what he thought about things, how he felt about

Tell me, who do you say that I am? (Matthew 16:15; Mark 8:29; Luke 9:20)

The Word became flesh and blood and moved into the neighborhood. (John 1:14, The Message)

17

people, how he responded to both adulations and censure, to both celebrations and the crucifixion.

Between the Christmas Jesus and the Easter Jesus is a rich, multi-layered story of encounters the human Jesus had with ordinary people, encounters that were apparently so radically life-changing that people quickly brought others to him. In the accounts of Jesus' mission and ministry in the Scriptures, we can learn what he taught and what he asked of those who followed him, and through integrating what we read into our lives, we can learn how to follow him.

We all bring our own perspective to an exploration of the life of Jesus. This perspective is formed from personal experience, what we have learned from others, cultural and religious influences, and our prejudices, blind spots, biases, hopes, and yearnings.

I have a well-worn, heavily marked copy of Marcus Borg's *Meeting Jesus Again for the First Time*. He writes about the image of Jesus that each of us carries. We all have a tendency to make Jesus over in our own image, perhaps preferring a childish image of him, the images we learned from a song, or our church's depiction of who he was. It's easy to miss the full New Testament picture of who he was and can be now.

Each era, too, emphasizes one aspect of Jesus' life over another, and each expression of Christ's church thinks its particular emphasis of ministry is a reflection of who Jesus really is. But none of us ever get the whole picture of Jesus, and none of us can ever trap him in our doctrinal boxes, though we may think we can. Jesus is so big that the more you know about him, the more you realize you don't know, and he is so mysterious that the more you know him—really know him—the more there is to know.

In a recent e-mail, my friend John Killinger asked, "Have you read *The Changing Faces of Jesus* by Geza Vermes?"[2]

I had not read the book, but I had spotted it when I was browsing in the bookstore at Grace Cathedral in California. Not wanting to load up my book bag any more than it already was for the flight back home to Houston, I'd quickly written down the title so that I could order it when I returned home.

John Killinger's e-mail prompted my memory, and because I respect him, his scholarship, and his writing so deeply, I quickly ordered the book. When it arrived and I began to read it, I was aghast.

As much as I love the study of the life of Jesus, how had I missed this book, this scholar, this man who is described as the world's leading scholar on the life of Christ?

The night of my discovery, I read an article written by biblical scholar Alan Culpepper, Dean of the McAfee School of Theology and renowned author of *Anatomy of the Fourth Gospel.* Right there in his essay were references to the work of Geza Vermes.

I find such synchronicities to be meaningful, mysterious, and reliable in finding my way through life.

Vermes helps us understand what he calls "the evolution of the image of Jesus," just as John Killinger helps us understand how our idea of salvation has unfolded and evolved in his book *The Changing Shape of Our Salvation.*[3]

The concept of Jesus I formed as a young child was a concept big enough for my childlike faith, but there came a time when this concept needed enlarging. If I were to put my faith in the Living Christ, I would have to expand my mind and my heart, and sometimes that process can be disconcerting.

Thanks be to God, when my parents first introduced me to Jesus, they also gave me permission to keep opening my mind and heart to the ever-expanding, increasingly deeper, and incredibly richer truths and mysteries of the historical person we call Jesus and the Living Christ.

What constantly draws me to want to know more about Jesus and know him more deeply is not so much my concern about the afterlife. I'm content to leave that in the hands of the Almighty. In the words of an old hymn, what continually *thrills my soul* is the difference trying to follow Jesus' life and teachings makes in my ordinary life, day by day. Here. Now.

When my old ideas and beliefs are challenged, I may be temporarily disoriented and even disturbed, but I am not frightened. Instead, I am thrilled because there is something else to learn, something more to experience. I know that what is true will always be true, and what is not true needs to be liberated from the constraints of my small mind. I keep meeting Jesus, and every time my image of Jesus expands, it is as if, in the words of Borg, I am meeting Jesus again for the first time.

In this book, I invite you to meet Jesus again, to open your mind and heart to a new unfolding, a deeper recognition, a more expansive point of view of Jesus. Each day, meet Jesus again in what

Indeed, for many Christians, especially in mainline churches, there came a time when their childhood image of Jesus no longer made a great deal of sense.
—Marcus Borg

Who is Jesus to me?

Who was Jesus to me when I was first introduced to him?

Who am I to the Living Christ?

he said and what he did. Take what you read in the Scriptures and in this book, and weave the ideas into your day. Who knows what new insight about your life might unfold.

Because I am a contemplative, I do what the seventeenth-century French lay brother known as Brother Lawrence taught us to do and "practice the Presence of Christ," using my imagination to picture Jesus with me. If you don't do that already, I encourage you to try it.

You don't have to wait until the "sweet bye and bye" to meet Jesus.

He's here, just like he said he'd be, meeting you right where you are.

I know. It's a mystery. And Mystery is Real, and it is Reality.

Remember what Jesus said? "I am with you always, to the very end of the age" (Matt 28:20b).

When Jesus' disciples reported to him what others were saying about him, Jesus turned the question back on them and said, "Who do *you* say that I am?" Consider how you might answer that question.

Many of us know the Christmas Jesus and the Easter Jesus, but all of us have gaps in our knowledge about the founder of our faith and what he thought. Even biblical scholars who have studied the Jesus story for a lifetime tell me that there are always new depths to plumb.

Is this Jesus whose life has inspired architectural and musical masterpieces, art and literary works, ministries of mercy and compassion, and also religious wars merely a historical figure? Was Jesus actually both human and God Incarnate? Is he a theory to be debated, or is he a Living Presence?

Is Jesus Savior if he isn't Lord?

Does following him today mean the same as it did in the first century?

What is the difference between Jesus the historical figure and Jesus the Living Christ?

Why do we call the church "the Body of Christ on earth"?

Is the Jesus of history and what he taught relevant to contemporary people?

Is there more to the Jesus story than staying out of hell and getting into heaven?

These questions and others provoke us, I hope, to reflect more deeply on the life and teachings of Jesus and to integrate what he said into our minds and hearts, and especially our imagination. Can what he did then change our lives now?

I must state my personal bias from the beginning: I do believe that it is possible to have a personal, vital, dynamic love relationship with the Living Christ now. I believe that because the Mystery of it all has engaged me at a soul level, challenging my intellect, my heart, and my will.

I believe that, for people like us who do not have the privilege of knowing the human Jesus, following him means taking the teachings of Jesus seriously by attempting to integrate them into my belief system and my daily actions. His teachings are big enough to challenge us, and following them has the potential to change lives.

I believe that when I cannot follow those teachings, it is possible to pray for the Living Christ to do in me and for me and through me what I cannot do for myself.

I believe that eternal life is far more than knowing facts about him. It is about quality of life more than length of life, whether on this side of death or afterward. As Jesus himself defined it, eternal life is knowing Christ, and that "knowing" is the knowledge of intimate experience (John 17:3).

I believe that in mysterious ways, the Living Christ does what Jesus did when he encountered individuals in the first century. Jesus healed, transformed, liberated, and empowered individuals he encountered, saving them from what had them enslaved and crippled, broken and incapacitated, and I believe that is what the Living Christ can do in us, with us, for us—and often in spite of us—now.

As a freshman at Baylor University, I slipped into the elevator at Ruth Collins Hall and leaned against the wall. Riding to the sixth floor after a late date, I pondered the poster on the wall that faced me.

There Jesus was, positioned like Uncle Sam with his finger pointing directly at me.

"Who do you say that I am?" was the caption, and I was riveted to that poster and its description of the workshops, speakers, and plenary sessions of Religious Emphasis Week on campus. In that moment, the Jesus story moved out of my childhood and the faith of my parents, and over the next years, that story would weave itself into my own journey of faith.

My late-night confrontation with Jesus' provocative question to his disciples was to move me down a lifelong path of curiosity about exactly who Jesus was. During that week, I began hearing something beyond the simple childhood stories about Jesus and the stories of my father's adult conversion. The speakers on campus challenged my thinking, stretching my mind beyond my childhood understandings and inviting me to expand my image of Jesus beyond someone who lived back in history whose death on the cross was my ticket out of hell.

At that moment in the elevator, I began forming my own faith in Christ, a faith based on an understanding of salvation as the process of becoming whole and healthy.

What About You?

1. In John 1:1-18, the "Prologue" of the Gospel of John, the writer makes bold claims about who Jesus is, setting up his earthly ministry. Later, John refers to the "signs and wonders" or "miraculous sign" of Jesus' work on earth. (See John 2:11; 20:30; 21:25.) What stands out to you most in the preface? What draws you toward Jesus in this passage? What makes you want to know more about him?

2. In John 1:35-42, John the writer describes the forming of Jesus' inner group, the disciples. What do you think made the two disciples John mentions in verse 37 leave John the Baptist and follow Jesus?

3. What do you think those two disciples thought and felt when Jesus turned around and asked them, "What do you want?"

4. From this initial encounter with the people who would become Jesus' inner circle, his invitation was to "follow him," which seems to be an invitation into a relationship. What do you think that was like for these first disciples of Jesus?

For Your Eyes Only
5. What makes you want to know more about Jesus?

6. When it comes to Jesus, would you call yourself curious, cautious, or committed—or a bit of all three?

Come to me, all of you who are weary and heavy-laden, and I will give you rest. Take my yoke upon you and learn of me, for my yoke is easy and my burden is light. (Matt 11:28-30)

Rest refers to interior quiet, tranquility, peace, rootedness of being one with the Divine Presence. Rest is our reassurance at the deepest level that everything is okay. The ultimate freedom is to rest in God in suffering, as well as in joy. God was just as present to Jesus on the cross, as on the mountain of the Transfiguration.

—Thomas Keating[4]

Yokefellow Spiritual Growth Group was begun by Dr. Cecil Osborne and informed by the teachings of Dr. Elton Trueblood. Members of the group are "yoked together" with a common intention of growing in faith, authenticity, honesty, and spiritual wholeness.

Chapter 1

The Great Invitation

Elton Trueblood was a noted and beloved twentieth-century American Quaker, author, theologian, former chaplain at both Harvard and Stanford universities, and founder of the Yokefellow Spiritual Growth Groups. In his autobiography, *While It Is Day*, Dr. Trueblood viewed Jesus' invitation in Matthew's Gospel (11:28-30) as Christ's clearest call to commitment. He wrote,

> I realized that the yoke metaphor involves what we/I must require if the vitality of the Christian faith is to be recovered. Being yoked with Christ may mean a great deal more, but at least it means being a participant rather than a spectator; it also means accepting a discipline which leads paradoxically to a new kind of freedom; it leads finally to fellowship because the yoke which we know best cannot be worn alone.[5]

I am not sure how I missed Jesus' great invitation in my years of participating in Sunday school, Vacation Bible School, and Bible sword drills, but I did. Perhaps in my child's mind, I focused on issuing the invitation to Jesus to come into my heart. I also learned to invite others to church so that they, too, could invite Jesus into their hearts.

Somehow, I had a big shift in understanding. The light began to dawn on the darkness that hovered over the deep of my unformed child's mind, and I began to realize that *Jesus* issued the invitations.

In those early years, I heard the invitation Jesus spoke to his disciples: "Follow me." But that was for the disciples who actually knew Jesus. I thought that invitation was special, *for them*, and I had the impression that it was an invitation that implied responsibility, service, sacrifice, and perhaps hardship. With my child's mind, following Jesus was for disciples and, perhaps, adults who were in what we called full-time missions and ministry.

As an adolescent, I sometimes worried that I would be invited to go into special service in missions and ministry. I wanted to live a normal life, however, and for me, that meant that I wouldn't go to some faraway place and endure difficulties as a missionary. I wanted to marry and have children and do what "normal" people did. Interestingly, my sister did want to hear the call of God to be a missionary, and she did want to go to faraway Africa. When it comes to religion and maybe everything else, the same message is heard, interpreted, and lived out in many ways by different people.

I'm sure that I had heard someone read Matthew 11:28-30 before, but on the night I first heard Jesus' invitation in Matthew 11:28-30, I was only twenty-six. Looking back on that night, I wonder how I could have felt so weary and heavy-laden at such a young age, but now I know that I felt the burden of trying to follow all the rules of my religious culture, some of which were not about doctrine so much as the social customs of my group. Perhaps I was weary of being such a good girl, behaving myself so that I wouldn't upset a church member, following the spoken and unspoken rules, and doing my duty, while something in me wanted to be free.

With a few years of depth analysis behind me, I have a clearer understanding of what made me so weary, and now I know that while I had, in good faith and a child's innocence, given my heart to Jesus and been baptized at the tender age of nine, my connection with the Living Christ was more about a connection with my parents' faith, the church as an organization or institution, and "the rules."

At the beginning of any movement, there is a powerful and transformative connection between the founder or originator of that movement and the first followers. As time goes on, the connections increase as the first followers bring in the next generation and the next, and when the founder of the movement dies, the first followers try to tell the stories that gave fire and energy to the movement, hoping to keep it alive. As the movement grows, it grows further away from the original relationship between the founder and the first followers, and then it becomes organized and institutionalized.

Today, more than 2,000 years since Jesus walked and talked on this earth, inspiring and changing people by his actual presence, many people are related not to the Living Christ who is at the center of our faith but to

- one of the leaders of the movement
- the institutional church
- a ritual
- a set of doctrines, laws and rules, or cultural and social norms

Depth analysis is, by definition, "exploring the depths" of a person, paying attention to dreams, inner motivations, slips of the tongue, physical symptoms, etc. Analysis means "to stir up from below," and the intention of depth analysis it to become conscious of what is unconscious. The process works to deal with the cause of things rather than the results, with the goal being to make more conscious decisions and to avoid being governed by that which one doesn't know about oneself.

- the organization
- a committee that serves the institution
- someone's self-serving idea of what the movement is
- the meetings, holy days, or social gatherings of the organization
- the members of the organization

Soon, when your connection is only to one of those peripheral touch points, the living, dynamic connection to the founder of the faith dissipates *unless there is an intentional effort to stay connected to that center.*

If the only connection you have is with a committee, a ritual, a rule, or a routine, and you don't have a vital relationship with the Living Christ, you're going to burn out, wear out, or opt out. Keeping the institution alive just for keeping the institution alive, without a connection to the reason for its being, is like trying to get life out of an empty husk.

In contemporary society, the term "Christian" has become so politicized and secularized that it has lost its original life-changing power, and people are leaving the church to seek meaning, belonging, spiritual nourishment, and sustenance—or simple relief!—beyond the institutional church that has in many places lost the connection to its very founder.

Many who have stayed within the institutional church are either trying to hold on to the past and the ways that used to work for them or are going through the motions, numbed by the repetitions and habits of a lifetime.

Jesus burst into a religious culture that had laid law upon law on the backs of its people, and he issued a radical, astonishing invitation.

"Come to me," he said, and then he gave a promise: "I will give you rest."

The second part of the invitation indicates that the "rest" Jesus promises is somehow linked with something to do. "Take my yoke upon you and learn of me," he says, but then he gives an assurance: "My yoke is easy, and my burden is light."

In Jesus' day, oxen were beasts of burden that pulled heavy loads, and ill-fitting yokes could injure and chafe the animals' necks. Taken at face value, it's hard for us to relate to oxen and yokes, but symbolically, the truth contained within Jesus' tender and compassionate invitation can change lives.

If the only connection you have is with a committee, a ritual, a rule, or a routine, and you don't have a vital relationship with the Living Christ, you're going to burn out, wear out, or opt out. Keeping the institution alive just for keeping the institution alive, without a connection to the reason for its being, is like trying to get life out of an empty husk.

A lovely legend says that the yokes Jesus carved in his father's carpentry shop fit the oxen perfectly, never chafing their necks as they pulled their loads and did their jobs.

The people of Jesus' day had their necks crammed into a religious culture that told them that if they followed the laws and rules and rituals well enough, worked hard enough to be good and righteous, and gave enough, God would bless them.

I know what it is like to stick my neck into the yokes of other peoples' expectations of me and my own self-designed and self-imposed impossible expectations. I know what it is like to do work that doesn't fit my personality, my temperament, my interests, or my skills, and I know what it is like to have to pull a load of burdens that have been imposed on me either by my own mistakes and failures or by others' mistakes and failures. I know what it is like to live in a religious yoke that has nothing to do with my soul's well-being or my spiritual life, and I know what it is like to live with a false or limiting image of who God is or who I am.

All of that will wear you out, sucking your life force and energy right out of your body, your heart, and your soul.

So it is that the people of Jesus' day heard his great invitation, and they flocked to him one by one and then in groups and massive crowds. Some of them were curious, just as some curiosity seekers come around today. Others were cautious, wanting to make sure that what he was offering was different from what they already had. And there were those who had come to the point of great need and were ready to commit from the beginning, just like there are today.

Jesus invited people into relationship with him. He seemed to want to teach others about the abundant life by spending time with them, eating in their homes, and having deep and meaningful conversations with them. When he said to the disciples, "Follow me," he was inviting them to observe him and read his life. Essentially, he was making himself vulnerable and available to their scrutiny, inviting them to test him to see if his talk matched his walk. When he invited people into relationship with him, it wasn't to build his ego or his fortune. Instead, Jesus wanted to give others what would make their lives whole and healthy. He wanted to save them from the forces that were robbing them of joy and peace.

Jesus didn't come just to show us the way to heaven when we die! He knew that salvation was about being whole and healthy in this life and that we are saved for a life of peace and fulfillment now. In a way, Jesus' life was a lesson about how to live the way God designed us to live.

The invitations Jesus gave were not about people coming around him to serve him. Of course, Jesus wanted the disciples and his other followers to do something, but the relationship with Jesus carried the exquisite possibility of *reciprocity*. Jesus had something to give them, and he wanted them to learn how to give to others as he gave.

John 10:10 is one of my favorite verses. In the margin, it is written in the King James Version, which is the way I learned it as a child. The New Revised Standard Version has nearly the same wording. I use the New International Translation for my devotional reading, and there the promise is translated "life to the full," while the Good News translation calls it "life in all its fullness." In *The Message*, Eugene Peterson renders John 10:10 like this: "I came so they can have real and eternal life, more and better life than they ever dreamed of."

What About You?

In Matthew 11:28-30, the writer includes one of the most famous of Jesus' sayings. Read it in at least two translations, and then imagine that you hear Jesus issue that invitation to you.

1. When was the last time you felt weary or burdened? What did you do to deal with those feelings?

2. Is there something in your life that causes you to feel weary and burdened on an ongoing basis? What is the cause or source of that burden?

I have come that they might have life, and have it more abundantly. (John 10:10)

3. In what ways have you tried to soothe yourself, deal with the problem, or forget about it? How has that worked?

4. What do you think Jesus meant when he said, "Come to me"?

5. Jesus said, "I will give you rest." What do you think that "rest" is?

6. Jesus used an image that is not familiar to us when he said, "Take my yoke upon you." Interpreted symbolically, what do you think he meant?

7. Jesus also describes his "yoke" as "easy" and his "burden" as "light." What could he have meant by that? What does that mean for us today?

8. What do you think Jesus meant by the term "abundant life"? Was he talking about spiritual qualities or material blessings?

9. In today's world with its "prosperity gospel" and love for the "power of positive thinking," it is easy to get confused about the abundant life. What is the difference between Jesus' perspective and the ideas of proponents of prosperity gospel and positive thinking? Are there some similarities?

10. Is the abundant life about "having it all"? Or was Jesus talking about more than that?

11. Read Galatians 5:22-23. Is there a connection between the abundant life and the fruit of the Spirit?

12. As you read Matthew 11:28-30, what is your emotional response to Jesus' invitation?

13. What "yokes" have you put around your neck that did not fit you?

14. What happened as a result of trying to work within a context that didn't fit you?

15. What does Jesus' term "rest" mean for you?

16. What are the implications of being "yoked" with Christ?

Chapter 2

The Greatest Verse

> For God so loved the world that he gave his only Son so that everyone who believes in him may not perish but may have eternal life. (John 3:16, NRSV)

There is it, the gospel in a nutshell.

Leave it to the writer of the Gospel of John to capture Jesus' definition of the good news in one verse that little children around the world have memorized for centuries and scholars have pondered for their whole lives.

When Jeannette Clift George was asked to choose one Scripture to recite in the movie about the life of Holocaust survivor Corrie ten Boom, she chose this verse.

Take it apart, phrase by phrase, and ponder the words in your heart, turning them over and over in your mind.

Don't miss that it begins with God's love. God's very nature is love. God cannot *not* love, because that is the essence of who God is. (See 1 John 4:8b. Note that this is repeated in 1 John 4:16b. Apparently, the writer wanted us to understand this idea.)

Don't miss that the reason for God's gift of his Son is God's love for us—not our sinfulness. This is important, and it's essential to start our theology here. In fact, it is the most important message I want to convey in this book.

Here is the good news: the outpouring of God's love for us caused God to initiate this radical thing we call the *Incarnation.* When human beings couldn't comprehend who God was and what God wanted to do in us, for us, and through us, God came to us in the person of Jesus. Jesus is the best picture of God we have, and this one verse captures the reason for the Incarnation. Love is the nature of God and the motivating force behind all of God's work.

Notice the inclusiveness of the word "everyone." Notice that God's intention is not that we perish but that we have eternal life.

We humans have a tendency to want others to perish, and I get nervous when other human beings start drawing exclusive lines. I am comforted, however, by these words from 2 Peter 3:9, speaking about God's nature: "The Lord . . . is patient with you, not wanting anyone to perish, but everyone to come to repentance."

"The Lord . . . is patient with you, not wanting anyone to perish, but everyone to come to repentance." (2 Pet 3:9)

When you have pondered this, substitute your name for "the world." Say it aloud, letting the impact of God's specific love for you sink deep into your heart. Indeed, God loves the whole world. It says so in this beloved verse, but when you say your own name, the particularity of God's love becomes more real, doesn't it?

Now fill in the names of your family and friends, the names of those you are praying for.

Finally, if you're serious about following Jesus and experiencing the abundant life, fill in the name of the person you love least.

How does that feel?

So what does it mean to "believe" in Jesus? Does it mean you give mental assent to the fact of Jesus, or that you recite one of the creeds, stating your belief in a certain list of doctrines, ideas, dogmas? Does it mean you repeat some words, a special formula, that someone has decided is the key to salvation? Does it mean you know facts about Jesus and agree with what he said?

What do people mean when they say that someone is a *believer*? And is what people today say it means the same as what Jesus meant when he used the word "believe"?

Sitting in the fellowship hall of St. Paul's United Methodist Church in Houston, I was mesmerized by the words of scholar Marcus Borg as he lectured from his book, *Speaking Christian: Why Christian Words Have Lost Their Meaning and Power, and How They Can Be Restored.*[6] Borg says that to "believe" in Jesus is not about giving intellectual assent to who he was or even whether you verbalize a creedal statement about believing that Jesus was the Son of God. Instead, Borg suggests, "to believe" is closer to "to belove."

To believe (belove) in Jesus is actually to respond to his great initiative of love and to the generosity of God *with love*. In fact, the word "believe" is more like "loving God back." (Read 1 John 4:19. The idea of loving God doesn't begin with us but is a response to God's love toward and for us.) I am not a Greek scholar, but when I heard Borg say that, it rang true to me. It also filled me with joy. Indeed, it felt liberating to me, as if my old ideas about what it meant to follow Jesus were released from the bondage of duty and responsibility and freed into the delight and wonder of a love relationship!

For a long time, I had interpreted the word "believe" to mean that I went beyond mental assent to attempting to follow the teachings of Jesus and imitate his spirit. Borg's new concept took me to an entirely new depth of relating to the human Jesus/the Living Christ.

Through my contemplative prayer practices, I have learned that when you pour out your heart toward God in love, you open the possibility of experiencing God's love for you. In fact, it is hard to separate loving God and being loved by God. That is one of the great secrets of the abundant life: loving God is the same thing as being loved by God.

Speaking at the Jung Center, Jungian analyst and Episcopal priest Pittman McGehee was asked a question about the Bible. While I don't remember the question or his answer, I do remember what he said at the end of his response to the question.

"It's a love story, after all, isn't it?"

The Bible, a *love story*?

Indeed it is.

What About You?

1. Read John 3:1-16, and think about the context of the passage.
   - What is the setting?

   - Who are the characters?

   - Who initiated the conversation?

   - Who was Nicodemus?

2. What do you think was the meaning behind Nicodemus's question? Why did he approach Jesus at night?

3. What did Jesus mean when he said to Nicodemus, "You must be born again"?

4. What do you think Nicodemus thought when he heard Jesus say the words in John 3:16?

5. Why were the words so revolutionary for a man like Nicodemus?

6. Is eternal life about living forever, or is it about the quality of life you can have if you live in relationship to the Living Christ?

7. Why is John 3:16 called "the gospel in a nutshell"?

For Your Eyes Only
8. It has been said that if you had been the only one on earth, God still would have come in the form of Jesus to show you how great God's love is and to give you eternal life. Do you believe that? Do you live as if you believe it?

9. It's also been said that God loves each of us as if we were the only one, and God loves all of us the same. Do you believe that? Who would you leave out?

10. Does the inclusiveness of God make you nervous? If so, why?

11. Here are some ways people love God: loving creation, sitting in silence, simply loving God, loving other people, worshiping with others who love God, caring for those who have needs, following God's instructions. In what ways do you love God?

Chapter 3

The Great Teachings

If you obey my commands, you will remain in my love, just as I have obeyed my Father's commands and remain in his love. (John 15:10)

I no longer call you servants. . . . I call you friends. (John 15:15)

Commandments and Teachings

Wait a minute.

Are these mixed messages from Jesus, recorded in the same chapter of the Gospel of John? In my Bible, those verses are not more than an inch apart, and yet they seem contradictory.

We're not his servants, but we are to follow his teachings. On the other hand, perhaps the seeming contradiction is part of the mystery of following Jesus, this God-man who is both divine and human.

Living into the ambiguity of faith is a challenge. It's part of the mystery, though, and it our puzzlement says more about us than it does about Jesus. He knew what he was teaching us, but we have to open our minds and hearts wider to grasp the mystery of his teachings.

It is said that the Gospel of John is like a pond that is shallow and safe enough at its edge for a child to play in, but out beyond the shallows it is deep enough for an elephant to swim in.

On some days I'm a child, and on others I'm an elephant.

Didn't Jesus come to free us from the burdens of the 645 laws that the religious leaders of his day had added to the Ten Commandments? Doesn't Paul, Jew of all Jews, declare that he had kept the law with impeccable discipline, only to discover the liberating power of the grace of the Living Christ? Wasn't it Paul who said, "For it is by grace that you have been saved, through faith—and this not from yourself, it is the gift of God—not by works, so that no one can boast" (Eph 2:8)? Paul also said, "It is for freedom that Christ has set us free. Stand firm, then, and *do not let yourself be burdened again by a yoke of slavery*" (Gal 5:1, my emphasis).

Albert Einstein said that we cannot solve today's problems with yesterday's solutions, and I think that his well-tested and proven

Living into the ambiguity of faith is a challenge.

observation is relevant to an understanding of what Jesus meant by asking us to *follow him*, what it means to be one of his disciples, the difference between freedom and license, and the interrelatedness of freedom with responsibility.

In the first place, following Jesus seems to require a differentiation of terms. Jesus did come to liberate people from whatever had them in bondage, and I happen to believe that a relationship with the Living Christ can accomplish liberation in our lives today. I have to confess, though, that I don't have a simplistic, one-size-fits-all formula or plan for how that happens for myself or anyone else.

I grew up singing the old hymn, "Jesus Saves," and I believe he can save, but what exactly does that mean? Is salvation an event or a process? Is salvation about staying out of hell and getting into heaven, or is there more to it?

We human beings enslave ourselves to so many things—work, other people, others' expectations, money, family, alcohol, drugs, food, sex, power, control, and on and on. We all have our idols. One distinction between idols and God is that idols demand, steal, and extract from us what gives us life, while God gives life to us, nourishing us as we surrender our lives. I believe that Jesus can save us from our addictions and our idolatries, but I have learned the hard way the scary counsel of Paul to the good people in the church at Philippi: "Continue to work out your salvation with fear and trembling . . ." (2:12b).

I confess that I know a lot about both fear and trembling. In fact, I know a *lot* more about them than I ever planned on knowing, but thankfully, Paul gives us comfort and support in the next verse: "for it is God who works in you to will and to act according to his good purpose" (2:13). (Remember that "fear," as it is used here, is about awe directed toward God and to the work of God. When I look back on my life and reflect on my process of salvation, I am truly awestruck at the ways in which God has worked.)

What does God's good purpose have to do with the original Law given to God's children and with the coming of Christ?

Let's put what Jesus asks of us in context. Before giving the Ten Commandments to the children of Israel, God established a covenant with them, beginning with Abram (later Abraham) as recorded in Genesis 12:1-3. From the beginning of this project, we see God desiring and trying to be in a relationship of love with the children of Israel, saying to them, "I will be your God and you will be my people."

The covenant relationship God established with Abraham and with the children of Israel was based on God's guidance and provisions for them, and implicit within the covenant agreement was the expectation that the children of Israel would allow God to lead them. Given the rebelliousness and self-will of the humans God created, sometimes I wonder if anyone ever asked God, "How's that working for you?"

God gave the Ten Commandments to the children of Israel through Moses to help them bring order to their lives. Frankly, we all still do better when we follow those commandments (see Exod 20:1-17). I've noticed as well that once we start breaking the first commandment, the one that says we should have no other gods before Yahweh, it's a lot easier to break the other nine.

There is more counsel for the children of Israel in the book of Deuteronomy, and one of those instructions has informed my spiritual pilgrimage for almost all of my adult life. In fact, it has become a guiding principle, a lamppost that has often provided illumination in a dark night or when I have had to make a big decision. "I have set before you today life and death, blessing and curses. Therefore, choose life . . ." (Deut 30:19). There is more to this idea in verse 20—the promise that comes with keeping the imperative. We are to choose life "so that you and your children may live and that you may love the LORD your God, listen to his voice, and hold fast to him."

Honestly, sometimes it's taken hard knocks to wake me up to the blessed privilege of making choices, and sometimes it's taken me a long time to discern the difference between practices, habits, behaviors, and attitudes that are life-giving and those that are death-dealing. Sometimes I've gotten confused and thought that some of my blessings were actually curses, and my curses blessings, but over time, God has been gracious to lead me through those dark nights of despair.

I've clung to Deuteronomy 30:19-20, and I've also clung to the words Jeremiah the prophet heard from God: "For I know the plans I have for you, declares the LORD, plans to prosper you and not to harm you, plans to give you hope and a future" (Jer 29:11).

With the perspective of history, we know that the children of Israel had a pattern of drawing near to God and obeying, and then turning away and rebelling, getting in trouble, or being taken captive, and then crying out to God to save them. If I hadn't done the same thing throughout my life, I could look at those self-willed people through the lenses of self-righteousness!

I have set before you today life and death, blessing and curses. Therefore, choose life . . . (Deut 30:19).

For I know the plans I have for you, declares the LORD, plans to prosper you and not to harm you, plans to give you hope and a future (Jer 29:11).

To the ones God had chosen for a unique relationship, God gave Jesus, and Jesus was the fulfillment of the hope and the future for people who knew what it was to cry out to God to save them.

We apples haven't fallen far from the tree, have we?

I know what it is like to cry out to God. I'm sure you do too.

What About You?

1. Read Deuteronomy 30:19. What choices did God give to the children of Israel? (Consider reading the context in Deuteronomy 30:11-20 or even the entire chapter.)

2. What does this verse tell us about personal responsibility?

3. What does it tell us about making choices?

4. Why was it important for the children of Israel to have this clear, straightforward statement from God?

5. This commandment (or invitation, depending on how you interpret it) from God follows what is called a "renewal of the covenant" between God and the children of Israel, as recorded in Deuteronomy 29. What is your understanding of "covenant"?

6. What is the difference between a *covenant* and a *contract*?

7. Why is this concept so important in the history of the Jews? Why is it important to us?

8. Read John 10:10 again (we covered it briefly in chapter 1). How would you define "abundant life" or "life to the full"?

9. How do you think Jesus defines it?

10. Is there a difference between "abundant" or "full" life, as recorded in John 10:10, and the "eternal" life Jesus talks about in John 3:16 and John 17:3?

11. What is the connection between God's invitation to the children of Israel to "choose life" and the purpose for which Jesus came—to give us abundant life and eternal life?

If a group of church members were asked to make a list of commandments Jesus gave, how many do you think they could list? How many could you list?

It's interesting to see what some people think Jesus said that he did not say. It's also interesting to look at his teachings and see that while he gave many *instructions*, he only called one of them a *commandment*. (We will get to his commandment in chapter 4.)

We are often troubled when we consider what Jesus asks of us. Sometimes it would be easier simply to keep the Ten Commandments and a few dietary laws, follow the ritual cleansing specifications, and hope for the best. And it would be much easier if we who call ourselves followers of Christ could check off a list of rules and laws, rituals and regulations and say that we had *kept the commandments* and were right with God.

With Jesus' coming, however, something began to change in how God dealt with human beings. Below, you'll find a list of what Jesus asked of his followers. Read it, and then reflect on it by answering the questions.

Jesus' Teachings

Let your light shine (Matt 5:16)

Forgive . . . seventy times seven (Matt 18:21-23)

Take courage (Mark 8:5)

Fear not (Matt 14:27b, Mark 8:50, Luke 12:32)

Seek first the kingdom of God (Matt 6:33)

Abide in me (John 15:4)

Love one another (John 15:12)

Do to others as you would have them do to you (Matt 7:12)

Feed the hungry (Matt 25:35)

Visit the prisoners (Matt 25:36b)

Love your neighbor as yourself (Matt 22:39)

Be reconciled to your brother (Matt 5:23-24)

Take on my yoke (Matt 11:29)

Learn from me (Matt 11:29)

Go and make disciples, baptizing and teaching (Matt 28:19-20)

Do not judge (Matt 7:1)

Heal the sick (Matt 10:8)

Raise the dead (Matt 10:8)

Cleanse those who have leprosy (Matt 10:8)

Drive out demons (Matt 10:8)

Love your enemies and pray for them (Matt 5:44)

Pray (Matt 6:5-13)

When you pray, go into your closet (Matt 6:6)

Don't do your acts of righteousness in public (Matt 6:5)

Do not hide your light under a bushel (Matt 5:14-15)

Let your Yes be Yes, and your No, No (Matt 5:37)

Love the Lord your God with all your heart, mind, and soul (Matt 22:37)

Do not store up for yourself treasures on earth (Matt 6:19)

What About You?

1. What is the difference between an *instruction* or *teaching* and a *commandment*?

2. Using the list of instructions or teachings Jesus gave his followers, respond to the following questions:

• Which is the hardest for you to follow?

• Which one had you forgotten?

• Which one, if followed, would make the world a better place?

• Which one, when you follow it, makes your life work better?

3. Compare Jesus' instructions to the Ten Commandments. How are they different? How are they alike?

4. How are the Old Testament people to whom God gave the Ten Commandments different from or similar to the New Testament people to whom Jesus spoke?

5. If you broke a law under the Jewish system, there was a prescribed punishment. How would you punish the breaking of one of Jesus' teachings?

6. Which of Jesus' instructions do you think is the most important?

7. Which is the only teaching Jesus called a "commandment"?

Is it possible that following Jesus is about is a shift in consciousness and orientation from keeping external laws, observing particular rites, and doing certain rituals to obeying what he asks in these instructions, motivated by a change of heart?

Perhaps the shift is away from our never-ending attempts to earn salvation by being good enough, working hard enough, trying often and fervently enough to an inward shift in the way we live our everyday lives. Perhaps when we are "in Christ" (Paul's term: see 2 Cor 5:17, 1 Cor 1:30, Rom 8:1, and Romans 16), living in step with his spirit (Gal 5:25), living in the ways of Jesus and the way of life (the yoke) that fits us best as human beings, we want to carry out Jesus' instructions.

Perhaps the abundant life has nothing to do with achieving, acquiring, or accomplishing in the outer world, but with the fullness of life that comes from an intimate, personal, dynamic love relationship with the Living Christ, a life that is lived out as we follow these teachings.

Could there be anything more different from these teachings than the norms of the world in which we live? Where Jesus said, "Love one another," the world says, "Take care of yourself." Where Jesus said, "Forgive, seventy times seven," the world says, "Don't get mad; get even." Try selling "Don't store up for yourselves treasures on earth" to a world that honors greed and avarice, applauds hoarding, and thinks it is okay to steal from others as long as it's legal.

The Golden Rule

How long has it been since you have heard a sermon on the Golden Rule? The world I see is often more full of behaviors that say, "Do to others *before* they do to you."

Let's face it. It's a challenge to follow Jesus. Our attempts to be his follower immediately force us to confront our selfishness, self-centeredness, pettiness, and self-absorption. I often reflect on a quote by British writer and philosopher G. K. Chesterton. "The Christian ideal has not been tried and found wanting," he said. "It has been found difficult and left untried."

Roberts Elementary School is nestled in the shadow of Rice University and the Texas Medical Center. Situated on a busy street, this school is surrounded by an impressive and attractive fence that is often adorned with various posters and streamers announcing an upcoming event.

One spring morning when I was driving past the school, trying to stay within the speed limit and get to an appointment on time, the words from colorful posters caught my eye.

No place for hate! were the words on the posters.

When I returned home, I drove back by the school and read the posters more carefully. Later, I researched this remarkable program on the Internet and discovered that it is a national program to stop bullying in schools.

So in everything, do to others what you would have them do to you, for this sums up the Law and the Prophets. (Matt 7:12)

Here is a simple, rule-of-thumb guide for behavior: Ask yourself what you want people to do for you, then grab the initiative and do it for them. Add up God's Law and Prophets and this is what you get. (Matt 7:12, The Message)

Do not do to others what would anger you if done to you by others.

—Socrates

45

Wouldn't it be interesting if adults could take the mind-set of "no place for hate" into the workplaces, their neighborhoods, their churches . . . and even their homes?

Reading about this program set me out on a mission, which led to a discovery of a children's book about the Golden Rule. When I gave a copy of that book to one of my granddaughters, she said, "Oh, I know about this! My principal repeats this every morning on the loudspeaker."

I was stunned and spent the rest of the day contemplating the idea that my grandchildren were learning the Golden Rule at public schools, and that they were being impressed with the principles of the "no place for hate" initiatives in their schools!

With later reflection, it occurred to me that it had been a long time since I had heard anyone mention the Golden Rule, much less offer it as a principle for life. Too much, we within the Christian community have been more concerned about imposing our way on others and straightening each other out. Too often, Christians have fallen into the rule that says, "Do unto others before they do unto you."

And yet, this Golden Rule, practiced in everyday life, might hold the secret to transforming relationships, and then, rippling outward, changing the world.

"Treating others as you want to be treated" is smart. In indicates and builds empathy and sensitivity to others. It fosters respect and compassion and can be a way to resolve conflict. It is simply good common sense.

The Golden Rule is not exclusive to Christianity, and, in fact, it is found in most religions; it is an ethical standard in most cultures. It is also good psychology, for it fosters the law of reciprocity in relationships and transactions. It is a valuable idea that permeates philosophy, promoting the idea that people are more than objects. In the understanding of social structures and sociology, the principle encourages treating all persons with respect and consideration—not just one's own group.

In some versions of the Golden Rule, the Rule is written from what a negative perspective: *Do not do to others what you do not want them to do to you.*

However it is written, all forms of the Golden Rule have one thing in common: they demand that people treat each other as they want to be treated.

The Golden Rule can done in small ways, at home and in the outside world.

Here are some simple ways that contribute to the good of the world:
- Think before you speak.
- Park between the lines on a parking lot, and don't take up more than one space.
- Think about how you want to be treated. How can you give more respect to others?
- Drive with care and concern for the other people on the highway.
- Speak politely to the strangers who help you at the drive-through, the cleaners, the grocery store.
- Stay off your cell phone when you are transacting business with clerks or other helpers.
- Consider how other people may feel about how your actions are affecting them. Develop or practice empathy.
- Face your prejudices and biases. Call them what they are. Give them up.
- Listen to what your loved ones are saying—without interrupting.
- Don't manipulate others to get your way.
- Discover what a co-worker, a friend or a family member really enjoys and find a way to provide that source of enjoyment for that person.
- When you notice that someone is having a hard day, look for a way to lighten his/her burden.
- Tip appropriately and even generously.
- Practice random acts of kindness for people who will never return the favor.
- Don't criticize. If you need to work out a problem, do so in a constructive way.
- Own your own flaws and mistakes. Make amends when you can. Fix what you have broken.
- Clean up after yourself.
- Stop talking fear talk. Stop listening to trash talk. Speak words of hope and faith.
- Be kind to everyone. Remember: everyone is having a hard time.
- Forgive. For your own sake, forgive.
- Love people and tell them you love them.

Post the Golden Rule on your wall. Repeat it to yourself, as you go about your day. If it's good enough for elementary school students, it's good enough for you!

What About You?

My friend laughed at me when I told him about the Golden Rule.
    "Ha!" he said. "You do that and you'll be a smudge on the road in my world!"

1. Is that true about your world?

2. Does it make you feel nervous to think about being kinder to people, especially the people who have hurt your feelings or who make it hard on you?

3. What do you think about making your life a "hate-free zone," where no bullying in any form is allowed?

4. When you have to confront a problem or defend yourself, can you do so and still practice the Golden Rule?

I am not willing to shrug my shoulders and say, "It's too hard; I can't do it." If Jesus came to give us abundant life and eternal life, then there has to be a way to access the quality of life he wants us to have. Perhaps the secret to that lies in a powerful and proven principle from the Twelve Steps of Alcoholics Anonymous, a principle captured in three simple words: first things first.

But before we proceed with putting first things first, here's a quote to pave the way: "Love is the only sane and satisfactory answer to the problem of human existence."

What About You?

1. Is that quote simply a sentimental idea? Why or why not?

2. How does love sometimes make us insane instead of sane?

3. Look again at the teachings of Jesus. What do they have to do with love?

Erich Fromm, renowned German psychologist and author of *The Art of Loving*, made that affirmation about the power of love. His book is a classic now, often chosen by people like me who, as a college student, believed in the power of love and wanted to love and be loved more than anything else in the world.[7]

I truly think Jesus gave us the secret to abundant life. I'm not inclined to declare that if you do "this," you will have "this," but I know for sure that there is something Jesus asked us to do that has the potential to change our lives. We humans are prone to complicating life with our rules and rituals, routines and responsibilities, all of which may be important and necessary. Jesus taught and lived in a culture that had been complicated with hundreds of rules for righteous living, rules that had become burdens that made life with God harder than it needed to be. In his genius, he spoke great wisdom in giving us a way of life in a simple commandment.

What About You?

1. What truths do you return to when life gets complicated?

2. How has your religious life cluttered up your spirituality?

Love is the only sane and satisfactory answer to the problem of human existence.

3. What do you think Jesus' bottom-line teaching would be, based on what you know now?

Chapter 4

The Greatest Commandment

Imagine that you are in a crowd of people, listening to Jesus teach. Perhaps this is your first time to hear him teach, or maybe you've been with him many times, trying to learn everything you can from this new kind of rabbi.

Would you stand around the edges of that crowd, or would you get as close as possible to the Rabbi Jesus?

What would you think and feel when the Sadducees and Pharisees interrupt Jesus, arguing with him over fine points of the law and trying to get him off message with their questions? There is hardly anything more annoying for a teacher or leader than someone who is determined to distract from his or her message.

Earlier in his teaching ministry, Jesus declared, "Don't think that I have come to abolish the Law or the Prophets; I have not come to abolish them, but to fulfill them" (Matt 5:17), but his opponents repeatedly challenged him for what he taught and did, such as healing people, gathering wheat on the Sabbath, and spending time with tax collectors and prostitutes.

Imagine your response if you were there on the scene when one of the experts in the Law tested Jesus with this question: "Teacher, what is the greatest commandment in the Law?"

Would you be duped either by the importance of this "expert" or by his question, thinking that it indicated a genuine interest or curiosity in what Jesus thought? Or would you see through the outward appearance to the inward motivation of the expert?

Perhaps a hush fell over the crowd when Jesus answered with the words of what is called the Greatest Commandment, recorded in Matthew 22:37-39: "Love the Lord your God with all your heart and with all your soul and with all your mind. This is the first and greatest commandment. And the second is like it: Love your neighbor as yourself." And then Jesus added a principle, the meaning of which is profound and practical. "All the Law and the Prophets hang on these two commandments" (v. 40).

There it is—the essence of Jesus' teachings.

Here is the key to the abundant life, the beginning and end of Jesus' ethics, and the secret to keeping all of his other teachings.

God is love. (1 John 4:8b)

Whoever lives in love, lives in God, and God in him. (1 John 4:16b)

There is no fear in love. But perfect love drives out fear . . . (1 John 4:18)

We love because he first loved us. (1 John 4:19)

Trust steadily in God, hope unswervingly, love extravagantly. And the best of the three is love. (1 Cor 13:13)

> Love the Lord your God with all your heart and with all your soul and with all your mind. This is the first and greatest commandment. And the second is like it: Love your neighbor as yourself. (Matt 22:37-39)

> If anyone boasts, "I love God," and goes right on hating his brother or sister, thinking nothing of it, he is a liar. If he won't love the person he can see, how can he love the God he can't see? The command we have from Christ is blunt: Loving God includes loving people. You've got to love both. (1 John 4:20-21)

Start here, Jesus says.

Spend the next year of your life integrating these spiritual practices—loving God and loving your neighbor as yourself—into your family life, your vocation, and your interactions with others, and see what happens.

Start here, even before you formulate your business plan, your career goals, your politics.

See what happens if you take this commandment seriously in daily life.

Jesus could play the part of the trickster well, and he never did it more smoothly than on this day recorded in Matthew 22 when the efforts to trap him escalated. It was a brilliant move for the Rabbi Jesus, especially when speaking with those who prided themselves on their knowledge of the Law, to go back to the Shema of Judaism, the foundational principle every observant Jew recited and every Jewish child learned at an early age: "Hear, O Israel: The Lord our God, the Lord is one. Love the Lord your God with all your heart and with all your soul and with all your strength" (Deut 6:4-5).

Jesus knew that the questioners who could not be silenced needed to remember this commandment to love God with their whole being. The commandment was so important, in fact, that God gave further instructions in Deuteronomy 6 about how to integrate it into a person's inner being so that the love of God would permeate the heart, radiating out in behavior that would reflect God's love.

> These commandments that I give you today are to be upon your hearts. Impress them on your children. Talk about them when you sit at home and when you walk along the road, when you lie down and when you get up. Tie them as symbols on your hands and bind them on your foreheads. Write them on the doorframes of your houses and on your gates. (Deut 6:4-9)

The new commandment and the new ethic that Jesus taught flowed from two life-changing principles. First, our love of God is to flow out of the individual in acts of love, compassion, mercy, and grace to others. Instead of relating to others out of duty, obligation, or rules, our interpersonal dynamics are to be motivated and shaped by our love for God, flowing naturally, organically, holistically out into love for others!

Second—and this is revolutionary—we are to love others *as we love ourselves.* Instead of teaching that we are to neglect ourselves or put ourselves last, Jesus comes along and suggests a principle that is paradoxical and deeply powerful. In fact, it has been suggested that this commandment is never broken. We actually do love others as we love ourselves.

The commandment doesn't say to love others *more* than we love ourselves. That could be idolatry or codependence.

It doesn't say to love others *less* than we love ourselves. That could be selfishness or inflation.

Instead, the commandment reveals the important principle that our love for God is intimately intertwined with our love for others and ourselves, and that our love for others and ourselves is a reflection of our love for God. This is powerful, and it has the potential to be life changing. It is a challenge big enough to last a lifetime, and it takes a willingness to wake up and be highly conscious and alert. Following this commandment requires us to take another look at what we mean when we say we "love," and it calls us to the Jesus way of loving ourselves and other people.

Most of us know what it is like to be obsessed with another person. We call that "falling in love," and it's probably not a good indicator of authentic love. We know what it is like to need someone else, to treat someone as an object, or to be treated as an object. We know about manipulation and duplicity that sometimes masquerade as love, and we know what it is like to pretend what we don't feel.

Carl Jung says that "where love is lacking, power and control rush in." In his simple statement of what he knew to be the greatest law among hundreds, Jesus confronted the tendency to base our interactions on keeping the rules or keeping up outward appearances.

This commandment truly is the secret of life, and here is another implication of it: if you're having trouble keeping one of Jesus' other teachings, such as forgiving someone who has offended you, caring for those who cannot care for themselves, loving other people, and giving up fear and taking on courage, *start with this commandment.*

Out of my good intentions, I may not be able to be as generous or merciful with others as I know God wants me to be, but if I start by practicing this greatest commandment, somehow God gives me the inner resources I need to do what I know I must do.

Out of my own broken heart or wounded pride, I may not be able to muster what I need to forgive someone who has hurt me or one of my loved ones. Knowing how dangerous non-forgiveness is and knowing that I should forgive, I may plaster a premature forgiveness over my hurt, only to plunge that hurt into the depths of my heart somewhere, leaving it to fester under the "shoulds" and "oughts" of my religious fervor. On the other hand, if I return to this great commandment, loving God first, then I can trust God's forgiveness to flow out of my heart naturally, in the right time and in the right way.

Out of my selfishness and self-centeredness, I may not be able to love others or myself, and when I cannot, if I return to the practice of loving God first, then I will be able to love myself and others appropriately.

It's relatively easy to have a set of rules and laws that you can check off if you follow them. It's harder to measure the effects of loving God, ourselves, and others? It gets complicated when there's no cut-and-dried punishment or reward system to keep tabs on each other's loving.

What About You?

1. What are the results of loving God and letting God love you?

2. How do you know when the love relationship between God and you is broken? Who decides how much you need to love God? How much is enough?

After washing the disciples' feet in that upper room before his death, Jesus told the disciples what they must do, and that time, too, he used the word "command." "A new command I give you: Love one another. As I have loved you, so you must love one another. By this all men will know that you are my disciples, if you love one another" (John 13:34).

"A new command I give you: Love one another. As I have loved you, so you must love one another. By this all men will know that you are my disciples, if you love one another" (John 13:34).

Jesus didn't say that his disciples would be known by their correct doctrine or by how closely they observed the law and kept the rituals, but by the love they had for each other. Apparently, Jesus placed a high value on love.

Before his dramatic Damascus road experience with the Spirit of Christ, the Apostle Paul was a zealot for his Jewish faith, keeping the letter of the Law and watching over the murder of those who followed the man Jesus. It was he, freed from the Law's tyranny, who wrote the famous and beautiful passage about love in 1 Corinthians 13:

> If I speak with human eloquence and angelic ecstasy but don't love, I'm nothing but the creaking of a rusty gate. If I speak God's Word with power, revealing all his mysteries and making everything plain as day, and if I have faith that says to a mountain, "Jump," and it jumps, but I don't love, I'm nothing. If I give everything I own to the poor and even go to the stake to be burned as a martyr, but I don't love, I've gotten nowhere. So, no matter what I say, what I believe, and what I do, I'm bankrupt without love. (1 Corinthians 13:1-1-3)

Somehow, if we get Jesus' greatest commandment working in our lives, life works as God designed it to work. In the cross below,

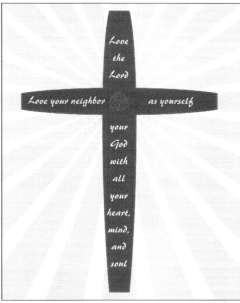

Consider committing to an experiment. Take on Jesus' great commandment in Matthew 22:37-39 for a period that works for you. It is said that it takes twenty-one days to form a habit. For some of us, it may take more than that. Keep a journal, noting your attempts to love God, love others, and love yourself. Consider using the "What About You" questions to guide your reflections.

notice that "Love the Lord your God with all your heart, mind, and soul" anchors us vertically in relationship with God. The horizontal beam, "Love your neighbor as yourself," encompasses our relationship to others. When you are grounded in loving God, you have the resources, the strength, and the motivation to love others as you love yourself.

On the same day I discovered the work of Geza Vermes in the bookstore of Grace Cathedral, another book seemed to leap off the shelf and land in my bag for the trip home.

I'd been teaching a class on Jesus for a year and was in the process of writing this book. In fact, the greatest commandment had been on my mind constantly all summer as I began to prepare the syllabus for a course I teach at my church titled "Fierce Love: Radical Measure for Desperate Times."

The book that caught my attention was *The Jesus Creed: Loving God, Loving Others,* written by Scot McKnight. The author teaches us "a new creed for life," how to put the great commandment into practice every day. In McKnight's words, what Jesus said should shape everything we say about Christian spirituality, since his teaching defines spiritual formation.

I couldn't agree more.

What About You?

1. When have you felt loved just for who you are?

2. Who has given love to you the most?

3. Write your own definition or description of love.

4. When you are trying to get others to love you or giving love to others, do you ever manipulate them? How well does that work? What blocks you from loving others and receiving others' love for you?

5. How do you know when you are loving God?

6. What is the difference in self-indulgence and loving oneself? How do you know which one you're doing?

7. What does it take for God to receive your love?

8. What evidence do you have that God loves you?

9. It has been said that we love God to the extent that we love the person we love least. Do you believe that to be true? Why or why not?

10. Would the people who are most important in your life say that you loved them well?

Chapter 5

The Greatest Adventure

When it comes to a relationship with Jesus, what is the difference between a curiosity seeker and an authentic seeker? a seeker and a wanderer? a seeker and a learner? a follower and a disciple? an apprentice and a disciple? What caused people to want to know and follow Jesus of Nazareth? What will cause people to want to know and follow the Living Christ today?

It's fascinating to think about the way people dropped what they were doing to follow Jesus. In most stories of Jesus choosing his followers, it seems that the people instantly obey his call. There must have been something magnetic and appealing about the human Jesus. Perhaps some truly did follow right away, but it's also possible that others observed him in and around his village, interacting with others, before they simply got up and started following him.

Jesus' invitation, first of all, was an invitation into a relationship with him. He invited people to follow him around and see who he really was, to eat with him, dialogue with him, and watch him as he interacted with others. Jesus didn't do his work within a protected environment where he could present only the best image of himself. Neither did he stay behind a church pulpit, speaking to people (or at them!) but not letting others see him away from his speaking post. This kind of vulnerability and transparency reveals the authenticity of Jesus. It also reveals something powerful about God: God makes himself known to us, and his ways are transparent to us if we have the eyes to see and the ears to hear.

In Jesus' day, a relationship with him meant that you could get close to him. He did have a crowd of curiosity seekers, but he also had close friendships with people such as Mary, Martha, and Lazarus, as well as Mary Magdalene. He related intimately to his disciples, and he had the inner circle of Peter, James, and John, who were with him at significant and peak experiences in his ministry. People in the first century could observe how he related to other people and see how he spent his time and his day-to-day life. They could converse with him as he listened to them. Those who were healed by his presence or his touch were changed forever by that direct encounter. Sometimes, don't you wish you could experience the actual physical presence of Jesus?

Come, follow me . . . and I will make you fishers of men. (Matt 4:19)

Jesus' friends and disciples watched him deal with conflict and controversy. They heard him teach about what it meant to be part of the kingdom of God, and they had the experience of being publicly identified with the human Jesus. Of course, that identification was both privilege and problem. The disciples had the experience of Jesus washing their feet, and his inner circle was there when he revealed his full splendor on the mountain hike when he was transfigured. They were there, too, in the Garden of Gethsemane, when he struggled mightily with the inevitability of his fate. Apparently, they were close enough to him that he also trusted him with the account of his earlier struggle when the adversary tempted him away from his mission and purpose.

Exploring the Scriptures
Read John 1:35-51.[9]

1. What made the disciples of John the Baptist leave him to follow Jesus?

2. What might those two disciples have thought when Jesus turned around and began a conversation with them?

3. Jesus asked them a powerful question: "What do you want?" Why did he start with a question? Why is that question so important?

4. What kind of answer did they give?

5. What does Jesus' response, "Come . . . and you will see," mean?

6. What are the implications of Jesus' invitation?

Read the following passages in which the other Gospel writers describe Jesus' calling of his disciples: Matthew 4:18-22; Mark 1:16-20; Luke 5:2-11.
7. How are these accounts alike? How are they different?

8. What was Jesus' specific invitation to these men?

9. What is the implication of Jesus' statement, "I will make you fishers of men"?

Read Mark 2:13-17 and Luke 5:27-32.
10. Jesus doesn't use the "fishers of men" imagery in these passages. Why not?

11. How is Matthew's story different from Mark's and Luke's (see Matt 9:9-13)?

12. What is the dictionary definition of the word *disciple*?

13. Do you think a follower and a disciple are the same?

14. In your own words, what do you think it means today to be a disciple of Christ?

15. What do you think were Jesus' criteria in choosing his disciples?

For Your Eyes Only
16. Imagine that you are with the human Jesus, and he asks you, "What do you want?" What would you say?

Today, we do not have the privilege and benefit of experiencing one-on-one encounters with the human Jesus like the people of the first century did. There are ways that we can experience the presence of what I refer to as "the Living Christ." Some call that mysterious reality "the Holy Spirit." I also like Matthew Fox's term, "the Cosmic Christ," because it expands my mind so that I imagine the presence of Christ not as my personal possession but as the presence of Christ throughout the world.

I experience the presence of Christ through the gift of my imagination, using that source of creativity to imagine the Living Christ with me. Other spiritual practices that help me maintain my connection with the Living Christ are Centering Prayer, the Welcoming Prayer, Lectio Divina, and Communion (also called the Eucharist or the Lord's Supper), worshiping with my family of faith, serving others in the name of Christ, and entering into the Gospel stories through the use of imagination.

Centering Prayer was developed by Thomas Keating, the Benedictine monk who has taught thousands of people to pray in a contemplative manner.

The **Welcoming Prayer** is another form of prayer developed by Thomas Keating. In this prayer, there is a focus on letting go of things that are inhibiting inner peace and welcoming the presence of Christ into those very areas of life that are most problematic.

Lectio Divina is a way of reading Scripture contemplatively, reflectively, slowly, and meditatively. In this practice, a passage is read three times, with a different intention for each time and time for quiet reflection after each reading.

For more descriptions of these practices, see my book *Dance Lessons: Moving to the Beat of God's Heart*

Through these practices, the locus of God's presence moves from being far away, beyond my reach, to being near me and within me.

During my first session of spiritual direction with Bishop Mike Pfeifer, he directed me to spend time with the exchange between Jesus and his first disciples, as recorded in John 1:35-51, when Jesus asked the two disciples who began to follow him, "What do you want?"

"What do you want?" Bishop Mike asked me. "What do you want in spiritual direction, and what do you want from Jesus?"

The questions stunned me. I'd spent a lifetime thinking about what Jesus wanted me to do and what he would ask of me. To think about what I was seeking and what I *wanted* was life changing for me.

William Glasser, the developer of the technique called "Reality Therapy," counseled the therapists he trained to ask their clients, "What do you want?"

Some people can answer the question instantly. For others, the answer requires time and reflection, courage and boldness. Sadly, some people are so constrained by others' expectations, committed to living another's agenda, defeated by life's demands, or crippled by an inability to access their hearts' desires that they cannot answer this question easily—or at all.

Dr. Glasser's therapists are trained to listen to the first response, and then ask further, "What do you *really* want?"

Often the deepest and most authentic desires are buried so deeply in our unconscious that it takes time, patience, and tenderness to allow them to surface into our conscious minds.

"What do you really want?" is a powerful question, for it not only takes the focus off what a person (or others in her life) thinks she ought to do but also gives her permission to access the power of desire. Our desires, after all, are often the impetus of God, pushing us to grow, to choose, to act, to become whole from within, and yet we s often either feel guilty about what we want or think we can't have what we want. We tend to label our desires as selfishness, and yet, in this passage in John 1 is a vital key to our wholeness.

What did I want? Answering that question changed my life.

What About You?

1. In the quiet and stillness of your heart, what do you want more than anything?

2. If you were the person who followed Jesus like John's disciple in John 1:35-51, what would you tell Jesus when he asked you what you wanted?

3. Choose which question is easier for you to answer: "What do I have to do today?" or "What do I want?" Why did you make that choice?

4. Realistically, no one can have everything he wants or imagines. Occasionally, time runs out on getting something we've always wanted. At other times, the cost of having what we want is too great. Do you have unfulfilled longings that you need to surrender to God?

5. Once you surrender and release those desires to God, what new desires surface? What is possible now that you have let go of something?

Chapter 6

The Great "I Am" Declaratives

I will ask the Father, and he will give you another Counselor to be with you forever—the Spirit of truth. (John 14:16)

I will not leave you as orphans; I will come to you . . . (John 14:18)

If anyone loves me, he will obey my teachings. My father will love him, and we will come to him and make our home in him. (John 14:23)

You learn who a person is by what he says about himself and what other people say about him. You also learn about a person by observing what she does. In the selected quotations of Jesus listed above, Jesus tells his disciples what he will do for them. At that point, they probably didn't realize he was talking about what he would do *after* the crucifixion and resurrection.

As Jesus went about his daily life, teaching and ministering to others, he spoke in symbols and images to communicate who he was. Those symbols meant something to his listeners, connecting his words with realities in their personal lives. The images, captured in what we know as the "I Am" statements, are both easily understood and deep enough for long years of reflection and study. In making his "I Am" statements, Jesus also connected his listeners to their heritage and history, reminding them of the time when God called Moses out of his life as a shepherd to be the great liberator of the children of Israel.

Stunned by the proposal and probably intimidated by the thought of going to Pharaoh and demanding the freedom of his people, Moses asked God, "Who shall I say sent me?" God replied, "Tell him that 'I Am' sent you."

Can you imagine Moses' reaction? I'm sure Moses felt puzzled by God's response, and yet, with profound simplicity, God expressed the fullness of God's nature, purpose, sovereignty, and power.

Explore Moses' story and the meaning of God's "I Am," as well as the meaning of Jesus' "I Am" statements. Use the "Exploring the Scriptures" questions as guides.

Exploring the Scriptures
Read Exodus 3.
1. When God told Moses what he was to do and say, God identified himself as "I Am Who I Am" and told Moses that when he spoke to Pharaoh, he should say that "I Am" sent him to liberate the children of Israel. Reflect on that name, "I Am Who I Am." What do you think it means?

Read Revelation 21:5.
2. Here, the Holy One says "I am . . . making all things new." What does that mean?

3. In both the Exodus and Revelation Scriptures, God is at work. In the first, God acts to liberate the people. In the second, what is God doing to "make things new"?

4. In the great "I Am" statements that Jesus made, he identified himself using images and symbols that were familiar to his listeners. Read each of these and then answer the questions that follow.

(a) I am the bread of life. (John 6:48)
(b) I am the light of the world. (John 8:12)
(c) I am the door. (John 10:9)
(d) I am the good shepherd. (John 10:11)
(e) I am the resurrection, and the life. (John 11:25)
(f) I am the way, the truth, and the life. (John 14:6)
(g) I am the true vine. (John 15:1)

• What do you think each of these images communicated to people in the first century?

• What do these images convey to you?

For Your Eyes Only
5. If, by entering into a personal, vital, dynamic love relationship with the Living Christ, you would have access to what is symbolized

But the Counselor, the Holy Spirit, whom the Father will send in my name, will teach you all things and remind you of everything I have said to you. (John 14:25)

Peace I leave with you; my peace I give you . . . . Do not let your hearts be troubled, and do not be afraid. (John 14:27)

by each of those images, which one would you most need or want today?

6. We call Jesus Great Physician, Lord, Redeemer, Savior, Friend, Son of God, Rabbi, Helper, Son of Man. Which do you most need him to be for you today?

When I was a child, I heard my mother sing these words of an old, simple hymn: "Spirit of the Living God, fall fresh on me." I heard her sing it often, not just at church but also while she worked in the kitchen, preparing lunch or canning fruit. I also heard my parents talk about "the movement of the Holy Spirit," often after a particularly meaningful worship service at our church. I heard my father preach about being guided by the Spirit of God, and I saw him struggle to follow what he perceived as God's will.

The Mystery of God's actual presence among us, working through us and available to us as a resource for good, was communicated through words and actions as a natural thing. Neither of my parents spoke in tongues, to my knowledge, and they didn't practice what the Apostle Paul called "the showy gifts." Instead, their devotion to Christ and their following him was a quieter expression of faith. For them, it was about "trusting and obeying" day by day. By their example, I learned early that it was natural to experience the Presence of God/the Living Christ/the Holy Spirit, and that following the guidance of that Mystery was a necessary practice!

What About You?

For each question, think about which of the three is easier for you to believe and why.

1. That Jesus lived long ago (in biblical times), that the Living Christ dwells in you now, or that you will be with Jesus one day in heaven.

2. That Jesus healed a blind man, that the Living Christ can heal your spiritual blindness now, or that you will see perfectly one day in heaven.

3. That Jesus walked on water when he lived on earth, that the Living Christ can walk across the stormy waters of your life and calm them, or that everything will be okay one day in heaven.

For them [the early Christian community after Jesus was no longer with them], this the post-Easter Jesus was the light that led them out of darkness, the spiritual food that nourished them in the midst of their journey, the way that led them from death to life.

—Marcus Borg[11]

. . . the Christian life is about entering into a relationship with that to which the Christian tradition points, which may be spoken of as God, the risen living Christ, or the Spirit. And a Christian is one who lives out his or her relationship to God within the framework of the Christian tradition. . . . My own journey has led beyond belief (and beyond doubt and disbelief) to an understanding of the Christian life as a relationship to the Spirit of God—a relationship that involves one in a journey of transformation.

—Marcus Borg

Part Two

Meeting Jesus in the Encounters

Introduction

Throughout the Scriptures, God is revealed as a relational being who seeks to walk and talk with the people God has made. So it is natural that in the Incarnation of God, revealed in Jesus, we see Jesus seeking and making friends, conversing with people, and involving himself in the lives of friends and family. As Jesus interacted with people, he was not remote from them, sitting on a throne or on a platform, removed from the action of daily life. Instead, he was out and about, pressed by the crowd, sought by seekers, and drawn to people who needed him.

Is Jesus' model of involvement with people, allowing them to see him up close and personal, a picture of how God relates to us? Is it possible for us to imagine that the Spirit of the Living Christ is out and about in the world with us, present to us in our everyday lives, illuminating the dark corners of confusion and guiding us through synchronicities, words of wisdom, the counsel of friends, and our inner knowing?

In his interactions with others, Jesus fit his treatment plan to the need, the teaching to the student, and his actions to the moment. As he affected others' lives, he did one of four things: He *healed* people physically, emotionally, and spiritually. He *liberated* people, freeing them from what had them constrained in favor of a fuller and more abundant life. He *transformed* people, moving within the circumstances of their lives to change what was limiting and harmful into what was good. He *empowered* people to become all that they were created to be.

While none of us can have the experience of walking and talking with the human Jesus, through the powers of imagination, we can enter into the Scriptures in such a way that the Living Christ can do for us what the human Jesus did for first-century seekers.

Many people find great meaning, direction, and assistance in following the ancient practice of *lectio divina*, using the imagination to picture themselves in the stories of the Gospel encounters or to picture Jesus with them in the present moment.

Others have encountered the Living Christ through the practice of Centering Prayer or other forms of contemplative prayer.

In the following lessons, see what unfolds for you in the Scriptures. Can you open your mind and imagination, your heart and your emotions to the possibility of an encounter with the Living Christ?

Chapter 7

Meeting Jesus in the Questions

The summons to sacred questioning—like the call to honesty, like the call to prayer—is a call to be true and let the chips fall where they may.

—David Dark,

I have some questions for you, and I want some straight answers. (God, to Job, Job 38:3b)

When I was a child, my mother called me "Meddlesome Mattie" because I asked so many questions. My father enjoyed my inquisitive nature, but now and then, I'm sure it got on his nerves to be plied with so many questions. My dad also skated on thin ice as the father of three daughters by joking that "with women, asking questions was curiosity or nosiness, but with men, it was intelligent investigation." He laughed as he said that, mostly because he knew it would get a reaction from one of us. Now I know that my habit of asking questions, like that of most children, was a way of connecting with my parents. If I could engage them in a conversation with my questions, then they were present to me, conversing with me, and engaging with me in a meaningful way.

Jesus was curious about people, and apparently he wanted to know them at an intimate level. He loved conversation with his friends, and he wanted to know what people thought. Jesus was a master of The Question, knowing when to ask and which question to ask of those who followed him, those who sought something from him, and those who challenged him.

That he asked so many questions reveals that he was a good teacher. He wanted others to think for themselves as well. Perhaps he wanted them to hear themselves talking; it seems that Jesus knew that some people don't know what they think or believe until they begin articulating it. There's something powerful about "hearing yourself think"; there's something life giving when another person values you enough to ask what you think.

Jesus didn't assume that others might be thinking what he was thinking or that they held his point of view. Nor did he simply lecture them, making pronouncements and issuing proclamations from a mountaintop or delivering speeches from a high altar. Instead, he engaged people in dialogue. Jesus had what I like to call "holy curiosity," and he was able to discern that quality, which has a childlike purity, in others.

There were times when Jesus said, "This is the way it is," and he was firm, clear, and straightforward with his teachings, but much of his teaching happened as he engaged people in a relationship through questions.

When others—either honest seekers or those who tried to trick him—questioned Jesus, he had the discernment to know when the question was authentic and when it was a trap. It's no small challenge in our interactions with others to discern the difference between questions that come from humility and respect and ones that come with a negative motivation. Jesus had the discernment to know the difference.

Recently, I have learned a great deal from a slow, reflective reading of David Dark's book, *The Sacredness of Questioning Everything*.[12] The book has been so important to me that I wrote a series of blog posts about it on my website. From the response to those posts, I have decided that there are people who do value the art of questioning, though sometimes it seems that most people simply want someone to give them "the answer." Dark wrote,

> I believe deliverance begins with questions. It begins with people who love questions, people who live with questions, and by questions, people who feel a deep joy when good questions are asked. . . . When we're exposed to the liveliness of holding everything up to the light of good questions—what I call "sacred questioning"—we discover that redemption is creeping into the way we think, believe, and see the world. This re-deeming (re-valuing) of what we've made of our lives, a redemption that perhaps begins with the insertion of a question mark beside whatever feels final and absolute and beyond questioning, gives our souls a bit of elbow room, a space in which to breathe and imagine again, as if for the first time. . . . When we have questions, illumination is possible. Otherwise we're closed and no light can enter.[13]

What About You?

1. How might you respond to the quote from David Dark?

2. How often do you ask questions related to your faith?

3. Do you feel that it's okay for you to ask such questions, or do they make you feel as if you're "not good enough" for God?

4. How can asking questions give you "a space in which to breathe and imagine again"? Why would this be a good thing?

Jesus asked many questions in his lifetime. What follows is a partial list. Read it and then do the activity.

Questions Jesus Asked

1. Can any of you by worrying add a single moment to your lifespan? (Matt 6:27)

2. Why do you notice the splinter in your brother's eye yet fail to perceive the wooden beam in your own eye? (Matt 7:2)

3. Why are you terrified? (Matt 8:26)

4. Why do you harbor evil thoughts? (Matt 9:4)

5. Who is my mother? Who are my brothers? (Matt 12:48)

6. Why did you doubt? (Matt 14:31)

7. How many loaves do you have? (Matt 15:34)

8. Do you not yet understand? (Matt 16:8)

9. But who do you say that I am? (Matt 16:15)

10. What profit is there for one to gain the whole world and forfeit his life? (Matt 16:26)

11. Can you drink the cup that I am going to drink? (Matt 20:22)

12. What do you want me to do for you? (Matt 20:32)

13. Did you never read the scriptures? (Matt 21:42)

14. Why are you testing me? (Matt 22:18)

15. Could you not watch for me one brief hour? (Matt 26:40)

16. Why were you looking for me? (Luke 2:49)

17. What are you thinking in your hearts? (Luke 5:22)

18. Why do you call me "Lord, Lord" and not do what I command? (Luke 6:46)

19. Where is your faith? (Luke 8:25)

20. What is your name? (Luke 8:30)

21. Who touched me? (Luke 8:45)

22. Do you want to be well? (John 5:6)

23. Do you love me? (John 21:16)

What About You?
1. Which of these pique your interest or your curiosity? You might put a check mark by those. What about these questions intrigues you?

2. Later, after you've thought about those questions, go back through them again and choose the five that interest you most. Mark them with a star or in some way that stands out for you. What makes these questions compelling?

4. Read through the list again and put an x by the ones that do not pique your interest. Why are these less interesting?

5. As you focus on your five questions, follow this plan.

• Rank the five in the order of your interest, with number 1 being the most; then read the Scripture context. What additional insight does the context give you?

• Imagine that Jesus is asking you that question today. How does that feel?

• Why did you chose that question?

• What do you think your answer to Jesus would be?

6. Consider working through these questions by writing your responses in a journal. Remember that we are transformed from the inside out, and sometimes the process takes time.

Do you have questions that you would like to ask God? Are there questions that no one has been able to answer to your satisfaction? Do some of Jesus' questions disturb you? Perhaps you have an answer that you would give to one of his questions, but you feel that it's not an appropriate answer. Maybe you even feel that your answers to Jesus' questions might displease him.

I've come to believe that some of my questions are given to me to keep me asking, seeking, and knocking and to keep me on the journey of faith. Sometimes I want to know the answer to something so much that I feel as if I will die if I cannot know the answer. But if we know all the answers, we don't need faith, do we?

Faith frees us to live into the questions and live with the questions. Faith keeps our minds and hearts, eyes and ears awake to the "faint whispers" of God's grace (Job 26:14).

Have patience with everything unresolved in your heart and try to love the questions themselves as if they were locked rooms or books written in a very foreign language. Don't search for the answers, which could not be given to you now, because you would not be able to live them. And the point is to live everything. Live the questions now. Perhaps then, someday far in the future, you will gradually, without even noticing it, live your way into the answer.

—Rainer Maria Rilke,
from *Letters to a Young Poet*[14]

Chapter 8

Meeting Jesus the Healer

Sometimes I am like the father who asked Jesus to heal his son. "I do believe," the distressed father said. "Help me overcome my unbelief." (Mark 9:24)

Sometimes I am like the woman who knows that if she can touch the hem of Jesus' garment, she will be healed (John 8:40-48). I have experienced inner healing of my mind, heart, and soul by reaching out to the Spirit of God in Centering Prayer and continuing to ask, seek, and knock on the heart of God for help and comfort and guidance. I know that the Spirit of God/the Living Christ works miracles in the inner kingdom of an open and available life.

Sometimes I am like the man Jesus healed of spiritual blindness. The man said to Jesus, "Lord, I believe," and then the man worshiped Jesus (John 9:35-41).

I want to believe in miracles. In fact, I do believe in miracles. I am confident, however, that it is not up to me to order God around about when to work a miracle. I stand before the Mystery with too much awe to presume that I can dictate to God how and when and in what measure God should work in a way that can be called "a miracle."

I also must confess that I am suspicious of those who make a lot of money and call attention to themselves, preying on those who are desperate for physical healing. I can ask for a miracle for healing, but I am compelled to leave the specifics of that miracle and the healing up to God. I am careful about how I talk about the work of the Almighty in creation. When I do experience a miracle, I hope to have the sight and sense to recognize it as a breakthrough of the supernatural power of God in everyday life.

I believe that God works in mysterious ways, and I believe that God is at work in creation and in and through human beings. I suspect that God would be able to work more freely if we humans were more open and cooperative with what God wants to do.

God did not create us as puppets. Instead, God dignified and burdened us with the power to choose, and some of us grapple mightily with our stubborn wills. We can cause ourselves and others difficulty and trouble when we choose to exercise our freedom.

Miracles are a retelling in small letters of the very same story which is written across the whole world in letters too large for some of us to see.

—C. S. Lewis

Something happened, and now I know . . . . He touched me and made me whole.

—Bill Gaither

The miracles of the church seem to me to rest not so much upon faces or voices or healing power coming suddenly near to us from afar off, but upon our perceptions being made finer, so that for a moment our eyes can see and our ears can hear what is there about us always.

—Willa Cather

I take the miracles Jesus performed in his earthly ministry just as they are recorded in the Gospels. I would rather spend my time drawing near to the Spirit of Christ and allowing that Spirit to work freely in my mind, heart, and will than debating over whether the miracles Jesus performed happened as written. I take Jesus' miracles at face value, but I also know that it won't make much difference if Jesus walked on water and calmed a storm for the disciples if I don't allow him to walk across the troubled waters of my inner life and calm the storm raging within me.

I love the stories of the miracles Jesus performed in the first century, but they remain as history lessons unless I allow the Spirit of the Living Christ to multiply what I give him for the good of others, just as he multiplied the loaves and fishes the little boy gave him the day the crowds gathered around him (John 6).

Jesus performed two kinds of miracles. In some of them, he changed one physical substance into something else or asserted his power over the forces of nature. In other situations, Jesus healed people.

On the next page are lists of the healing miracles Jesus performed. Before you study the individual miracles more deeply, consider the following questions.

What About You?

1. What do you think about the miracles of Jesus? What do you want to believe about those miracles?

2. Does your belief or lack of belief in the healing power of Jesus today limit your life in any way? Do you believe that your faith or lack of faith limits God and God's work?

3. What is the difference between believing in *miracles* and believing in *magical thinking*?

I believe that Jesus everything the Bible says he did; just because I don't understand how he did them doesn't mean he didn't do them. I believe that Jesus had a depth of understanding of the laws of nature that we don't have, and he was therefore able to work with those laws in supernatural ways.

For those who are willing to make an effort, great miracles and wonderful treasures are in store.
—Isaac Bashevis Singer

After all, I don't see why I am always asking for private, individual, selfish miracles when every year there are miracles like white dogwood.
—Anne Morrow Lindberg

Healing Miracles of Jesus

The Miracle	Matthew	Mark	Luke	John
Official's son				4:46-54
Possessed man		1:21-27	4:33-37	
Peter's mother-in-law	8:14-15	1:29-31	4:38-39	
Many at sunset	8:16-17	1:32-39	4:40-41	
Leper	8:1-4	1:40-45	5:12-15	
Paralytic	9:1-8	2:1-12	5:18-26	
Man at Bethesda				5:1-17
Withered hand	12:9-13	3:1-6	6:6-11	
Crowd in Galilee	4:23-25			
Centurion's son	8:5-13		7:1-10	
Widow's son			7:11-17	
Two demoniacs	8:28-34	5:1-20	8:26-39	
Jairus's daughter-1	9:18-19	5:22-24	8:41-42	
Unclean woman	9:20-22	5:24-34	8:49-56	
Jairus's daughter-2	9:23-26	5:35-43	8:49-56	
Two blind men	9:27-31			
Mute man	9:32-34			
Touching clothes	14:34-36	6:53-56		
Crowd in Galilee	9:35			
Few in Nazareth		6:1-6		
Gentile's daughter	15:21-28	7:24-30		
Deaf man		7:31-37		
Multitude	15:29-31			
Epileptic boy	17:14-21	9:14-29	9:37-42	
Blind man				9:1-41
Blind/mute man	12:22-24		11:14-15	
Man of Bethsaida		8:22-26		
Stooped woman			13:10-17	
Man with dropsy			14:1-16	
Lazarus raised				11:1-45
Ten lepers			17:11-19	
Crowds in Judea	19:1-2			
Bartimaeus	20:29-34	10:46-52	18:35-43	
Many in Jerusalem	21:14			
Ear of Malchus			22:47-53	18:10-11
Resurrection	28:1-10	16:1-20	24:1-53	20:1-31

Exploring the Scriptures

Read Mark 5:21-43 (also recorded in Matt 9:18-26 and Luke 8:41-56).[15]

1. What *questions* are asked in this story?

2. What is Jesus' attitude toward Jairus and toward the woman in the crowd?

3. What does his sensitivity to the woman who touched him tell you about Jesus?

4. With which character in this story do you most easily identify?

5. How is this incident relevant for us today?

Read Mark 5:1-20 (also recorded in Matt 8:28-34 and Luke 8:26-37).[16]

6. There are two important questions asked in this passage. What are they?

7. Why is Jesus' question to the demoniac so crucial in this story?

8. In today's world, who would "the demon-possessed man" be?

9. Why were the people so upset when Jesus cast the demons into the swine?

10. What does this incident say about Jesus' priorities?

11. How is this incident relevant for us today?

Read John 5:1-15.[17]
12. Jesus' question to this particular man is life changing. Why do you think he asked it?

13. The man obviously had a physical problem. What was his deeper problem?

14. Jesus was direct with this man, telling him what to do. Why do you think he took that approach with him?

15. Do you think the man considered not obeying Jesus' command to him?

16. How is this incident relevant for us today?

Read Mark 2:1-12 (also found in Matthew 9:1-8 and Luke 5:17-26).[18]

17. The Pharisees' questions indicate a conflict between Jesus and "the establishment" that continues until the crucifixion. Why do you think the Pharisees cared more about the law than the person?

18. How did Jesus know what the Pharisees were thinking?

19. Given their narrow point of view, could they have truly answered Jesus' question?

20. What does the friends' compassion teach us about caring for others?

21. How is this incident relevant for us today?

22. We do not have direct access to the human Jesus and his healing touch. What do you think about his healing miracles as recorded in the Bible? Are they simply nice stories about amazing things that happened in history, or is there some relevance for us today? If so, what is the relevance?

23. How do some people today distort the issues of healing and physical miracles? How do some people misuse Jesus' name in relation to people either getting well or dying from illness or injury? How might their actions diminish the authentic power of a personal relationship with the Living Christ?

24. Given the historical accounts of Jesus' healing miracles as well as the ways some people distort them today, how can we as believers pray for healing? How have you seen God respond to such prayers?

For Your Eyes Only
25. Which of Jesus' healing stories affects you most deeply? Why?

26. If you could ask the Living Christ to heal one aspect of your life, what would it be?

27. If there is something in your life that is not likely to change, how might the *acceptance* of that aspect be a form of healing?

28. Carl Jung said that many of our problems are never solved, but we can learn to live with them in a new way. How does that resonate with you? Is it liberating or depressing?

29. From the point of view of the Living Christ, which may or may not be the same as your point of view, what do you think he would like to heal in you?

In Jesus' encounters with individuals as recorded in the four Gospels, he affected each person's life in the specific way that person needed: whether healing, transformation, liberation, or empowerment. To lift these stories out of the pages of the Bible and make them relevant to your life today, spend a few days with each story, making it yours by imagining yourself as one of the characters. Here are some steps that may help you:

1. Go through all the characters in the story, including the character of "the crowd" or "one of the disciples," imagining what it was like to be in that setting. Picture the surroundings. Imagine the sights, sounds, aromas, tastes, or sensations on your skin that the persons might have experienced.

Imagine what it was like to look into Jesus' eyes. How does he look at you? What is the expression in his eyes? What does his voice sound like? How do you feel, up close and personal with him?

Also try to imagine what it was like to be Jesus in each setting.

2. Now write about the story and your imaginings. What new thoughts have come to you? What might the Living Christ be doing in your life today?

3. Take the story with you throughout your day. When you return to it, what else does it say or mean?

4. Ask God to reveal something to you about yourself and something about God through this story. What might those revelations be?

Chapter 9

Meeting Jesus the Liberator

When I was a little girl, I walked into the auditorium of a large conference center with my mother just prior to a gathering of women from all over the state of New Mexico. Across the front of the auditorium was a large banner, emblazoned with the words, "Jesus Is the Answer."

Out of my mouth popped the words, "Well, what's the question?"

My mother had a highly developed skill. She could continue carrying on a conversation with the adults in front of her while at the same time pinching the tender flesh on the back of my arm. As she carried out this torture, she smiled as if she were perfectly poised and in control.

I would love to think that the words that popped out of my mouth were evidence that I had an unusually developed spirituality for a child my age, or that I was precocious, but most likely I was speaking out of a child's innocence. The way my mother pinched me, you would have thought that I was a smart-mouth kid!

I have never forgotten either my mother's pinch or my response to the banner over the front of that auditorium, and frankly, my resistance to simplistic bromides and pithy proclamations about the Holy One has remained strong.

I was brought up to view what is sacred carefully and with reverence. As a tender and impressionable little girl, I heard the story of my father's dramatic and life-changing conversion experience, and I heard him plead with others to give their hearts to Christ. I also heard him preach about the power of being saved from what separates us *from* God and the power of being saved *for* freedom in Christ.

Later, when I was a college student, I read *The Cost of Discipleship* by Dietrich Bonhoeffer, and I learned the difference between cheap grace and costly grace. All of that and much more in my heritage and history made a profound impression on me.

Indeed, our freedom in Christ is a free gift of grace, but it is a costly gift. We have been granted freedom, both from what binds us and for the abundant life, but freedom isn't easy, and the way of Christ costs us. Freedom in Christ isn't a license to keep doing what

So if the Son sets you free, you will be free indeed. (John 8:36)

Now the Lord is the Spirit, and where the Spirit of the Lord is, there is freedom. (2 Cor 3:17)

we've always done, and it carries with it both the gift of abundant life and the burden of responsibility.

There is freedom in Christ, but it is also true that there is no easy walk to freedom. Some people within the religious world forget the cost of freedom and want to make our freedom easy, like entertainment.

I think about the people Jesus healed and liberated. Each of them had to return to their lives and live out their liberation in the context of family and friends. Even if Jesus liberates you, you have to live out your freedom.

What About You?

1. What does it mean to be "free in Christ"?

2. If Jesus saves us/liberates us, from what are we liberated?

3. If Jesus saves us/liberates us, for what are we set free?

4. From what character defect, burden, responsibility, or memory would you like to be freed?

5. Is what binds you the result of your own choices, or is it the result of others' choices?

6. What would "freedom in Christ" look like for you in daily life?

It is for freedom that Christ has set us free. Stand firm, then, and do not let yourselves be burdened again by a yoke of slavery.
(Gal 5:1)

Exploring the Scriptures
Read John 8:1-11.[19]

1. Where was Jesus right before his encounter with the woman who was caught in adultery? Why does John want us to know where he had been?

2. What is significant about the fact that the action in this event takes place in "the temple courts"?

3. Where was the man or men who had also been "caught in adultery"?

4. Why do you think this story has been told as the story of the "woman caught in adultery"?

5. How do you think the human Jesus could tell the difference between a question asked by a true seeker and a question asked by someone trying to trap him?

6. What did Jesus ask the woman? Why do you think he asked her that question?

7. How hard do you think it was for the woman to leave her life of sin?

8. How would you say Jesus defines sin?

9. Why did Jesus put compassion above following the law?

10. From what was this woman freed? For what was she freed?

Read John 11:1-44.[20]
11. Why did Jesus not go straight to his friend Lazarus when he heard that he was sick?

12. Why do you think Mary and Martha felt free to chastise Jesus for not coming sooner?

13. What do Jesus' tears tell you about him (v. 35)?

14. What does his weeping tell you about the nature of God?

15. What purpose does Jesus' prayer of thanksgiving serve in verses 41-42?

16. How did other people participate in this liberating miracle Jesus performed?

17. From what was Lazarus liberated? For what was he liberated?

For Your Eyes Only
18. Is there a part of your life in which you feel bound by something? What is that like for you?

19. Is there something in your life that needs to be forgiven? What would it take for you to feel forgiven?

20. Which definition of sin comes closest to your idea of sin? Why?
• breaking one of God's laws
• separation from God
• messing up
• missing the mark
• doing something really bad
• falling short of God's standards

21. What is the difference between true guilt and false guilt?

22. Thomas Keating says that if we still feel guilty or ashamed ten minutes after confessing our sins, we are confessing to the wrong god. What do you think about that?

23. How could the Living Christ liberate you today? From what? For what?

24. Read Galatians 5:1, 13-15. What does it mean to be "free"?

25. To apply the story to our lives, we might interpret Lazarus's death wrappings in one of the following ways:
• other peoples' unrealistic expectations
• failures, mistakes, losses
• fears
• guilt and shame
• defense mechanisms
• character defects
• prejudices and biases
• anger or hate
• flawed and false self-image
• one's unrealistic expectations of oneself

Which of those death wrappings has you in its grips?

26. Describe a time in your life when you experienced God's liberating mercy, grace, love, and peace. What was that like for you?

27. How would you describe to a friend what it means to be "free in Christ"?

28. What do you think it means to be "free from the law"?

Through many dangers, toils and snares
I have already come
'Twas grace that brought me safe thus far,
And grace will lead me home.

—John Newton,
from "Amazing Grace"

Chapter 10

Meeting the Transforming Jesus

. . . be transformed by the renewing of your mind. (Rom 12:2b)

And we, who with unveiled faces all reflect the Lord's glory, are being transformed into his likeness with every-increasing glory, which comes from the Lord, who is the Spirit. (2 Cor 3:18)

Many elements contribute to the spiritual formation of a human being. We are shaped and formed by our earliest care givers, experiences that either help or hinder us, others' influences and teachings, and the opportunities we either have or don't have, for whatever reason. For some, the elements that form our faith are positive and life giving; for others, these elements crush ours spirits, making faith hard.

Anyone who contributes to the religious education of a child has a powerful impact on the formation of faith, but whatever the child's religious upbringing (or lack of it), most people get to midlife by conforming to the outer world's instructions, doctrines, rules, and rituals. At some point in a person's life, generally at midlife though not always, she gets an opportunity—through a hunger, a crisis, an awakening, or an event—that has the potential to reform and transform her.

It is significant that Jesus performed his first miracle at a wedding, transforming the common, ordinary element of water into something that sparkles—wine (John 2). That first miracle is highly symbolic for those of us who attempt to follow Jesus.

That same power in Jesus seems to be available to us through open and receptive prayer. It is a transforming power that has the potential to change us from the inside out. True and lasting change always happens at the deepest level, and that seems to be where the Living Christ works best, operating like the life force works invisibly within a bud to produce a flower.

Years ago, I discovered a Scripture that gave me hope in a dark time. I memorized Romans 8:11 in the translation I had, which was the New International Version. I like it as well in Eugene Peterson's *The Message*:

> It stands to reason, doesn't it, that if the alive-and-present God who raised Jesus from the dead moves into your life, he'll do the same thing in you that he did in Jesus, bringing you alive to himself? When God lives and breathes in you (and he does, as surely

as he did in Jesus), you are delivered from that dead life. With his Spirit living in you, your body will be as alive as Christ's!

I have learned that when I am able to surrender what is insufficient, inadequate, damaged, or wounding to the Living Christ, he can take what I have given him and work within me either to transform what I have surrendered to him or to transform me.

Transformation happens when we change our minds, when our hearts are changed, or when our stubborn wills soften enough for change to happen. Transformation can happen in an instant, but my experience tells me that for most of us, it happens step by step, over time.

For example, in the life of Nicodemus, as explored in the following Scripture, the change in his life began with his approaching Jesus by night, and we can wonder what it was that made him seek out Jesus and what it was that made him go by cover of night.

Was it curiosity that led Nicodemus to Jesus? Was he trying to check him out for the religious authorities, or was there a hunger in him that drove him out into the night to Jesus? Had he come to something like a mid-life crisis that was causing him to wrestle with his religious practices and spiritual realities? Did he want something more than he had? Who, having gone through mid-life, whenever that passage occurs, doesn't understand the words of Dante Alighieri in *The Divine Comedy*: "In the middle of our life's journey /I found myself in a dark wood, /having lost the way."

Being transformed—changed from within—often begins in the middle of a dark night of the soul, a dark time in your life or a time when you feel that you have lost your way.

The cover of night has always fascinated me. Of course, there could be an explanation so simple as the fact that at nightfall, he was finally finished with his day's work, but it seems more likely that it was easier for him to go under the cloak of darkness to check out the new and troubling rabbi than it was for him to go in the daylight, exposing himself to possible censure or criticism by his family or the religious authorities.

Whatever the reason for Nicodemus's night journey to Jesus, we can see that transformation often brings us out of the dark and into the light. We are usually satisfied with where we are and how we are until, for whatever reason, we find ourselves "in the dark" and yearning for light.

In my experience, transformation begins with an event. In the instances in the Scriptures in this chapter, transformation began when each individual encountered Jesus.

Then, each one was changed over time. As that encounter with Jesus and integrating his teachings into daily life unfolded within the person, transformation happened.

Often, too, transformation unfolds as the new understanding of oneself and God are in dialogue with one's old thoughts, habits, behaviors. Sometimes, transformation requires several wrestling matches with God—often in the middle of what I call "night school"—and like Jacob wrestling with the angel, there's often some wounding that happens with the wrestling.

Exploring the Scriptures
Read John 3:1-21.[21]

1. Why do you think Nicodemus went to Jesus under the cover of darkness?

2. What evidence of *faith* do you see in Nicodemus?

3. Were the questions Nicodemus asked Jesus true seeking questions, or was he trying to trap Jesus? Explain your response.

4. What did being "born again" mean to Nicodemus?

5. What do you think Jesus' definition of being "born again" was/is?

6. In simple terms, what did it mean for Nicodemus to be born again? What would that decision have cost him?

7. Read John 7:50-52 and John 19:38-42. Though the Gospel writer doesn't tell how Nicodemus responded to Jesus' words in that nighttime visit, what conclusions can you draw about his response to Jesus, based on these two references?

8. How would you say that being "born again" and "being transformed" are synonymous? What outer evidence might indicate that this miracle has happened to a person?

9. How is the term "born again" sometimes trivialized and weakened in today's world?

10. Do you think that Nicodemus went to Jesus because he was spiritually searching, or was he simply curious about Jesus?

11. How do you think Nicodemus was transformed?

12. Read John 19:38-42. What do you think happened to Nicodemus between the after-dark visit with Jesus and this event?

In the transformation process that occurred within Thomas, often called Doubting Thomas, change began with a powerful experience with the resurrected Christ who met Thomas the point of his need. By making his wounds visible and tangible to Thomas, the resurrected Christ must surely have astounded Thomas, shocking him by his vulnerability and with his availability.

Often, the Living Christ grants people who are new on the journey of faith special occurrences and unusual experiences that inspire and activate imagination, courage and faith. Later, when there are the necessary periods of testing, it is common to long for the kinds of experiences that first jarred us out of our old ways of being and inspired us into the new journey of transformation.

Keith Hosey, my great teacher, often cautioned against getting too attached to a mystical experience that occurred early in one's journey. The masters in the spiritual life know that the dark nights of the soul and the times when it feels as if "nothing is happening" are necessary events in the life of faith.

Read John 20:24-31.[22]

13. Why do you think the resurrected Christ appeared to the disciples?

14. Was there something wrong with Thomas's insistence on evidence that Jesus had risen?

15. Do you think that the Living Christ accommodates himself to our particular needs today?

16. What is the difference between honest doubts/questions and cynicism/skepticism?

17. Thomas changed within. How do you think that felt to him?

18. Was the transformation in Thomas from doubter to believer accomplished through a change of mind or a change of heart?

19. What do you think is the meaning of the term "wounded healer"? Why can someone who has been wounded be such a powerful healer?

20. How was Thomas transformed? How did what Jesus did for him "save" him?

There is no question that Mary Magdalene experienced a radical transformation when she met Jesus. However, another transformation has occurred for Mary Magdalene in the collective consciousness since people have awakened to the realization that there are no grounds for labeling Mary Magdalene a "prostitute"! Sometimes transformation happens in the ways in which people see, and sometimes, seeing correctly evolves over time—even thirteen centuries!

Read John 20:1-18.[23]
21. Why do you think Mary Magdalene stayed at the tomb?

22. In the sixth century, Pope Gregory labeled Mary Magdalene a prostitute when he couldn't figure out the differences among the many "Marys" in the Gospels. He simply conflated them all,

decided that the demons Jesus cast out of Mary Magdalene were sexual, and deemed her a prostitute! Why do you think that label stuck?

23. Why do you think Jesus chose to appear first to Mary Magdalene after the resurrection? How was she transformed by her encounter with Jesus at the empty tomb?

24. There is evidence that Jesus healed Mary Magdalene (see Luke 8:2). Obviously, his power in her life was transforming, or he would not have entrusted her with the task of taking the news of his resurrection to the disciples. How did Jesus liberate her? How did he empower her?

25. Mary Magdalene was transformed by her relationship with Jesus. Complete this sentence by filling in the blanks: Mary Magdalene was transformed from her life as a _____ to a life as a _____.

26. How is Mary Magdalene still being transformed today?

For Your Eyes Only
27. Is there a part of you that is like Nicodemus? When does that part of you "show up" in your everyday life?

28. What does it mean in your personal life for you to be "born again"?

29. Is it possible that a person can have many "new births" and "rebirths"? Explain.

30. Do you think people are transformed all at once or over time? What has been your experience of transformation?

31. If the Living Christ could transform one thing about your current life, what would it be?

32. What doubts do you have about whether or not the Living Christ is still alive and active in the world or in your life today?

33. What would it take for you to access the power of transformation in your life?

34. What is the difference between "putting God to the test" and asking for some kind of evidence that God is near, God is active, and God cares about you?

35. With which of the characters in these stories do you most closely identify? Why?

36. What part of you is like Thomas, who needs proof in order to believe?

37. What part of you is like Mary Magdalene, needing to be freed from some chains that are holding you hostage? What label do you need to remove from yourself?

Chapter 11

Meeting the Empowering Jesus

What is power, anyway? What kinds of power are there?

The dictionary says that to *empower* someone is to grant or give them authority or power. My mind quickly offers all kinds of examples of power that human beings have, either because they are born with that power or they gain it by learning, growing, achieving, or acquiring. Some people assume power, acting as if they have it or "faking it until they make it."

Are you comfortable talking about the kinds of power you have? Why or why not?

There is financial power, certainly, and it can open doors for people. There's the power that comes from position, family, natural gifts or attributes, and opportunity. There is earned power, gained from education or experience, and there is personal power that some people have naturally and some try to mimic, such as personality, temperament, or seductive abilities.

In what settings do you feel most powerful? What power do you have over other people? In what setting do you feel powerless? Who has power over you? How does that affect your daily life?

There is power gone awry, misplaced and misused power. There is the corruption of power, the abuse of power, and the problem of overpowering others. Some know what it is like to be powerless, and a reflective observation of human history reveals that the cycles of power repeat, so that those who are in power for a period are over-thrown by the powerless, who have become powerful by ways that are often violent and destructive.

Are you aware when another person is overpowering you? How do you react? Are you aware when you misuse your own power or when you use more or less power than the situation demands?

There is the power of genius and the power that comes from developing your talents, and there is the spiritual power that Jesus breathed into his disciples, a power that gave them the ability to act on his behalf, in his character, and under his will.

Are you ever afraid of your own power? Do you back away from the responsibility of owning your own power? Do you prefer for

> You will receive power when the Holy Spirit comes on you . . . . (Acts 1:8)

> dunamis—the mighty and miraculous power of God at work in creation, through individuals

> I am not ashamed of the gospel, because it is the power of God for the salvation for everyone who believes . . . . (Rom 1:16)

Jesus . . . breathed on them and said, "Receive the Holy Spirit." (John 20:22)

Sometimes our light goes out, but is blown again into instant flame by an encounter with another human being. Each of us owes the deepest thanks to those who have rekindled this inner light.

—Albert Schweitzer

others to take the lead in your life, or do you feel comfortable owning your life, your power, and your choices?

Jesus, as God, empowered other people to become more than they knew they could be. Jesus saw what was lying dormant or unrecognized in others, and, through his actions toward them, he changed their lives, empowering them to do what they never dreamed they could do.

When Jesus breathed on the disciples so that they received the Holy Spirit, he gave them the power that would change them, and then, as they engaged with other people, the same inner power that came from the Source was available to change others.

Jesus gave others something that empowered them from within.

Perhaps you have had the experience of being empowered to do something you never imagined you could do. Perhaps someone—a human instrument—saw something in you that you couldn't see and inspired you to do what you didn't know you could do.

Who has empowered you in your life? Do you believe that the person was an instrument of God's grace, mediating power and empowerment to you?

Albert Schweitzer said, "Sometimes our light goes out, but is blown again into instant flame by an encounter with another human being. Each of us owes the deepest thanks to those who have rekindled this inner light."

Most likely, you recall someone who has empowered you to be more than you knew you could be. Perhaps it was a teacher or a friend, a parent, grandparent or an aunt or uncle who saw the potential in you before you did and through encouragement or by providing either an opportunity or financial provision, empowered you to access your giftedness, discover a talent, develop a natural skill or simply believe in yourself.

Paradoxically, in the fascinating economy of life, God sometimes works through difficulties, tragedies or inadequacies to strengthen and empower a person to be and become far more than his or her circumstances would normally have provided. It is interesting to observe how for some people, hardship makes for strength and uncommon courage, while others buckle under their fate or give up into a life of bitterness.

I've often wondered how it was that Jesus seemed to know how to empower people, and how many missed the gift of his empowerment because of any number of excuses.

Exploring the Scriptures

Read Matthew 16:13-20 (also recorded in Mark 8:27-29 and Luke 9:18-20).

1. What did Jesus sense in Simon Peter that caused him to say what he did in verses 17-19?

2. What do you think Simon Peter felt when he heard those words from Jesus?

3. What was going on within Simon Peter, the fisherman, that made him realize who Jesus was?

Read Matthew 26:31-35 (also recorded in Mark 14:27-31 and Luke 22:33-34).

4. What was it about Peter that made Jesus predict Peter's betrayal of him?

5. Did Jesus make a mistake earlier when he gave Peter such power?

Read Matthew 26:69-75 (also recorded in Mark 14:66-72; Luke 22:53-62; and John 18:16-25, 27).

6. After what had happened in Peter and to him, why did he betray Jesus?

7. How do you think Jesus felt, knowing what Peter had done?

Read John 21:15-25.
8. Why do you think Jesus gave Peter another chance?

9. Jesus admonished Peter to love his sheep and tend his lambs. What does this mean?

10. Exactly what power did Jesus give Peter?

11. What happens when power takes over in any person, any institution, any relationship?

Read John 4:1-42.
12. Why did Jesus initiate a conversation with this woman, given the restrictions about a Jew talking to a Samaritan and a man talking to a woman?

13. What was it about her that made him move into an intellectual discussion of theology?

14. What changed this woman's perspective?

15. Why don't we know her name?

16. How did Jesus empower this woman?

17. What do you think about the fact that she, this nameless woman, had so much influence within her community?

18. What do you think about the fact that this woman has been called "the first evangelist"?

For Your Eyes Only
19. When you think about *power*, what reactions do you have?

20. What kinds of power do you have in your own life? What kinds do you lack?

21. In what ways does a relationship with the Living Christ *empower* a person today?

22. How is being forgiven *empowering*?

23. What is the difference between spiritual power and the power we see wielded in the world?

24. When have you felt the *dunamis*/power of God working in you, for you, through you?

25. What part of Jesus' ministry calls to you at this time in your life? What do you most need from him—his healing, liberating, transforming, or empowering power?

Part Three

Meeting Jesus the Teacher

Introduction

The life of the human Jesus was formed—spiritually, emotionally, physically, and relationally—within the context of his family and the Jewish culture of his day. His religious culture was shaped by a heavy emphasis on teaching, and rabbis oversaw much of his religious education. The teachings included conversations about the weighty matters of the law, the rituals and traditions, and of course the nature of God.

Jesus seemed to be a natural teacher, teaching both by words and by what he did. He let his life speak, and those who had eyes to see and ears to hear could learn the wisdom of God through him. Jesus spoke to the crowds and also mentored his disciples, initiating them personally into the ways of God. He was particularly transparent with his inner circle, revealing to them the deepest truths about God and himself. He taught in different settings, such as a mountaintop or by a lake; nature often provided his classroom.

The teaching methods Jesus used matched the message and the learners. He was a masterful teacher, knowing when to engage the left brain through discourses and when to engage the right brain, activating his listeners' imaginations with parables, aphorisms, and allegories. Jesus didn't back away from difficult and complex issues, and sometimes he stunned people with his hard sayings.

If you consult a concordance under "truth," focusing on the Gospel citations, you may be astounded to see how many times Jesus said, "I tell you the truth." (In the King James Version, he says, "Verily, verily.") Jesus spoke with a confidence and poise that drew the crowds and honest seekers (the curious, the cautious, and the committed) and also threatened the religious leaders of his day who were accustomed to speaking for God.

If you grew up in Sunday school, you probably know the story of Jesus' staying in Jerusalem after the Passover feast when he was only twelve and worrying his parents, Mary and Joseph. When his parents found him *after three days*, he was sitting among the teachers in the temple courts, listening to them and asking them questions. "Everyone who heard him was amazed at his understanding and his answers," reports the Gospel writer Luke. (See Luke 2:41-51.) Everyone was amazed, but Jesus' parents had an understandable human reaction. No matter how smart that young boy was, and even if he was *Jesus*, he had the full human experience of a scolding from his mother! I love it that Luke includes this story in his account of Jesus' life.

The source of Jesus' authority in teaching was no less than God, his Father, and he was clear about that. Many times Jesus said, boldly and directly, "I tell you the truth," but he also emphasized repeatedly that "the Son can do nothing by himself; he can do only what he sees his Father doing because whatever the Father does the Son does also" (John 5:19).

John gives a window into the tender love relationship Jesus had with his heavenly Father in John 14:31, where Jesus says, ". . . but the world must learn that I love the Father and that I do exactly what my Father has commanded me." Always, Jesus pointed back to his Father as the source, revealing his humility and submission to God the Father. But Jesus' declaration that "I and the Father are one" (John 10:30), a revelation he made naturally and confidently because it was the truth, alarmed the religious leaders of his day, irritating and frustrating them and ultimately pushing them to condemn Jesus.

In his tender prayer at the end of his ministry, recorded in John 17, Jesus prays an astounding petition for his disciples and "for those who will believe": he asks ". . . that they may be one as we are one" (John 17:11b, 22b). It is an awe-inspiring idea that we, today, can be one with God as Jesus was one with God. Some people doubt that, and others shrink back from the challenge of it, but those who are willing to open their minds and hearts to that reality can find ultimate meaning and purpose in life. The reality of life with God and the possibility of an intimate, personal, vital, and dynamic love relationship with the Living Christ is what Jesus attempted to teach when he talked about the kingdom of God/heaven and how to enter it.

Jesus taught about who God was, attempting to correct the distortions people had about his heavenly Father and what life with God was all about. Jesus taught servant leadership, and he taught what it meant to be friends with him and with each other. By his actions and words, he taught the nature of authentic love that is possible in kingdom living. "Love one another as I have loved you," he told his disciples, reminding them that love was the evidence of their discipleship (John 15:12).

A disciple, by definition, is a "disciplined learner." Many of us want to rest on the idea of the security of the believer, which affirms that if we have accepted Christ as our personal savior, we will go to heaven when we die. If we are true followers of Jesus, there's much more than the afterlife, and that abundance is found in following the teachings of Jesus, apprenticing ourselves to the Living Christ, learning what Jesus taught, and then implementing the truths into our daily activities, our relationships, and our devotional lives. To be a disciplined learner of Jesus' teachings is one of the most exciting ventures available to us ordinary, everyday pilgrims.

In fact, the venture can transform our lives. It can heal us at a deep, spiritual level. Incorporating the teachings of Jesus into our minds and hearts can liberate us, and it can empower us to live the life we are intended to live, to be fully human and to be fully alive as never before.

What About You?

1. What is the difference between *fact* and *truth*? Give examples.

2. What did Jesus teach—fact or truth?

3. When might facts contradict truth?

4. What is required to believe facts?

Love one another as I have loved you. (John 15:12)

5. What is required to believe truth?

6. What is the difference between facts and a person's interpretation of facts?

7. What is the difference between *truth* and *opinion*?

8. What is the difference between truth and one's opinion of that truth?

9. What is the difference between *teaching* and *indoctrinating*; giving information and persuading; teaching facts and teaching people?

10. What is the definition of the word *education*? What is the etymology of the word?

11. What was Jesus' goal in his teaching?

Chapter 12

Meeting Jesus in the Parables

Expect to be disturbed when you read the parables of Jesus. Better yet, *hope* to be disturbed. Hope that the living truth at the core of the parables will penetrate your defenses, shake up your prejudices, and drive the blinders from your eyes so that you can see the activity of God right in front of you. Don't you love an adventure that won't leave you the same as you were when you started?

"In the long, quiet years of growing up in Nazareth, Jesus was given the task of reconciling the world back to a new understanding of the divine nature." With those words, my friend and teacher, beloved preacher, and priest John Claypool begins his popular book, *Stories Jesus Still Tells: The Parables.*[27] I am fascinated that John's title is in the present tense. He found that the parables Jesus told continue to convey the sparks of truth that light the way for us in the darkness. Claypool's comment may be gentler than Susan Colón's, but the truth remains: something as radical as Jesus' teachings had to be conveyed in a way that upset the status quo of thoughts and behaviors but also delivered in a way that would connect with his listeners' lived experience.

Jesus the teacher knew that a story using everyday, familiar images would engage the people's right brains, catch them off guard with a surprise or a startling metaphor, and perhaps shake up an old way of thinking. He wanted to open their minds and hearts to a new way of seeing the world, understanding God, and discerning the ways of God. Jesus needed a way to convey the power and reality of the kingdom of God to ordinary people, and the parable turned out to be the perfect vehicle for such a task.

Jesus spent those long growing-up years observing his parents as they went about their daily tasks. He observed the adults in his village who carried out their business and planted their crops. In those years, Jesus learned about how people seek for things that are lost, and he saw people struggle to find the balance between living their own lives and living within families and communities.

Schooled in the rabbinic tradition of the *midrash,* Jesus was accustomed to exploring one of the texts from the Torah or listening to a rabbi expound a scriptural text or one of the rabbinic parables.

The parables were oral events (and language events) delivered by a poetic prophet.
—C. F. Burney[24]

When a metaphor contains a radically new vision of world it gives absolutely no information until after the hearer has entered into it and experienced it from inside itself.
—John Dominic Crossan[25]

The parables of Jesus in the synoptic gospels upset the religious applecart, rearrange fixed categories of social and moral hierarchy, and provide puzzlement and sometimes fury. What is to be done with these stories that are homey yet alienating, foundational to Christianity yet persistently iconoclastic?
—Susan E. Colón[26]

Matthew, Mark, and Luke are called the "Synoptic Gospels." Synoptic means "to see with one eye." Those three Gospel accounts tell what Jesus did. Then John comes along and says, "And this is what it meant."

John used allegory, images, and symbols to communicate deep truths about Jesus' teachings; the other Gospel writers revealed those deep truths in the parables Jesus taught.

It was natural for him to speak about the divine using earthy and earth-bound stories and images.

Jesus observed that people had the wrong idea about who God was and what God was doing, and so he learned to tell simple, almost childlike stories to reboot their imaginations and clarify their vision. Jesus understood that if he told a story, the child in his listeners would understand the story, and he was clear that if they wanted to enter the kingdom of God, they had to become as little children. That is still true for us today. For some of us, it is a larger task than it is for others.

Generally, Jesus wanted to convey one central truth that was contained within his parable, but there was often more than one. When we read them today, sometimes their meanings are clear. At other times, we have to turn the stories over in our minds, as if we are examining a precious diamond with many facets. The truth contained within a parable may affect one person in a particular way, while another person has a completely different experience with it. All of us, however, can find meaning in the parables, and all of us may apply them in different ways.

On the next page is a list of the parables Jesus told. As you scan the list, consider choosing one that you will read every day for the next week. As you do that, continue to refer to the "What About You?" questions. Note whether your answers change or your understanding deepens. You may choose to read all the parables and then go back and choose your favorites, as I do at the end of this chapter. Whatever method you use, familiarize yourself with these stories. Integrate them into your everyday world, and see how your perspective shifts.

	Event	Matthew	Mark	Luke
1	The Growing Seed		Mk 4:26-29	
2	The Two Debtors			Lk 7:41-43
3	The Lamp under a Bushel	Mt 5:14-15	Mk 4:21-25	Lk 8:16-18
4	Parable of the Good Samaritan			Lk 10:30-37
5	The Friend at Night			Lk 11:5-8
6	The Rich Fool			Lk 12:16-21
7	The Wise and the Foolish Builders	Mt 7:24-27		Lk 6:46-49
8	New Wine into Old Wine-skins	Mt 9:17-17	Mk 2:21-22	Lk 5:37-39
9	Parable of the Strong Man	Mt 12:29-29	Mk 3:27-27	Lk 11:21-22
10	Parable of the Sower	Mt 13:3-9	Mk 4:3-9	Lk 8:5-8
11	The Tares	Mt 13:24-30		
12	The Barren Fig Tree			Lk 13:6-9
13	Parable of the Mustard Seed	Mt 13:31-32	Mk 4:30-32	Lk 13:18-19
14	The Leaven	Mt 13:33-33		Lk 13:20-21
15	Parable of the Pearl	Mt 13:44-46		
16	Drawing in the Net	Mt 13:47-50		
17	The Hidden Treasure	Mt 13:44-44		
18	Counting the Cost			Lk 14:28-33
19	The Lost Sheep	Mt 18:10-14		Lk 15:4-6
20	The Unforgiving Servant	Mt 18:23-35		
21	The Lost Coin			Lk 15:8-9
22	Parable of the Prodigal Son			Lk 15:11-32
23	The Unjust Steward			Lk 16:1-13
24	Rich Man and Lazarus			Lk 16:19-31
25	The Master and Servant			Lk 17:7-10
26	The Unjust Judge			Lk 18:1-9
27	Pharisees and the Publican			Lk 18:10-14
28	The Workers in the Vineyard	Mt 20:1-16		
29	The Two Sons	Mt 21:28-32		
30	The Wicked Husbandmen	Mt 21:33-41	Mk 12:1-9	Lk 20:9-16
31	The Great Banquet	Mt 22:1-14		Lk 14:15-24
32	The Budding Fig Tree	Mt 24:32-35	Mk 13:28-31	Lk 21:29-33
33	The Faithful Servant	Mt 24:42-51	Mk 13:34-37	Lk 12:35-48
34	The Ten Virgins	Mt 25:1-13		
35	The Talents or Minas	Mt 25:14-30		Lk 19:12-27
36	The Sheep and the Goats	Mt 25:31-46		
37	Parable of the Wedding Feast			Lk 14:7-14

What About You?

1. As you read a parable, analyze it as you would any short story. Use questions like these:

- What is the setting?

- To whom is the parable told?

- Who are the characters, or what are the items?

- What is the plot or the problem?

- What is unsettling about this story?

2. What is the central truth of this parable? What did Jesus want us to know?

3. What does this parable teach about God?

4. What does this parable reveal about living in the kingdom of God?

5. Does this parable show you anything about your own life?

Listed below are questions pertaining to my favorite parables. You may want to apply some of these questions to your favorite parables.

Exploring the Scriptures
Read Luke 15:11-31.[28]
1. Who does the father in the parable represent?

2. For which character do you have the most empathy? the least?

3. What do you think Jesus wanted us to know by telling this parable?

4. What does this parable teach about the nature of God?

Read Luke 15:1-10.

5. Why did Jesus make such a point about "lost things"—sheep, coins, sons?

6. What was Jesus trying to communicate about God's relationship with lost things?

7. How do you feel about the fact that Jesus gives so much meaning to what is lost?

8. Is there a part of yourself that you have lost? What would it take to find it?

Read Luke 10:25-37.

9. What two questions prompted Jesus' telling of this parable?

10. Who are the main characters in this parable?

11. What do you think is the *central truth* of this parable?

12. Which part would you play in this parable? Which part would you *want* to be?

13. What meaning does this parable have for your daily life?

Read Mark 4:26-34.
14. In these two parables, Jesus compares "the kingdom of heaven" to small things, using gardening and farming images. How does translate for contemporary city dwellers?

15. How would you apply this parable in your own life?

16. Why would Jesus compare something as enormous as the kingdom of God to small things?

Read Matthew 13:44-45.
17. What is the treasure in a field or the pearl of great value?

18. What is the central truth of this parable?

Because human beings spend the first part of life conforming and adapting to the outer world, to parents, peers and authorities figures, there is a neglect among most people of the True Self, the Self that is at the core of every human being. This isn't a bad thing; it's just the way we grow.

At some point, often at the mid-life passage, a crisis, a hunger or an awakening often is the catalyst for turning inward, seeking the inner kingdom where the True Self is discovered, accessed and honored. Sometimes that quest to be guided from within instead of living from the outside in requires a rigorous process of time, energy and money.

The pearl is often the symbol of the soul or the True Self, and it is the pearl of great price because the quest for it is costly.

For more about this, see my book *Joint Venture: Practical Spirituality for Everyday Pilgrims.*

19. Could the treasure in the field or the pearl of great price be your True Self? Explain.

Read Matthew 18:21-35.
20. Why did Jesus tell this parable?

21. What feelings does it evoke in you?

22. What is the central truth in this parable?

Read Matthew 20:1-16.
23. What do you like about this parable?

24. What do you not like?

25. What point is Jesus trying to make, and why?

For Your Eyes Only

26. Which of these parables spoke to you most?

27. Did any of them disturb you? If so, why?

28. Are these parables relevant to today's culture? Why or why not?

29. What did you learn about the kingdom of God in these parables?

Chapter 13

Meeting Jesus in the Sermons

"Preach the gospel always and, if necessary, use words."

Those words that are attributed to St. Francis of Assisi remind us that how we live is itself a sermon. What we do proclaims more loudly than our words what we really believe, and yet there are times when it is necessary to use words. Jesus was a master of knowing when and how to use words.

I am a third-generation minister's wife, and so I have heard many sermons in my lifetime. I've heard some that I still remember because the message was so profound and life changing. I've heard some that made me cringe for one reason or another, and I've heard some that left me feeling as if I had been standing (or sitting, most likely) on holy ground. I've also thought a lot about sermons, and I've reflected deeply on the human instruments who have delivered them. While I cannot ever say that I preach, I have stood behind my share of pulpits and delivered what I hope were proclamations of the love, joy, and peace of God.

Whatever your history with sermons and preachers, I invite you to think about your own experience. As you do, ponder this: during every sermon that is delivered, every person in the congregation is listening for what he wants to hear, censoring what he doesn't want to hear, and wanting to hear something entirely different from what the person on the pew in front of him wants to hear. It's tough to deliver a sermon, knowing that what you say may or may not be what people hear.

What About You?

1. What is the difference between a speech, a lecture, a sermon, and a sales pitch?

2. What is the real purpose of a sermon?

The sermon you enjoy most is not likely to be the one that will do you the most good.

—Anonymous

To be always relevant, you have to say things which are eternal.

—Simone Weil

3. What feelings are evoked by sermons?

4. When you hear a sermon that makes you uncomfortable, which is the most likely reason? What do you do when this happens?
- I disagree with the sermon.
- The topic makes me squirm.
- I don't understand what I heard.
- The message and the messenger don't match up.
- I don't like the way I feel when I leave.
- What I heard doesn't fit anything I've ever heard before.

5. When you hear a sermon, what do you want? Below are some possibilities; add others as necessary.
- I want to learn something new.
- I want to be inspired.
- I want to be encouraged.
- I want to see what I agree with and what I disagree with.
- I want practical tools for my everyday life.
- I want to feel closer to God, or at least be shown how to get there.
- I want to be shown how I can improve my life.
- I want to be made to feel guilty.
- I want to be shown how to experience forgiveness, mercy, grace, peace.
- I want to know how to experience the Living Christ and follow him.

While Jesus taught people in informal settings in which he told stories and used short statements to make profound points, he also taught in longer teachings, which scholars called *sermons* or *discourses.*

Matthew and John contain the primary discourses—sermons—of Jesus. If you have time, check out the parallel accounts that Mark and Luke give of Matthew's discourses. The author of Mark, the first written account of Jesus' life, was primarily interested in action, so he emphasized what Jesus did. Both Mark and Luke, however, contain portions of Jesus' discourses. Matthew, writing to Jewish readers, wanted to capture what Jesus taught. And John interpreted what Jesus did and wrote from a deeper, more mystical perspective.

Here is a list of Jesus' discourses in Matthew:

Matthew 5–7—The Sermon on the Mount (the most well-known discourse)
Matthew 10—The Mission Discourse
Matthew 13—Parables of the Kingdom of Heaven, or Parabolic Discourse
Matthew 18—Discourse on the Church
Matthew 23–25—Discourse on the End Times

Consider reading each discourse, noting what catches your attention, what disturbs you, or what surprises you. Pay attention to Jesus' audience as well. These questions can help you reflect.

Exploring the Scriptures
1. What in this sermon is relevant to today's culture?

2. What kinds of responses do you suppose Jesus evoked when he delivered these words?

3. What in the sermons could have gotten him in trouble with the religious leaders of his day?

Here is a list of Jesus' "Farewell Discourses" in John:

John 13
John 14
John 15
John 16
John 17

These questions can help you reflect on Jesus' words in John.

Exploring the Scriptures
1. What do you find most meaningful in these words of Jesus?

2. To whom did Jesus deliver these messages?

3. What is the difference between the discourses in Matthew and those in John in tone, intention, and meaning?

4. Which discourse gives you the most comfort?

5. In all of Jesus' sermons, what do you wish he had *not* said?

If you study Jesus' sermons, you can glean clear direction for formulating an ethical system that begins with an intimate relationship with him. He also offers guidance for how to relate to other people.

What About You?

From the lists of sermons, choose a portion and spend the next several days making it personal to you. Follow these steps.

1. Read the passage at least once a day.

2. Imagine what it would have been like to hear Jesus saying these words to you. How did his voice sound? What expressions did he make? Did he look you in the eye?

3. After reflecting, ask yourself these questions:
   • Now that I have spent time with this teaching, am I any different?

   • What behavior do I need to change?

   • Do I still want to be Jesus' follower?

4. Read and reflect on the following quotation. Write your response below or in your journal.

> The question should not be "What would Jesus do?" but rather, more dangerously, "What would Jesus have me do?" The onus is not on Jesus but on us, for Jesus did not come to ask semidivine human beings to do impossible things. He came to ask human beings to live up to their full humanity; he wants us to live in the full implication of our human gifts, and that is far more demanding. (Reverend Peter J. Gomes, *The Scandalous Gospel of Jesus*)

Chapter 14

Meeting Jesus in the Sermon on the Mount

It continues to astound and disturb me that the understanding of what it means to be a Christian is increasingly distorted in cultural and political discourse. Instead of calling myself a Christian now, I often say that I am attempting to be a follower of Christ. Eugene Peterson, beloved teacher and author of *The Message*, as well as a five-volume series on spiritual theology, refers to "the Jesus way." The great spiritual writer of the twentieth century, Thomas Merton, once described himself as "one loved by Christ." Our definitions and self-designations are important, for they reveal our reference point and our identity, all of which then reveal what we do and why we do it.

Indeed, following the Ten Commandments is a good thing. In fact, life in any culture goes best when those commandments are not merely nailed to a courtroom wall but inscribed within our hearts and lived out, naturally, in our everyday lives.

Matthew 5, 6, and 7 contain what we know as The Sermon on the Mount, in which Jesus gives his important teachings about what it means to live the Jesus way. Sometimes I ponder what the world might look like if, within my community of faith, we spent a year trying to internalize this magnificent sermon and incorporate its teachings into our daily lives.

If you go back to the Ten Commandments and, in fact, the Torah—the first five books of the Old Testament—you see that God sets boundaries and limits for the people to help them learn how to live in the covenant relationship God wanted to establish with them. At a particular stage in faith formation, all of us need to know the rules, the rituals, and the guidelines of our environment, our relationships with others, and our relationships with God. Those guidelines need to be straightforward and clear: do this and don't do that.

In the Sermon on the Mount, Jesus spoke to a people group who had lived under the law for centuries, and they had finally come to a place in their development when they were able to live the Jesus way.

Seek first his kingdom and his righteousness, and all these things will be given to you as well. (Matt 6:33)

The meteoric ascendancy of interest in spirituality in recent decades is largely fueled by a profound dissatisfaction with approaches to life that are either aridly rationalistic, consisting of definitions, explanations, diagrams and instructions . . . or impersonally functional, consisting of slogans, goals, incentives and programs . . . . There comes a time for most of us when we discover a deep desire within us to live from the heart what we already know in our heads and so with our hands.

—Eugene Peterson[29]

125

For further reading on The Sermon on the Mount:

• *Mount and Mountain, vol. 2: A Reverend and a Rabbi Talk About the Sermon on the Mount* by Michael Smith and Rami Shapiro (Smyth & Helwys Publishing, 2013)

• *The Ladder of the Beatitudes* by Jim Forest (Orbis Books, 1999)

• *The Sermon on the Mount: A Foundation for Understanding* by Robert A. Guelich (Word Books, 1982)

But then again, I may assume too much. Some of them were ready for the Jesus way, but some of them were not. It's like that today, isn't it?

And before I think that I'm ready for the Jesus way, but others might not be, I must confess that on some days, I want to live the Jesus way with all my heart. On other days, though, I get tired and discouraged, and I want what I want when I want it, like my four-year-old daughter.

Specific things about Jesus draw me to living the Jesus way. First, when I study the life of the human Jesus, I see utter authenticity. He is what he is—transparent, vulnerable, centered, and grounded in his purpose and mission in his earthly life. Second, the human Jesus has an intimacy with the Father that I crave. I believe we are intended to live in oneness with the Father. This is the source of Jesus' confidence, courage, wisdom, and love. Jesus also has the ability to be deeply intimate with his friends while still maintaining his own identity. He obviously loves deeply, and he loves with "giving love" instead of "needing love." Fourth, Jesus is fully in the moment. He is present to people and to what is going on when it is going on. Finally, Jesus lives what he teaches. His walk matches his talk.

Putting aside the divinity of Jesus for a moment, I have to say that the human Jesus draws me, compels me, and inspires me. In the terms of depth analysis, it has been said that the human Jesus is the symbol of the True Self. In other words, he shows us what it is like to be fully who one is and to do what one is sent here to do. In walking the Jesus way, we put ourselves on the holy path to becoming fully who we are intended to be.

The Sermon on the Mount, then, is filled with a description of how we can be followers of the way of Jesus. It does contain some strong directives, and if you return to the directives in chapter 3, "The Great Imperatives," you will find that many of them come from the Sermon on the Mount.

Chapter 15 offers an exploration of the Beatitudes, which are found at the beginning of the Sermon on the Mount, but in this chapter, I ask you to take a broad view of the entire sermon. Countless volumes have been written about the Sermon on the Mount. I hope you will seek out some of these writings to enhance your study. Above all, familiarize yourself with what Jesus actually said in the sermon. After all, none of us wants to get caught telling someone we are Christians simply *because we follow the Ten Commandments*!

Exploring the Scriptures

The Sermon on the Mount, recorded in Matthew 5, 6, and 7, contains some of Jesus' most important teachings, particularly those related to ethical and moral issues. We would expect Matthew, writing to the Jewish community, to record Jesus' teachings about such things.

Read Matthew 5:13-47.

1. In these verses, Jesus addresses difficult issues. Because it was his intent to free people from the bondage of legalism, it is important that we don't use these verses to create more laws, and yet reasonable laws are necessary for a civil society. Was Jesus speaking to anyone or specifically to followers of the Jesus' Way ?

2. Jesus taught about an *internal* relationship with God that will be *expressed* in the way human beings relate to and treat each other. What principles does he teach in these sections of Matthew 5?

   • 5:13-16

   • 5:17-20

   • 5:21-26

   • 5:27-30

   • 5:31-32

> The Sermon on the Mount is not about Morality. It is about Jesus.
> —Henri Nouwen[30]

• 5:33-37

• 5:38-42

• 5:43-48

3. Did anything you read in those passages disturb you?

Read Matthew 6.
4. Jesus teaches more important principles for living the abundant life in this chapter. As you read this chapter, what part of it inspires you? What part of it encourages you?

5. Matthew 6:33 is one of the most important verses in this chapter. In practical terms, what do you think it means to "seek first the kingdom of God"?

Read Matthew 7.
6. In Matthew 7:1-5, Jesus makes a bold statement about judgment. What are its implications in daily life?

7. Do you think verse 6 contradicts verses 1-5?

8. What does Jesus mean in verses 7-8? Have you ever tried this? Has it worked for you? If it hasn't, what do you think about Jesus' words here?

9. What is the narrow gate in verses 13-14?

10. How do you feel about what Jesus says in Matthew 7:15-23? What is the good news in these verses?

11. In Matthew 7:24-29, Jesus makes a connection between following him and building a house—a clearly understood visual image. Given all that he has said in this Sermon on the Mount, what is the solid foundation on which we are to build our lives?

For Your Eyes Only

12. What is the hardest part about this lesson for you?

13. If you could choose one part of these chapters to integrate into your daily life for this month or this year, what would you choose?

14. Do you believe that "the Christ-within," as the Apostle Paul expressed it, can help you live the "blessed" life described in the Sermon on the Mount? Explain.

Contained within the verses of this famous sermon is one of the great secrets of kingdom living that Jesus entrusted to his disciples and followers. In chapter 4 ("The Greatest Commandment"), there is an image of a cross. Note that in each of these cross images, the part of the Scripture that anchors the cross in the ground is the part about the primary relationship with Christ. The crossbeam, then, has to do with our relationship with others, the world, and ourselves. Remember that when we are grounded first in God—in God's presence, purpose, love, and power—then we are empowered and freed to love others as ourselves.

Let's visualize another cross with the words of Matthew 6:33. The "Seek first the kingdom of God and his righteousness" are written on the vertical beam of the cross, grounded firmly in the earth. On the horizontal crossbeam are the words, "and all these things will be added to you."

Here's one of the secrets of kingdom living: At the beginning of the day or a project, take a minute to "seek God first." When you are confused and don't know what to do, "seek God first." When you are out of sorts or feel alienated from God or others, do what you know to do to connect yourself with the presence of God, who is never disconnected from you. When you do that—when you seek God first—you are putting first things first.

All recovering people rely on this foundational slogan of Alcoholics Anonymous: "first things first." Once you have done that in a prayer of surrender, a prayer of abandonment to God, a prayer of intention, or a prayer of remembrance, then you are free to *trust God and do the next thing.*

Often, we think it's up to us to make ourselves holy or spiritual or sober, when in truth, it is God at work in us, bringing about good. Sometimes we flail away at our problems, trying to solve them, resolve conflicts, make things happen, and bring about our own miracles, when the secret to the abundant life is contained within Matthew 6:33.

Seek first the kingdom of God And all these things will be added to you

I carry on a debate with myself as to which one of my favorite imperatives comes first in my life. Since Jesus designated Matthew 22:37-39 as the greatest one, I'd better go with it as the most important, but it is my conviction, born out of life's experiences, choices, and mistakes, that Matthew 6:33 is a close second. If Jesus' teachings are like a brilliant multi-faceted diamond, perhaps these two teachings are so closely connected that it is hard to see one without the other. I do know this: following Matthew 6:33 is integral to keeping or following Jesus' other teachings, and I know that if I do not keep Matthew 22:37-39 uppermost in my consciousness, I have the tendency either to revert to rule keeping or to give up on following the Jesus way because, in my own power, it is too hard.

What About You?

1. From what you know so far, how would you define the "kingdom of God" Jesus talks about?

2. What kind of kingdom is it? How is it different from the kingdoms we inhabit on earth?

3. Practically, how does a person put the kingdom of God first? Is it an attitude we adopt? Are there behaviors, practices, and habits that go along with it? How does the statement "first things first" apply to seeking God's kingdom first?

4. Is following the teachings of Jesus too hard, given the imperfections in our lives?

5. How does the love of God, which we are to receive and give, help us follow the ethical and moral teachings of Jesus?

6. Why is the church, which is the community of faith and the Body of Christ on earth, so important in the forming of our faith and helping us live out the Jesus way?

7. What do you need most to help you live the Jesus way?

Chapter 15

Meeting Jesus in the Beatitudes

There is a moment in the worship service that my tradition calls "the Lord's Supper," when the officiant serves the cup of wine or grape juice and says, "This is the blood of the New Covenant" or "The blood of Christ, shed for you."

It takes my breath away every time.

I take that moment seriously, for it makes me aware once again that I have chosen to participate in an observance of remembering. It is in that moment when I remember that I have been released from the burden of trying to earn God's love, grace, mercy, approval, favor, or salvation by being good enough, following the rules closely enough, or being righteous enough.

It is in that moment when I remember that I have been freed from the burden of the law, and freed for the abundant life of love, joy, peace, and the other fruit of the Spirit of Christ, who dwells within me.

It is in that moment when I remember that I am joining with followers of Christ around the globe who participate in this ritual of grace in many different ways, and in that participation with others, I am part of the mysterious, mystical Body of Christ on earth.

In that moment, as well, I remember that it is not enough for me to receive the grace only for myself, but that the grace I have been given is to be lived out in acts of love, mercy, compassion, and grace toward others.

Left to the law, all of us can become hard-hearted with pride, self-righteousness, and an inflated sense of our own holiness. In the new covenant that was established with Christ and in the new kingdom of love, the acts of mercy, compassion, generosity, and love toward others flow naturally from the inside out. Instead of trying to look good and keep up appearances, the new covenant calls us to live from our hearts. That is the Jesus way.

Jesus had harsh words for those whose outer behavior might look good but whose hearts were full of hate, anger, greed, envy, resentment, duplicity, and other afflictive emotions or intentions. I shudder when I read Matthew 23, especially Matthew 23:25-27:

This is a brand new covenant that I will make with Israel when the time comes. I will put my law within them—write it on their hearts!—and be their God. And they will be my people. (Jer 31:33)

I will give them an undivided heart and put a new spirit in them; I will remove from them their heart of stone and give them a heart of flesh. Then they will follow my decrees and be careful to keep my laws. They will be my people, and I will be their God. (Ezek 11:19-20)

Woe to you, teachers of the law and Pharisees, you hypocrites! You clean the outside of the cup and dish, but inside they are full of greed and self-indulgence . . . . Woe to you, teachers of the law and Pharisees, you hypocrites! You are like white-washed tombs, which look beautiful on the outside but on the inside are full of dead men's bones and everything unclean.

A quote on my desk calendar made me smile, but it was a wry smile. "If there is anybody in this land who thoroughly believes that the meek shall inherit the earth, they have not often let their presence be known" (W. E. B. Du Bois).

When I take my focus off what matters most in my life and forget to place loving God at the center of my agenda, it seems easier to live under the law, with a checklist I can use to monitor my good behavior, than to live from the inside out, empowered by the love of God. At least my *ego* believes it is easier to do that.

My True Self, however, knows that, driven by my need to polish the outside of myself and inflate my ego, I will be miserable. My True Self knows that the way of Jesus is the way of happiness, the way of surrender to God.

Jesus began his Sermon on the Mount with a beautiful description of the qualities of a person who follows the Jesus way. The old way was that people tried to earn favor with God by following the law. The new way, the way of the new covenant, is that the qualities described in the Beatitudes flow from us naturally when we are in harmony, in sync, in intimate relationship with the Living Christ. Instead of living as if you have to cause God to love you or bless you—or protect you from bad things happening to you—the Beatitudes are the attitudes of being that result from the fact that God already loves you.

Doesn't it make your heart tender to know that there's nothing you can do to make God stop loving you? Doesn't it soften your heart to know that there's nothing you can do to make God love you any more than God already does?

Exploring the Scriptures
Read Matthew 5:1-12 (also found in Luke 6:20-23).

I will make an everlasting covenant with them; I will never stop doing good to them, and I will inspire them to fear me so that they will never turn away from me. I will rejoice in doing them good . . . . (Jer 32:40-41)

1. Over the next week, read these verses each day, and note if one speaks to you more than the others. Why is this one so meaningful to you?

2. Go to www.biblegateway.com and read the Beatitudes in other translations. For example, read the King James version, the Good News version, and *The Message*. Notice which translation speaks most directly to you. Why do you think that is?

3. Read the Ten Commandments in Exodus 20:1-17. How are these commandments different from the Beatitudes?

4. Read Exodus 19 to get a sense of the background of why God spoke the Ten Commandments to Moses to give to the children of Israel. What is the difference between the crowd to whom the commandments were given and those to whom Jesus spoke the Beatitudes?

5. What is the difference between the Ten Commandments and the Beatitudes?

6. Will keeping the commandments listed in Exodus bring about the state of being described in the Beatitudes?

7. Are the Beatitudes laws to follow or a description of those who live in an intimate relationship with Christ? Explain your response.

8. How could a contemporary person, formed in our culture, live in the spirit of the Beatitudes?

Many years ago, a friend who was a member of Al-Anon introduced me to the Twelve Steps of Alcoholics Anonymous. At the time, membership in either AA or Al-Anon was shrouded in secrecy, and I had to promise that I would not tell anyone that I had seen the Twelve Steps of the recovery program. Today, information about AA and the Twelve Steps is available on the Internet, and volumes of books for any number of addictions contain the steps.

From the time I first saw them, I knew that I needed the Twelve Steps, though I had not yet heard the word *codependency*, and I knew instantly that the steps were biblical. Many times, I have taught the Twelve Steps with a biblical base, within my church, and it gives me great joy when I hear of a Twelve Step group that meets within a church facility and is blessed by the church leaders.

Those Twelve Steps, the AA recovery program, and the Beatitudes, as well as the larger Sermon on the Mount, go hand in hand. They are all about the following attributes of the Jesus way:
• humility
• honesty
• the ability to surrender to God and to the plan of recovery, or the Jesus way
• a willingness to be taught, guided, led, counseled
• the ability to grieve—to be authentically sorry—for the harm you have caused others
• a willingness to ask forgiveness and to forgive
• the capacity for empathy and mercy for others who suffer
• the ability to be "sold out" to your plan of sobriety or the Jesus way

• a commitment to keeping "first things first," including a daily spiritual practice
• a willingness to be used by God as an instrument of hope and healing in the lives of others

What About You?

1. How do the qualities expressed in the Beatitudes compare or contrast with the unspoken "rules" of our culture (such as get even, compete and defeat, take care of number one, get all you can, don't let anyone stop you, winner takes all, win at all costs)?

2. Can you express the qualities of the Beatitudes without the Presence of Christ in your life? Why?

3. Are the qualities of the Beatitudes the result of love and of keeping the Great Commandment? Why?

4. How do these qualities compare with the fruit of the Spirit, as expressed by Paul in Galatians 5:22-23?

5. How much are these Beatitudes valued, practiced, or taught in today's culture?

6. How important are these qualities in your life? Why?

7. Which quality do you most want? Which one is less appealing to you?

8. Can serious followers of Christ ignore the Sermon on the Mount? Why or why not?

Chapter 16

Meeting Jesus in the Hard Sayings

Following Jesus is complicated. It's harder than I thought it would be.

As I said in the introduction to Part 1, I love Baby Jesus. Don't you? I love sweet Jesus, meek and mild, and I love to sing "Fairest Lord Jesus," especially when the choir swells on the last stanza.

It makes me feel warm and safe to think of being with Jesus in the sweet bye and bye, but sometimes the things Jesus said and did disturb and confound me. I don't like to admit it, but the truth is that sometimes I want an easy gospel. I want to feel good, and I don't want to be uncomfortable. I don't want to feel put-upon, and I don't want Jesus to burden me, and yet I must face the reality that if I'm to follow Jesus, it's going to be hard.

Following Jesus is hard because I want things to go my way, for my benefit. It's hard because the kind of love Jesus lived pushes against my selfishness and self-centeredness. Jesus' disciples struggled, too, and I'm thankful that the Gospel writers didn't edit either those struggles or Jesus' struggles out of their account. A sanitized version of the Gospels wouldn't have any muscle to it.

Jesus isn't just for me and my people. He burst into a particular culture with a revolutionary message that turned the value system of his day upside down and inside out. Jesus' message is just as radical (going to the root of things) and revolutionary (turning things around) today as it was in the first century.

I confess that, though I don't want to do this, I pick and choose the parts of Jesus' teachings and message that I like, the parts that make me feel good and the parts that soothe my ego. Honestly, I'm still discovering things Jesus said that I had "overlooked" or "forgotten," things that are too hard to follow because I'm not yet either mature or courageous enough, or things that I don't understand. I know it's not what a serious follower of Jesus does, but I sometimes slip into a state of forgetfulness and mindlessness.

I do well sitting here at my computer, writing about Jesus and thinking about how I want to follow Jesus, but, when confronted with demands that are too costly or walking my talk or being obedient, I wonder about myself. Jesus upset the religious and social

Teach me your way, O God, that I may walk in your truth; give me an undivided heart to revere your name. (Ps 86:11)

Don't be flip with the sacred. Banter and silliness give no honor to God. Don't reduce holy mysteries to slogans. In trying to be relevant, you're only being cute and inviting sacrilege. (Matt 7:6)

The hard way is the easy way. (AA slogan)

Lord, make me pure, but not yet.

—Augustine

norms of his culture. He offended people, and sometimes his own family and followers found him thoroughly disconcerting and perhaps even embarrassing. Jesus spoke about God in terms of intimacy with God, and that scandalized folks, especially the ones who wanted to keep the Lord far away, high and lifted up, away from daily life.

Jesus did scandalize people, but for those who were his true followers—for the ones who understood—his message and his presence brought peace, joy, and love. In Jesus, people came to know God as they never had before.

When I encounter the sayings of Jesus called "the hard sayings," I pull back a little. Sometimes I pull away because I don't understand what he is saying, but at other times I do understand, and the words are too hard.

The following list includes some of the hard sayings of Jesus. The questions that follow will help you explore your own thoughts about these sayings.

The Hard Sayings of Jesus

Eating the flesh and drinking the blood of the Son of Man	John 6:53
Not the righteous but sinners	Mark 2:17
The Sabbath for man	Mark 2:27-28
Not dead but sleeping	Mark 5:39
Flavorless salt	Mark 9:50
The jot and tittle shall not pass	Matthew 5:17-20
Being angry with your brother	Matthew 5:22
Adultery in the heart	Matthew 5:28
Plucking out the right eye	Matthew 5:29
Divorce and remarriage	Mark 10:11-12
Eunuchs for the kingdom of heaven	Matthew 19:12
Not swearing	Matthew 5:34
Turn the other cheek	Matthew 5:39
Love your enemies	Matthew 5:44
Be perfect	Matthew 5:48
Non-forgiveness	Matthew 18:35
Temptation	Matthew 16:13
Pearls before swine	Matthew 7:6
Sin against the Holy Spirit	Luke 12:10
Seeking a sign	Mark 8:12; Luke 11:29-30
Seeing and not perceiving	Mark 4:11-12
Don't go among the Gentiles	Matthew 10:5-6
Let the children be fed	Mark 7:27
Greater than John the Baptist?	Matthew 11:11

Violence and the kingdom	Matthew 11:12; Luke 16:16
Hating one's parents	Luke 14:26
Casting fire on the earth	Luke 12:49
Not peace but a sword	Matthew 10:34
The Father and the son, Matthew 11:27	
You are Peter	Matthew 16:18-19
Take up your cross	Mark 8:34
The kingdom coming with power	Mark 9:1
For or against	Mark 9:40; cf. Luke 9:50
Son of man has nowhere to lay his head	Matthew 8:20; Luke 9:58
Let the dead bury their dead	Luke 9:60
Don't look back!	Luke 9:62
Whom to fear?	Luke 12:4-5; Matthew 10:28
The elder brother's refusal	Luke 15:25-28
Why do you call me good?	Mark 10:18; Luke 18:19
Sell what you have	Mark 10;21
Give for alms what is within	Luke 11:41
The camel, the rich man, and the eye of a needle	Mark 10:25
Serving God and mammon	Matthew 6:24; Luke 16:13
Using unrighteous means to make friends	Luke 16:9
The great chasm	Luke 16:26
Where is faith?	Luke 18:8
Fair pay/right living	Matthew 20:14-15
The first will be last	Matt 19:30; 20:16; Mark 10:31; Luke 13:30
Many are called; few are chosen	Matthew 22:14
The wedding garment	Matthew 22:12
Cursing the fig tree	Mark 11:14
Faith that removes mountains	Matthew 17:20; Mark 1:23; Luke 17:6
Render to Caesar	Mark 12:17
Call no man your father	Matthew 23:9
You brood of vipers	Matthew 23:33
The eagles gathered together	Matthew 24:28; Luke 17:37
I do not know you	Matthew 25:11-12
This is my body; this is my blood	Mark 14:22-24
Let him who has no sword buy one	Luke 22:36
Friend, why are you here?	Matthew 26:50
You will see the Son of Man	Matthew 26:63-64; Mark 14:61-62; Luke 22:67-70
Why have you forsaken me?	Mark 14:34; cf. Matthew 27:46

It's not the words in the Bible that I don't understand that bother me. It's what I do understand that bothers me.
—Mark Twain

If anyone had asked me in the past, "Who is the center of your life?" I would have answered without much hesitation, "Jesus, who called me to follow him." But now I do not dare say that so easily. The struggle to become a full member of a community of faith has proved to be a struggle to let go of many idols along the way and to choose again and again to follow Jesus and him alone.
—Henri Nouwen[32]

Exploring the Scriptures

1. Scan the list of the hard sayings of Jesus. Put a check mark next to the ones that catch your attention.

2. Read the context of each hard saying. What comes before and after the verse that contains the hard saying? To whom was this said?

3. Choose at least five of the hard sayings and answer these questions about them:
  • What makes it so hard?

  • Why does it bother me more than some of the others?

  • What impact, if any, does it have on my faith or my personal daily life?

  • Is the statement hard because it is hard to understand? hard to apply? hard to follow? offensive? seems harsh, judgmental, unloving? all of the above?

4. Typically, what do most people do with these hard sayings?

5. How can these hard sayings be misused, even among Christians?

6. Can you say that grace and love are mingled in with these hard sayings? If so, how? If not, what do you mean?

7. Jesus said that the greatest commandment was to "Love the Lord with all your heart, mind, and soul, and your neighbor as yourself." Is this also the hardest commandment?

What About You?

8. What do the following Scriptures say about our human difficulty in dealing with the hard sayings of Jesus?

> But for right now, friends, I'm completely frustrated by your un-spiritual dealings with each other and with God. You're acting like infants in relation to Christ, capable of nothing much more than nursing at the breast. Well, then, I'll nurse you since you don't seem capable of anything more. As long as you grab for what makes you feel good or makes you look important, are you really much different than a babe at the breast, content only when everything's going your way? (1 Cor 3:1-4, *The Message*)

> I have a lot more to say about this, but it is hard to get it across to you since you've picked up this bad habit of not listening. By this time you ought to be teachers yourselves, yet here I find you need someone to sit down with you and go over the basics on God again, starting from square one—baby's milk, when you should have been on solid food long ago! Milk is for beginners, inexperienced in God's ways; solid food is for the mature, who have some practice in telling right from wrong. (Heb 5:11-14, *The Message*)

It will simplify our discussion if we admit the truth at the outset that the teaching of Jesus is difficult and unacceptable because it runs counter to those elements in human nature which the twentieth century has in common with the first—such things as laziness, greed, the love of pleasure, the instinct to hit back and the like. The teachings as a whole show that Jesus was well aware of this and recognized that here and nowhere else lay the obstacle that had to be surmounted.

—F. F. Bruce[33]

What makes Jesus' sayings so hard?

- They are hard because he made people think.
- They are hard because what he said made people rethink some of their assumptions and reconsider some of the things on which they had based their lives.
- They are hard because we live in a completely different culture from the culture of Jesus' day. He spoke in a different language—Aramaic—and the words of the New Testament were written in Greek.
- Some of his sayings are hard to understand, but some of them are easy to understand, and we don't like what we understand.
- They are hard because they may ask us to change, and we often would rather die as we are than change to become who we are meant to be.
- They are hard because they are true, and the harder something is, the more likely it is to be genuine or true.

My ego self wants it easy, but Jesus intends the growth of the soul.

My ego wants comfort, but my True Self and Christ within want my wholeness.

My ego wants to feel good and look good, but Christ within is interested in authentic peace and inward joy, lived out in acts of love, compassion, and mercy.

The yoke of Jesus may be easy and his burden light, but it can take a long time to wrest our necks from the yokes we've always worn and give up carrying the burdens we've learned to accommodate and even "love." Jesus' hard sayings run counter to my well-entrenched and often hardened prejudices, biases, presuppositions, and traditional assumptions about life and human relations. But to make them easy would be to obscure their meaning and power.

My life experience has taught me that only as I draw near to God, abide in Christ, and allow him to abide in me am I able to live the Jesus way. Only as I seek first his presence in my inner life do I even come close to knowing how to interpret the hard sayings of Jesus. Only as I love him first and let him love me do I have the strength, ability, endurance, faithfulness, and persistence to apply what Jesus said in my everyday life.

God does not ask of us a maturity that we have not yet attained, but once we have grown up, there is the expectation that we are able to live up to the high standard of love Jesus sets, which means that we don't quake in the face of doing hard things. In fact, some people even see the big challenges as opportunities to rise to the occasion.

What do you think? Is the Jesus way worth it?

Jesus did many other miraculous signs in the presence of his disciples, which are not recorded in this book. But these are written that you may believe that Jesus is the Christ, the Son of God, and that by believing you may have life in his name. (John 20:30-31)

Jesus did many other things as well. If every one of them were written down, I suppose that even the whole world would not have room for the books that would be written. (John 21:25)

There are only two ways to live your life. One is as though nothing is a miracle. The other is as though everything is a miracle.
—Albert Einstein

Part Four

Meeting Jesus in the Miracles

Introduction

"I need a miracle!"

How many times have you heard someone say those words? Have you ever said them?

Have you ever experienced what you would call a miracle? What was that like?

In the accounts of Jesus' life recorded in the four Gospels, he performed miracles that fall into two categories. Some miracles met a human need, either by healing, exorcising a demon, or raising someone from death into life. Other miracles transformed an element of nature in some way. In all of his miracles, Jesus gave his Father the credit for the power to perform them. The miracles Jesus performed were not done not for his purposes but to meet definite needs of others. Neither did Jesus perform a miracle to satisfy the tests of the Pharisees and teachers of the law.

I don't get to orchestrate, organize, or set the timetable for what I think God should do in my life. When I have experienced what appear to be breakthroughs of the supernatural and the synchronicities I believe are God's handiwork, they usually come as a surprise, and often just when I am about to give up! I've learned, too, that "praying harder" is not the key to activating the miraculous. Instead, an open heart and mind and a willingness to surrender to God's love create the opportunity for God to work in me/for me/through me/with me.

Jesus' miracles were not confined to a single sphere of life, so they could never be considered trickery. Jesus' miracles were performed on nature, on human beings, and on demons. The miracles were done openly in front of spectators and witnesses. They did not always involve the faith of the person healed but were sometimes done in spite of the lack of faith. Jesus performed his miracles so that people would believe in him.

Sometimes Jesus approached the person in need of healing. Sometimes the person approached Jesus. Sometimes friends or a family member brought a person to Jesus for healing or went to him on behalf of someone. Sometimes Jesus' healing miracles were connected with sin, but not always.

Notice, especially, that while Jesus wanted people to believe in him and respond to God's work in their lives, he never asked for anything in return. In fact, he sometimes told the person not to tell anyone what he had done for them.

It may be helpful for us to get a sense of Jesus' life before he went about performing miracles. It seems that he was unusual from the beginning. We will explore the unusual birth of Jesus later, but for review, read the account of the announcement of Mary's pregnancy and Jesus' birth in Luke 1:26-56 and Luke 2:1-20. I love this tender, beautiful story of the Incarnation, and I am especially drawn to the account of Jesus' advent into an earthly plane in the Prologue to the Gospel of John (John 1:1-18).

One of my favorite Scriptures is John 1:14: "The Word became flesh and made his dwelling among us." I especially like Eugene Peterson's rendering of that verse in *The Message*: "The Word became a man and moved into the neighborhood."

Another appropriate background passage for the miracles of Jesus is Luke 2:21-40, when Jesus' faithful Jewish parents took him to the temple to "present him to the Lord." There, old and faithful Simeon took the baby in his arms and blessed him, crying out with joy and confirming to Jesus' parents that this was an unusual child.

Read as well the account of Jesus' trip to Jerusalem when he was twelve, as Luke records it in Luke 2:41-52. All of these stories form the foundation for who Jesus was as he began performing miracles.

Exploring the Scriptures
Read Luke 2:41-52.[35]

1. What kind of parents were Mary and Joseph?

2. What might Mary and Joseph have said to each other during the three days they looked for Jesus in Jerusalem?

The Gospels use four Greek words to characterize Jesus' miracles:

1. **Dunamis** emphasizes that the mighty power of God has entered our world as displayed in Jesus' miracles (see Matt 11:21; Mark 6:2, 5, 14; 9:39; Acts 13:10).

2. **Teras** means "wonder" and underscores the extraordinary character of Jesus' miracles. It is always used with some other word (such as "signs and wonders") so that we will not think of the miracles simply as dazzling demonstrations (see Mark 13:22; John 4:48).

3. **Ergon** means "works" and is used both for Jesus' miracles and for his ordinary deeds of mercy (see John 5:20, 36; 7:3; 10:25).

4. **Semeion** means "sign" and indicates that Jesus' miracles were to teach us a spiritual truth (see John 2:11; 4:54; 6:2; 11:47).

A miracle is more than something unusual (though in ordinary speech we often call such events miracles). A true miracle is something beyond man's intellectual or scientific ability to accomplish. It is not natural, even though it may be unusual; a miracle is supernatural (that is, from God or Satan). It is more than a highly improbably event; it injects a new element (the supernatural) into the natural order of things.

—C. S. Lewis[34]

3. What did Luke mean when he said that Jesus' parents were "astonished" when they saw their son talking to his teachers?

4. What tone of voice might Mary have used when she asked Jesus why he had treated them as he did?

5. Why didn't they understand what he had done?

6. Luke says that after this incident, Jesus went back home to Nazareth with his parents and was obedient to them. What does that mean?

7. Mary's "pondering those things in her heart" is a well-known statement from this story. What do you think this means?

For Your Eyes Only
8. Have you ever asked a question about God or an adult topic and either embarrassed your parents or caused an adult to shame you for asking such a thing?

9. Have you ever wanted to ask something but were afraid to? Have you ever had to hide your curiosity?

10. What does the curious child in you want to know today?

Remember my young friend who cried out in the middle of a formal Christmas Eve service, "Who is this *Jesus person* they keep talking about?"

This Jesus person walked on water and made blind people see.

He turned water into wine and made a lame man walk.

This Jesus person raised Lazarus from death.

He has taken my fears and turned them into energies for good.

He has taken my broken heart and made something useful out of my wounds.

This Jesus person has taken my mistakes and flaws and given me abundant life.

Chapter 17

Meeting Jesus at the Beginning

In Luke 4:18-19, Luke records Jesus' mission statement, spoken by him in the synagogue in Nazareth.

As Luke tells it, Jesus had just come back from his forty days in the desert, the place where the Spirit of God had led him following his baptism (see Luke 3:21-22; 4:1-29). Quoting the prophet Isaiah, Jesus identified himself in the place where he had lived. Judging from the people's extreme reaction, there must have been something powerful about what he said and the way he said it.

Eugene Peterson writes Jesus' mission statement like this in *The Message*:

> God's Spirit is on me;
> he's chosen me to preach the Message of good news to the poor,
> Sent me to announce pardon to prisoners and
> recovery of sight to the blind,
> To set the burdened and battered free,
> to announce, "This is God's year to act!"

That Jesus person was bold, wasn't he?

I have always been impressed by what happened after the people drove him out of town. Surely his ability to walk right through them and be on his way must have stunned the crowd, fascinating some and infuriating others. *How did he do that?* That Jesus person stirred things up, didn't he?

I have always been fascinated by what it must have been like for Mary and Joseph to parent this child, and what it must have been like for his siblings.

Sometimes it's a problem when there's an exceptional child in the family, and since Jesus apparently had the human experience of growing up in a family, I'm guessing life got interesting.

A lovely legend says that when Jesus was working in Joseph's carpentry shop, he carved little birds and then, when he blew his breath on them, they came alive and flew away. I love that story because I like to think about the boy Jesus and what he must have been like. Having raised children, I'm fascinated by how he grew, what mischief he might have gotten into, how he related to his

The Spirit of the Lord is on me, because he has anointed me to preach good news to the poor. He has sent me to proclaim freedom for the prisoners, and recovery of sight for the blind, to release the oppressed, to proclaim the favorable year of the Lord. (Luke 4:18-19)

150

friends in the village, and what Mary must have pondered in her heart as she watched him sleep at night.

What was it like to be the mother of the human Jesus, watching over him and caring for him?

It also intrigues me that the first miracle Jesus performed was at a party, and that it was to meet not the need of a desperate or dying person but the need of a family who would be embarrassed because they had run out of wine! And as a mother, I love that his mother instigated this first miracle. How was she able to get him to do what she asked him to do? After all, *he was Jesus!* (As a Baptist, I also have to chuckle that Jesus turned that water into wine and not punch or grape juice.)

Exploring the Scriptures
Read John 2:1-11.[36]
1. What was the predicament at the wedding?

2. Why do you think Jesus was invited to this wedding? What does that say about him?

3. What prompted Mary to ask Jesus to help with the hosts' problem?

4. What is your reaction to Jesus' response to his mother in verse 4?

5. Why did Mary ignore Jesus' response and give her own orders to the servants?

6. How do you think Jesus felt when his mother essentially put him on the spot?

7. Why did the servants do what Jesus told them to do?

8. Why did Jesus perform his first miracle, which didn't save someone's life, heal a sick person, or raise a dead person to life, but merely saved a family from embarrassment and met the needs of wedding guests? What does this tell us about Jesus?

9. If wine is symbolic of joy and celebration, what does this first miracle signal?

For Your Eyes Only
10. What in your life is incomplete or inadequate, like the water in the water jars?

11. What do you need to surrender to the Living Christ in order to let him help you?

12. In what ways do you need the Living Christ to turn water into wine for you?

      To literalize a gospel story is to trivialize it. To see this story (or any story of Jesus) only as an event that happened in the first century in a small village far away is to leave it back in history or trapped on the pages of your Bible. To see the meaning behind every part of this story is to allow the Spirit of the Living Christ to lift it off those pages and move it deeply into your life.

      Rather than mere water pots used for ritual cleansing in a Jewish household, the pots are symbols of something greater. Seen symbolically, they represent the inadequacy of the law to bring grace and peace, love and joy. The wine is symbolic of the sparkle of life that Jesus brought. That Jesus performed this first recorded miracle at a wedding feast can symbolize the new life, the fresh start, he brings. The wedding feast itself symbolizes our abundant life with Christ. What truths can you find in the stories of Jesus' other miracles?

What do you want?
(John 1:38b)

Chapter 18

Meeting Jesus—An Overview of the Miracles

What difference does it make that Jesus walked across the water in the first century if we do not allow the Living Christ to walk across the waters of our lives and calm our fears now?

What difference does it make that Jesus turned the water into wine in the first century if we do not allow the Living Christ to take what is imperfect, incomplete, common, and ordinary and transform what we have into something like "the best wine of all"?

What difference does it make that Jesus raised Lazarus from the dead in the first century if we do not allow the Living Christ to work in the depths of our inner lives and bring back to life the parts that have died?

This chapter offers an overview of Jesus' miracles. Working with these stories could take a lifetime. You can simply scan this chapter and the stories, or you can work them into your life, kneading them into your mind and heart like good yeast into dough. I encourage you to do the latter.

The Miracles of Jesus in the Four Gospels[37]

No.	Miracle	Matthew	Mark	Luke	John
1	Marriage at Cana				Jn 2:1-11
2	Exorcism at the Synagogue in Capernaum		Mk 1:21-28	Lk 4:31-37	
3	Miraculous Draught of Fishes			Lk 5:1-11	
4	Young Man from Nain			Lk 7:11-17	
5	Cleansing a Leper	Mt 8:1-4	Mk 1:40-45	Lk 5:12-16	
6	The Centurion's Servant	Mt 8:5-13		Lk 7:1-10	Jn 4:46-54
7	Healing the Mother of Peter's Wife	Mt 8:14-17	Mk 1:29-31	Lk 4:38-41	
8	Exorcising at Sunset	Mt 8:16-17	Mk 1:32-34	Lk 4:40-41	
9	Calming the Storm	Mt 8:23-27	Mk 4:35-41	Lk 8:22-25	
10	Gerasene/Gadarene Demoniac	Mt 8:28-34	Mk 5:1-20	Lk 8:26-39	
11	Paralytic at Capernaum	Mt 9:1-8	Mk 2:1-12	Lk 5:17-26	
12	Daughter of Jairus	Mt 9:18-26	Mk 5:21-43	Lk 8:40-56	
13	Bleeding Woman	Mt 9:20-22	Mk 5:24-34	Lk 8:43-48	
14	Two Blind Men at Galilee	Mt 9:27-31			

No.	Miracle	Matthew	Mark	Luke	John
15	Exorcising a Mute	Mt 9:32-34			
16	Paralytic at Bethesda				Jn 5:1-18
17	Man with Withered Hand	Mt 12:9-13	Mk 3:1-6	Lk 6:6-11	
18	Exorcising the Blind and Mute Man	Mt 12:22-28	Mk 3:20-30	Lk 11:14-23	
19	Infirm Woman			Lk 13:10-17	
20	Feeding the 5,000	Mt 14:13-21	Mk 6:31-34	Lk 9:10-17	Jn 6:5-15
21	Walking on Water	Mt 14:22-33	Mk 6:45-52		Jn 6:16-21
22	Healing in Gennesaret	Mt 14:34-36	Mk 6:53-56		
23	Canaanite Woman's Daughter	Mt 15:21-28	Mk 7:24-30		
24	Deaf mute of Decapolis		Mk 7:31-37		
25	Feeding the 4,000	Mt 15:32-39	Mk 8:1-9		
26	Blind Man of Bethsaida		Mk 8:22-26		
27	Transfiguration of Jesus	Mt 17:1-13	Mk 9:2-13	Lk 9:28-36	
28	Boy Possessed by a Demon	Mt 17:14-21	Mk 9:14-29	Lk 9:37-49	
29	Coin in the Fish's Mouth	Mt 17:24-27			
30	Man with Dropsy			Lk 14:1-6	
31	Cleansing Ten Lepers			Lk 17:11-19	
32	Blind at Birth				Jn 9:1-12
33	Blind Near Jericho	Mt 20:29-34	Mk 10:46-52	Lk 18:35-43	
34	Raising of Lazarus				Jn 11:1-44
35	Cursing the Fig Tree	Mt 21:18-22	Mk 11:12-14		
36	Healing the Ear of a Servant			Lk 22:49-51	
37	Catch of 153 Fish				Jn 21:1-24

Exploring the Scriptures

Choose a miracle, read the story several times and, if you desire, in more than one translation. Then consider the following questions about each miracle you study.

I. Healing Miracles or Cures

In the chart of Jesus' miracles, these are the healing miracles: 5, 6, 7, 11, 12, 13, 14, 16, 17, 19, 22, 23, 24, 26, 30, 31, 32, 33, and 36.

1. As simply as possible, state what happened in this incident.

2. Who was there when this miracle was performed? Who witnessed the miracle?

3. Did the person who was healed seek Jesus, or did Jesus go to the person himself?

4. Did Jesus tell the person not to tell what had happened to him/her in this incident? If so, why do you think he said that?

5. Does this miracle relate to your life in any way?

6. Which miracle touches you most? Why?

II. Exorcisms
In the chart of Jesus' miracles, these are the exorcisms: 2, 8, 10, 15, 18, and 28.
1. What is the dictionary definition of exorcism?

2. What are the differences among these healings? How are they alike?

3. What relevance might these stories have for people today?

4. Which story is most meaningful to you?

5. How do you think Jesus felt about the people from whom he cast out demons?

III. Resurrections of the Dead
In the chart of Jesus' miracles, 4 and 34 are the resurrection miracles.
1. What did it mean to the people in these stories when their loved ones were raised from death?

2. How can these miracles give meaning to our lives today?

IV. In-depth Study
Choose one of the miracles, and read it every day—in several translations if possible (see biblegateway.com). Then answer the following questions about it in your journal.

1. What first caught your interest about this miracle?

2. What touches you most deeply about Jesus' treatment of the sick or troubled person in this story?

3. With which person do you most identify? In what ways do you identify with this person?

4. Imagine that Jesus is healing you as he healed the person in the story. What does that feel like to you?

5. After studying the miracle for several days, what conclusions have you drawn from it?

For Your Eyes Only

1. What difference does it make in your personal life to interpret these miracles literally? What difference does it make to interpret them symbolically?

2. If the Living Christ could/would perform a healing miracle for you, what would it be?

3. In what ways are you "possessed" by fear, guilt/shame, insecurity, or hate/anger?

4. What part of you has "died"? How could the Living Christ bring that part of you back to life?

5. What do you think the term "inner healing" means? How do you think the Living Christ can bring you inner healing? How is that connected with salvation?

What About You?

1. If you could have been present at one of the miracles Jesus performed, which one would it be? Why did you choose that one?

2. What human need did Jesus meet in performing that particular miracle?

3. How might Jesus' miracles have affected those who witnessed them?

4. After reflecting on these miracles, how are they relevant to people who live today?

5. If someone asked if you believe that Jesus actually performed the miracles, what would you say?

6. If someone asked if you believe that miracles still occur today, and that God/the Living Christ works them, what would you say?

7. It has been said that "wisdom begins with wonder." How did studying Jesus' miracles help you feel a sense of wonder? What makes you curious?

Chapter 19

Meeting Jesus in the Storms

One day, I joined friends for lunch after a worship service of beautiful music and the lighting of the Advent candle. We were in a festive mood until a woman in the group leaned forward and changed the subject to the topics on the evening news. Quickly, the discussion turned into a recounting of the scary and scandalous until finally it felt as if the oxygen had been sucked out of the room.

"This world is just going crazy," someone said, "and there are so many dangers out there."

Earlier, I'd pondered *Time*'s cover article, "The Decade from Hell" (7 December 2009) and its list of the terrible things that occurred in the world in the decade that was coming to a close. Even if you weren't directly involved in one of the major crises of the decade, just hearing about each one over and over produces stress. No wonder we're all so anxious!

My lingering response was to wonder how we in the human family have contributed to the troubles either directly or by inertia, apathy, and irresponsibility. I also wondered if we could work together to avoid some of these disasters.

Then I had another thought. *Aren't we who call ourselves Christian supposed to be the ones with hope, the ones who have the good news?*

Surely the Christians in the first century knew about dangers. Simply by identifying themselves with Jesus, they were vulnerable. Perhaps Mark, the first of the Gospel writers, wrote about Jesus' calming the storm to calm the storms of fear in the hearts of these earliest followers of Jesus.

All three writers of the Synoptic Gospels include the story of Jesus calming the storm. Matthew, Mark, and John include the story of Jesus walking on water. In these accounts, Jesus works with nature to calm the disciples' fear when they get caught in a storm. Read the accounts of Jesus' calming the storm in Matthew 8:23-27; Mark 4:35-41; and Luke 8:22-25. What similarities do you find in these accounts? What differences?

In this event, Jesus and the disciples were at sea when a storm came up that was so bad the waves broke over the boat. Jesus, however, was asleep!

> Sometimes God calms the storms, and sometimes he calms his child in the storm.
> —Anonymous

> Oh, God, the storm is so big, and my boat is so small.
> —Anonymous

> Take courage! Do not be afraid. (Mark 6:50)

Terrified, the disciples woke him up and asked, "Don't you care if we drown?"

External situations toss us about—the economy, pandemics and endless threats of terrorists, wars and rumors of wars, strife in families and within the family of faith. We worry about our jobs, our families, our health, and our insurance! With the storms that batter us from without and the doubts and fears that assail us from within, it is no wonder we are afraid! Sometimes it feels as if God has gone to sleep and we are, like the disciples, left to wonder if God cares if we drown in our predicaments.

Awakened, Jesus calmed the storm and then asked the disciples, "Do you still have no faith?" I wonder how they felt, given what they had seen and experienced with Jesus.

When a new storm rocks my boat, I sometimes panic and wonder if God is still with me or if I am going to have to weather it alone in my small boat on the great big ocean of life.

The other storm story is recorded in Matthew 14:22-32; Mark 6:45-51; and John 6:16-21. Read each of these and notice the similarities and differences.

In this story, Jesus had gone up the mountain to pray. The disciples had taken their boat into the middle of the lake. A storm came up that was so bad the disciples strained at the oars. Jesus saw their difficulty and walked to them on the water, but the disciples thought he was a ghost and were terrified.

This story makes me wonder how many times God is with me but I am unable to see him because I am so blinded by my fears and worries. I love the moment when Jesus said, "Take courage! It is I! Don't be afraid." And I especially love when Jesus climbed into the boat with them and the storm died down.

What About You?

1. Since we do not get to walk and talk with the actual Jesus, how can we experience a relationship with the Living Christ? How does a person "practice the presence of Christ"?

2. What storms are currently tossing the "boat of your life" around? What waves of crisis or personal turmoil threaten to overturn your boat?

3. What kinds of things have you turned to in order to calm yourself? What efforts have worked only momentarily or haven't worked at all?

4. If the Living Christ were to approach you, as Jesus walked on the water toward the disciples, would you recognize him? If so, how?

What can we do, other than wring our hands and flail about in fear, when life is hard and we are afraid? These storm stories challenge us, and Jesus challenges us to be people of faith in the midst of life.

Perhaps one of the greatest miracles the Living Christ works in us is turning our fear into courage. I've learned that I can cooperate with that miracle. Sometimes I feel that I have to wake up the Living Christ, but more often the truth is that he has to wake me! In order for the Living Christ to work this miracle of courage in our inner lives, we must do our part.

We must wake up to the reality that Christ is with us. Perhaps "waking Jesus up" means waking up our sleepy selves to the reality of Christ's presence with us. But how do we do that? Practicing the presence of Christ in daily life keeps us awake to Christ's presence. Being with other followers of Christ, studying the Gospels, and knowing what Jesus did and said keep us awake to him.

Indeed, Jesus said, "Go and tell," but he also said, "Abide in me and I will abide in you." He told us to forgive, feed the hungry, care for the wounded, and love one another. When we consciously try to do what he told us to do, we keep him alive in our lives.

We *must persevere, and we must encourage others to persevere.* We are often so weary and overwhelmed with our troubles and traumas that we don't feel like we can go on. In a sermon after the tragedy of September 11, 2001, Alan Jones, the dean of Grace Cathedral in San Francisco, quoted Samuel Becket, who said in *The Unnamable*, "I cannot go on; I will go on."[38]

There is something heroic about suiting up and showing up to meet the challenges of our lives. We can attune ourselves to troubles and traumas. We can listen to expressions of hate or fear. We can talk about doubt and terror. Or we can choose to attune ourselves to the mysterious presence of the Living God who is with us in our storms, saying, "Take courage! I am with you!"

We must remember who we are. We are Easter people, so we are not life/death people but life/death/life people. We live under a divine imperative to proclaim hope and to live as people of radical courage and uncommon love. We don't just sing the great anthems of hope and then revert to our fears; instead, we must always be prepared to give an answer to everyone who asks us to give a reason for our hope.

Here's the reason: *Emmanuel has taken on human form and moved into the neighborhood.* And so we proclaim to each other: Take courage! *God is with us.*

Chapter 20

Meeting Jesus with the Loaves and Fishes

In the account of Jesus' temptations, Jesus refuses the Adversary's taunting challenge to turn the rocks on the ground into bread. Jesus must have been hungry, for he had been in the wilderness for forty days. During that time, he had many opportunities to wrestle with what kind of Messiah he was going to be.

He had, after all, heard the voice of his Father saying, "This is my beloved Son, in whom I am well pleased," as he was lifted up out of the baptismal waters of the Jordan River by his cousin, John the Baptist.

Those words of God at his baptism, clearly discernible to Jesus, came from a coronation formula from Jesus' Jewish heritage that carried great meaning for him. We find that formula in Isaiah 42:1, where the blessing was bestowed on the servant of the Lord: "Here is my servant, whom I uphold, my chosen, in whom my soul delights; I have put my spirit upon him; he will bring forth justice to the nations (Isa 42:1)."

From a biblical perspective, blessing is not about being privileged or special. Instead, it implies empowerment for service and is bestowed by one with authority. Jesus knew all of that, just as he knew the words that he read as his mission statement. I've wondered if the words of the great prophet Isaiah rumbled around in Jesus' mind and attention during those forty days he spent in the wilderness after his baptism.

When the Adversary, the one who opposes, tempted Jesus to turn rocks into bread, Jesus had the opportunity to define his mission even more clearly. Through being tempted with a mission focused on sensationalism, power, or meeting physical needs, Jesus knew more clearly who he was and what he was sent here to do.

Sometimes you don't know what you believe until you are confronted with the opposite of what you believe.

That Jesus could have done anything that the Adversary put before him, but chose not to, makes a powerful point about the miracles he did perform: God works in mysterious ways, his wonders to perform, *but on his terms, his timetable, and for the purpose he has in mind.*

I can pray for a miracle and or for a breakthrough of God's supernatural power, but I must remember that God chooses when and where and how much to work, and in what ways God will work. It's dangerous to try to force the Almighty into your mold to suit your purposes, on your timetable, according to your desires, even if you *know for sure and without a doubt* that your request will bring God all the glory!

It's dangerous to trifle with God.

The story of Jesus' multiplying the loaves and fishes for the huge crowd of hungry listeners is often taught to children.

I remember how much I loved the fact that a child helped Jesus by giving him his loaves and fishes. I was intrigued that the child offered what little he had to Jesus, while the disciples wanted to send the crowd home.

But when I was a child, I heard the story out of context. The Gospel writers position this miracle of right after the beheading of Jesus' cousin John the Baptist. Surely that terrible event concerned and alarmed the disciples and greatly troubled Jesus. As the disciples gathered around him, the crowds began to approach, and Jesus said to them, "Come with me by yourselves to a quiet place, and get some rest." Jesus' attentiveness to his disciples' need for space away from the crowds, for solitude and reflection on what was happening, reveals his tenderness and empathy for them.

The crowds followed, however, as they attempted to find solitude, and Jesus had compassion on them. All of us are created with the need to connect with the transcendent, with the Power that is greater than ourselves. Jesus knew this about people, and he knew that it was his mission to connect with them at a soul level.

Perhaps Jesus' compassion motivated every miracle he performed, and that is what the Adversary never understood. Neither did the Adversary comprehend that Jesus' mission was to reveal the compassion at the heart of God. Jesus wasn't drawing people to himself to give them the buzz of a momentary sensation.

That day, he moved into the crowd and taught them many things. Late in the afternoon, the people got hungry, but when the disciples wanted to sent them away, Jesus took a small basket of food from a young boy, gave thanks to the Father, and then, through the mysterious ways known only to God, Jesus multiplied the loaves and fishes to meet the needs of the crowd.

Exploring the Scriptures[39]

1. Read the biblical account of this miracle in Matthew 14:13-21; Mark 6:31-44; Luke 9:10-17; and John 6:5-15. What are the similarities? What are the differences?

2. What do you think caused all four Gospel writers to include this event in their narratives of Jesus' life and ministry?

3. If you had been there that day, who might you have been—an onlooker, one of the disciples, a curiosity seeker, an honest seeker, the boy's mother, the boy with the loaves and fishes? Who would you have wanted to be?

4. Whether a talent or personal resources, what can you give to the Living Christ for use in the lives of others?

5. What reasons do you withhold what you have from the Living Christ?

It is meaningful to me that even Jesus experienced the need to be apart, and I believe that he connected with the Father in his times of solitude and silence. He drew what he needed from God to return to the crowds and to his disciples and give them what they needed.

Human need is pervasive, constant, and unrelenting. Human need is a bottomless pit. The poor are always with us, and that includes the parts of our inner landscapes that are impoverished. Jesus knew this, and he knew that he had to be selective in responding to the needs of the crowds who clamored for his time and attention.

We are not Jesus, but we are asked to participate with the Living Christ as he alleviates suffering and need. We have to know our limits, and we have to be sensitive to the guidance of God, but here are some principles from this story:

• We can stay awake and aware to peoples' needs.
• We can be willing to be God's instruments in giving aid and help.
• We can give what we have as if we are giving it to God.
• We cannot give what we do not have.
• We can focus on God's generosity and trust God with what we give.
• Fear blinds us to what God can do.
• God calls us to act out of courage and faith.

Here's what I know to be true: following Jesus isn't for the faint of heart, and we need each other along the path. Perhaps it is a miracle when we step outside ourselves and trust each other, trust God, and trust the process to unfold as it will. We never know when we will be asked to participate with the Living Christ in the miracle he wants to perform among us!

Chapter 21

Meeting Jesus in Everyday Miracles

Recently, I've read and heard reports about the increasing number of people who call themselves atheists. And more and more people check "none" on forms that ask for a religious affiliation. Those people are called "nones." Think about it. In a country that some call "a Christian nation," people are choosing to be "nones."

Truthfully, I can understand why people are disenchanted and disgusted with public displays of religion (PDRs, perhaps?).

PDRs remind me of Jesus' other teaching about prayer, where he instructs the disciples not to pray on the street corner "to be seen by men" (Matt 6:5-8). Jesus seemed to have issues with "practicing your righteousness before men." Consider reading or rereading Matthew 23. I warn you: reading it is like walking through a field of garlic.

Here's what I know about following Jesus: if you take seriously "the Jesus way," and if you try to integrate the principles, teachings, commandments, and patterns that Jesus modeled in his earthly life, miracles of transformation can occur.

In the margins of this chapter, I cited some of Jesus' teachings that have challenged me most. Sometimes, trying to do what Jesus asked in those verses has given me trouble—both because of the behavior of others and because of my own stubborn will.

Sometimes I want to be right more than I want to get along with other people. Sometimes I cling to my worries and fear because they are familiar to me, and I don't know what I'd do without them. Sometimes I don't want to forgive; sadly, sometimes holding a grudge feels good. Sometimes I act as if I trust my own efforts more than I trust God, and sometimes I don't want to love other people, especially my enemies.

I'm not proud of it, but I have a tendency to climb up on the judgment seat, which is a self-appointed position, and act as if it is my job to pronounce judgments, issue edicts, and act as if I know what everyone else on earth should do. Even worse, I sometimes carry those judgments in my heart, silently enjoying the repetitive process of criticizing, condemning, and assigning blame.

Love your enemies and pray for those who persecute you. (Matt 5:44)

Therefore, if you are offering your gift at the altar and there remember that your brother has something against you, leave your gift there in front of the altar. First go and be reconciled to your brother; then come and offer your gift. (Matt 5:23-24)

The miracle of God's mercy, forgiveness, and grace begins to manifest itself when I am brought to my knees, humbled and sometimes humiliated by the reality of my self-will run riot. This self-will wants what I want when I want it, no matter how it affects other people. The miracle continues if I cooperate with the Corrective Power, known as the Disturber or the Holy Spirit, who has brought to my attention—through other peoples' reactions to me, my own restless spirit, or the mess I've made—that I need to change my ways instead of trying to change other people.

When I follow the biblical model and work through the Twelve Steps, implementing the power of that process, I cooperate with the miracle-making work of the Living Christ in making things right again. When I have the courage to begin the process of taking a fearless and searching moral inventory of my own attitudes, afflictive emotions, and harmful behaviors, admitting to myself and another person the exact nature of my wrongs, confessing my sins to God, and then, as appropriate, making amends for the harm I have done, I give God/the Living Christ/the Holy Spirit room and freedom to work a miracle.

It is a miracle when the Living Christ
• works the work of forgiveness in families and among friends.
• brings me out of the bondage of my self-will and into humility.
• gives me compassion for others instead of judgment.
• helps me live in courage and trust instead of worry and fear.
• helps me move beyond my selfishness to authentic love for others.

Indeed, there are dramatic events that we call miracles, but in daily life, we can practice the teachings of Jesus and break resentments sometimes held for generations. This is when we can see miracles happen.

When we have come to the end of our abilities and actions and fall on our faces in failures and disappointment, admitting our finite limitations, surrendering will and life to God as we understand him, the miracle-working power of the Living Christ can began to work, often at an unseen level.

Many things have not worked out as I wanted them to work out. I have had losses that I have lamented for a lifetime. Even the people Jesus healed ultimately died. And yet the sun keeps rising every morning.

The tides keep going out and coming in, and there are enough occasions of grace when things do work out, when the prodigal comes home, the relationship is restored, what was wrong gets turned around, that I've decided to hedge my bets on the power of the one who turned water into wine.

Often, transformation begins with the recognition of how far apart our image of ourselves is from other's image of us.

Transformation can begin when you are willing to take a hard but loving look at the places in your life where your talk doesn't match your walk, and for those of us in the religious establishment, transformation can begin when you are willing to face the places where the outside of your life doesn't match the inside.

If you're bold and brave enough to do it, take a look at Matthew 23, and then beam a light into your own life and see what muddy, brackish or stagnant waters might be made clean and clear, and in what ways what is broken or messy or unpleasant in your life can be transformed into something beautiful.

Transformation starts with telling the truth to yourself.

Exploring the Scriptures
Read Matthew 23—preferably from The Message

1. What problem did Jesus address in verses 1-4?

2. What are the results of following people who tell you to do something that they themselves don't do?

3. Why is it important for a person to walk what she talks?

4. What difference does it make for a person to do right because it is right? What about those who do right to gain points with others?

> Do not judge, or you too will be judged. For in the same way you judge others, you will be judged, and with the measure you use, it will be measured to you. (Matt 7:1-2)

5. What Jesus teaches in verse 12 seems to be such an obvious truth that one would think it would be unnecessary for him to have to say it. Why don't people know the truth about this teaching?

My command is this: Love one another, as I have loved you. (John 15:12)

6. In what ways do religious people "shut the door of the kingdom of heaven" for others?

7. In what specific ways do religious people hinder other people's relationships with God (v. 15)?

Let my trust be in Your mercy, not in myself. Let my hope be in Your love, not in health, or strength, or ability or human resources. If I trust You, everything else will become, for me, strength, health, and support. Everything will bring me to heaven. If I do not trust You, everything will be my destruction.
—Thomas Merton[40]

8. Eugene Peterson calls religious hypocrites "frauds." Jesus saved his harshest criticism for religious frauds. What is Jesus' charge against those frauds in vv. 15-22? What contemporary examples of this can you relate?

9. In *The Message*, Peterson renders Jesus' "Woe to you," spoken to the religious leaders, as "You're hopeless!" What is it about being a religious fraud that brings about woe or hopelessness?

10. What is Jesus' charge against the frauds in vv. 23-26?

11. According to Jesus, what are the most important matters of the law?

12. Why is it easier to measure out a tenth of spices than it is to give justice, mercy and faithfulness?

13. In verses 25-28 Jesus gives two vivid and horrifying visual images of the sin of hypocrisy. If you used these images to explain hypocrisy to a middle-schooler, what would you say?

14. If sin is separation from God, how does hypocrisy separate us from God? Or is it a symptom of that separation?

15. What is the hypocrisy Jesus addresses in vv. 29-32?

16. Verses 33-36 contain some of Jesus' harshest language. Why do you think Jesus is so passionate about the state of the religious leaders? Why does he save his most severe judgment for the religious establishment?

17. What tenderness do you see from Jesus in vv. 37-39?

18. In the Old Testament, God's wrath and judgment were not intended to destroy but seem to be spoken out of deep anguish for the children of God and the state into which they had gone. God's redemptive love often carries with it that anguish, but the judgment

is intended to bring people back to God. Do you see redemptive love in this chapter?

For Your Eyes Only

19. Which one of the "woes" of Jesus hits you, personally, hardest?

20. In what places are you most likely to be hypocritical? How does that feel?

21. Do you know when you are pretending a spirituality that isn't real? How do you know?

22. What is the hope for those who don't walk their talk?

Part Five

Meeting the Praying Jesus

Introduction

Prayer, like Jesus, is complicated. And it's also simple. Both things are true.

Perhaps it is better to say that prayer is part of the mystery of life with God. The truth is that my prayer life is rather simple and uncomplicated, even when I'm wrestling through the night with an issue that has me in its grips. And the truth is that my relationship with the Living Christ is clean and clear and almost childlike. That doesn't mean it is easy or simplistic, but it is life giving.

The Jesus way of prayer is the one I have chosen to follow.

The Jesus way of prayer is the way of loving God with all my heart, mind, and soul, and asking for what I need to love my neighbor as myself. It is the way of seeking first the kingdom of God. The Jesus way is not about my telling God what to do for me. Instead, the Jesus way is about being still and quiet enough to discern what God is trying to do, and then asking for what I need to cooperate with what God is doing.

The Jesus way of prayer is the way of surrender to the Father's will, and the words of that way are "Thy will be done." The wrestling I do in prayer is usually about my difficulty in accepting something I cannot change, and accessing the courage I need to change the things I can change. I am familiar with the idea of the "self-will run riot," and in the school of prayer, I've had lots of lessons, tutorials, and night school classes dealing with my self-will. Still, I want what I want when I want it.

The Jesus way of prayer is most often the way of solitude and silence, the way of listening for the still, small voice of the Holy One. When Jesus drew apart to the other side of the lake or mountainside to pray, I imagine that the words of the psalmist, recorded in Psalm 46:10, were in his mind: "Be still and know that I am God."

For prayer is nothing else than being on terms of friendship with God.
—Saint Teresa

Come near to God and he will come near to you. (James 4:8)

The Jesus way of prayer is the way of gratitude. Before Jesus called Lazarus from his grave, he thanked God that God had heard him (see John 11:41). Before Jesus multiplied the loaves and fish, he thanked God.

The Jesus way of prayer is the way of John 15, the way of abiding in Christ and allowing him to abide in me. It is the way of intimacy with God. The Jesus way of prayer is the way of the Lord's Prayer. The Jesus way of petition in prayer is the way of John 17. When I pray for others and myself the same petitions Jesus prayed for his disciples, I know that I am praying with Jesus rather than against him.

As a facilitator of Centering Prayer workshops and a longtime practitioner of this method of contemplative prayer, I often quote one of my most important teachers, Thomas Keating, the Benedictine monk who formulated this method of praying. How do we know if we are praying "right" or if our prayers are "effective"? Keating says, "Intention is everything."

Indeed, when it comes to praying, what is in our hearts matters most. God told Samuel, "The LORD does not look at the things man looks at. Man looks at the outward appearance, but the LORD looks at the heart" (1 Sam 16:7). And the writer of Proverbs says, "Guard your heart with all diligence, for it is the wellspring of life" (Prov 4:23).

Chapter 22

Meeting Jesus in the Secret Room

Luke introduces what we typically call "The Lord's Prayer" by telling that one of Jesus' disciples said to him, "Lord, teach us to pray" (Luke 11:1-4).

Do you think the disciples had observed Jesus in prayer? What made this disciple curious about the way Jesus prayed? I wonder if the disciples had heard Jesus praying. Were they beginning to connect the amazing deeds Jesus did with what they observed in his prayers?

Matthew sets Jesus' teaching about prayer in a context that contrasts his way of praying with the way the disciples likely saw others pray. Perhaps they, too, struggled with public praying and with prayer groups.

When I discovered contemplative prayer and, most specifically, the way of praying known as Centering Prayer, the practice of prayer finally came alive to me.

Read Matthew 6:5-8 in the translation you normally use. Then read Eugene Peterson's version in *The Message*:

> And when you come before God, don't turn that into a theatrical production either. All these people making a regular show out of their prayers, hoping for stardom! Do you think God sits in a box seat?
>
> Here's what I want you to do: Find a quiet, secluded place so you won't be tempted to role-play before God. Just be there as simply and honestly as you can manage. The focus will shift from you to God, and you will begin to sense his grace.
>
> The world is full of so-called prayer warriors who are prayer-ignorant. They're full of formulas and programs and advice, peddling techniques for getting what you want from God. Don't fall for that nonsense. This is your Father you are dealing with, and he knows better than you what you need. With a God like this loving you, you can pray very simply.

When you pray, go into your room, close the door, and pray to your Father, who is unseen. (Matt 6:6)

We do not know how to pray as we ought. (Rom 8:26)

What About You?

1. Why did Jesus need to pray?

2. How do you define prayer?

3. What has been your experience with prayer?

4. Why did Jesus speak so strongly about hypocrisy and public praying?

5. Was Jesus talking about an actual and literal *secret room* to which one should go for prayer, or is this symbolic of something else?

6. What do you do if you don't have a secret room or a secluded place?

7. How can you "pray without ceasing," as Paul instructed in 1 Thessalonians 5:17, and stay in that secret room or secluded place?

My prayer life changed forever when I was introduced to the concept of "practicing the presence of Christ" as formulated by Brother Lawrence, "the prayer of the heart," and the method of Centering Prayer.

Nothing has aided my understanding of Jesus' teachings about the kingdom of God more than discovering the Scripture where Jesus says that "the kingdom of God is within" (Luke 17:21), and no book has been more important to me in understanding this than the classic, *The Kingdom Within*, by John Sanford.[41]

I was introduced to this concept of the kingdom within as a member of the Yokefellow Spiritual Growth Groups, and when I heard Thomas Keating teach about "going into the secret room of your heart," I knew that prayer is communion with the Spirit of God. I knew that it takes place at a deep level in the human being, and that "going within" is one of the most important tasks of a praying person. Admittedly, "going within" is not something we teach in our American culture that is focused on the external world—doing jobs, tasks, and routines that help us achieve, acquire, and accumulate outer-world things.

In that outer-world mode, even our prayers and prayer groups are often focused on getting God to do what we have written on our prayer lists. Instead of our being conformed to the image of Christ, we work hard to get God to adapt and conform to our desires, our agendas, and our activities, praying "thy will be done, of course" as we do it.

It is wonderful to have a secret room or a quiet, secluded place for prayer. Who wouldn't like that? I have loved my time at the Quiet House at Laity Lodge in the Hill Country of Texas. I value quiet study, where I can close the door and practice Centering Prayer in the pre-dawn hours of the day.

But here is the secret of transforming prayer: the Jesus way of praying takes place at the inner level, symbolically expressed as "the heart," where you and God meet. In that connection, "abiding in Jesus," you open your mind and heart to the indwelling presence of God, who then gives you what you need to live your life moment by moment.

The way we pray without ceasing is the way of Jesus, and it is the way of staying connected to the vine (see John 15), whether you are on the subway, surrounded by hundreds of people, or in the middle of a busy store. In this deep intimacy with God, which takes place within what we call the heart, at least four things happen.

First, the practice of Centering Prayer or other forms of meditation and contemplative prayer gives what Thomas Keating calls "the Divine Therapist" permission to heal the wounds of a lifetime at the unseen level. I have experienced this process, and I know that the consistent practice of Centering Prayer can do just what Keating says.

Second, in this deep intimacy with God, God speaks to you from within, guiding you in subtle ways and in some ways that are not so subtle.

Third, in this intimacy with God, over time you begin to want what God wants. Most people spend their lives asking God for what they want and then "claiming" Jesus' guidance to ask, seek, and knock, interpreting that Scripture as if it means we are supposed to wear God down with our requests. Jesus, however, most likely used the psalms as his prayer book, and he probably knew what the psalmist knew as a secret to "effective" praying: "Delight yourself in the LORD, and he will give you the desires of your heart" (Ps 37:4).

When I was a child, all I could see was that God would somehow, by some magical thinking or magical doing, give me what I desired. The secret of that verse is that the more we delight in God, the more our desires will conform with God's desires for us, so that gradually, over time, we begin to want what God wants for us. So it is that when we pray, we are praying "in his name."

Praying "in Jesus' name" doesn't mean we tack on that phrase at the end of our list of petitions like a slogan. Instead, praying in his name means that we pray in his character or that we pray what God wants because we have taken the time to delight in God and have allowed God to shape our desires.

The fourth thing that happens when we nurture this intimacy with God in the secret place of our inner life is that we begin to see the fingerprints of God more clearly and more often. Instead of looking outside ourselves for "signs" of God's activity, we allow ourselves to be guided by the Spirit, who dwells within.

Exploring the Scriptures
Read Matthew 6:5-8.
1. Describe the kind of prayer life Jesus did *not* want his disciples to have.

2. Describe the prayer life he *did* want for the disciples.

3. What is your reaction to Jesus' words, "Your father knows what you need before you ask"? Do you believe this?

4. Do you think you can trust that God will give you what you need before you ask for it? In what part of your life do you trust God to do this? In what part of your life do you have the most trouble trusting that God will do this?

5. What evidence do you have that God is trustworthy?

Read Luke 11:1-13.
6. How is this teaching different from Jesus' teaching about prayer in Matthew?

7. What does Jesus emphasize in the verses after the Lord's Prayer? Why do you think he does this?

8. Is what we are to ask for, and what the Holy Spirit wants to give us, spiritual abundance or our own agenda?

9. Describe your personal prayer life.

10. How would you like your prayer life to be different?

11. Who would be a good resource for you in nurturing your prayer life?

12. Which of these statements resonates most deeply with you as being *true*? Why?

- Prayer is relationship with God.

- Prayer is communication with God, flowing from God to us and from us to God.

- Prayer is about practicing the presence of Christ.

- Prayer is surrender.

dialogue

I'm so afraid
I don't have enough
What I have isn't good enough!
and the still small Voice whispers,
"Give me what you do have.
See what I can do with what you give me."

You don't understand—do you?
Aren't you far away, distant,
remote? Do you even care
that I am so afraid?
and the still small Voice whispers,
"I do see you . . . I always see you."

How can I know that you
will help me? I cry out to you—
I plead with you—I beg.
God, don't you know how I hate
begging?
and the still small Voice whispers,
"Take courage."

This is it. This is the Big One.
This one will take me down.
Don't you even care?
and the still small Voice whispers,
"It is I."

I can't see you, it's so dark! And I
am so afraid. In fact, I'm terrified.
and the still small Voice says,
"Don't be afraid. Come to me."

Do I dare take one step . . . and then the next?
Yes? No? Maybe?
Yes

Chapter 23

Meeting Jesus in the Lord's Prayer I

The Lord's Prayer is Christianity's greatest prayer.
It is also Christianity's strangest prayer.
It is prayed by all Christians,
but it never mentions Christ.
It is prayed on Sundays,
but it never mentions Sundays.
It is called the "Lord's Prayer",
but it never mentions Lord.
—John Dominic Crossan[42]

I have had six awakenings involving what I was brought up to call "The Lord's Prayer." Each incident that precipitated my awakening occurred when I had been on a serious quest for a deeper experience of the personal Christ for several years. I wanted to pray as Jesus prayed. Perhaps these incidents caught my attention because they were part of my process of learning and because my desire drew the experiences to me.

The first incident occurred when I heard the speaker at a Rotary Club event. I don't remember the topic, but I remember how the group of Rotarians (all men at that time) stood solemnly and prayed the Lord's Prayer together. Before that time, I hadn't heard those words prayed outside a church setting.

"What are they doing with our prayer?" I thought to myself.

It wasn't that I thought Christians owned the Lord's Prayer, but it sounded and felt strange to me in that secular setting. It sounded hollow, somehow, and perfunctory, but I worked hard not to judge. Who was I to know what was in their hearts or minds?

The second incident occurred when I heard that there were orders of the religious whose lives were devoted to praying the Lord's Prayer all through the day. The idea of that fascinated me, and I decided that I would start by praying the prayer in the morning and at night, but also while I walked my set miles around the neighborhood. Often, I thought about those religious people, far away in a monastery or convent, and I felt a sense of solidarity with them.

Another time, I stood with a circle of people who were members of a recovery group. At the end of their meeting, they held hands as they prayed the Lord's Prayer. I don't know what surprised me about that, but something piqued my interest. Somehow, I connected with the prayer and the process of recovery, and it touched something deep in me.

The fourth time I was stunned by the Lord's Prayer, I had asked some of the women in a Bible study I teach to pray the prayer in languages other than English. Before they began, I made the point that around the world, every day, people are praying this prayer—either in solitude or in community with others—in many different languages. As the women each prayed—in Russian, French, Portuguese, Spanish, and Italian—something that felt like a holy hush enveloped those of us in that room.

Most of us in my Baptist tradition do not pray the Lord's Prayer regularly in our worship services. Twice—once at the Benedictine monastery in Snowmass, Colorado, and again at the National Cathedral in Washington, DC—while praying the Lord's Prayer within liturgical settings, joining my voice with the voices of people I don't know but who seemed to take this greatest prayer seriously, I was moved almost to tears. The feeling of unity with my brothers and sisters in Christ who are nevertheless strangers to me has been so powerful that just recalling it brings that sense of worship back to me. I have felt that same power in the prayer when I repeat those words at Palmer Episcopal Church in Houston, when I join my daughter and her family for worship.

One more moment with this prayer almost brings me to my knees, and it is when the family of faith to which I belong stands together and sings Albert Hay Malotte's arrangement of the Lord's Prayer. It means so much to me to sing this prayer within my church community.

What About You?

1. Do you remember the first time you heard someone pray the Lord's Prayer?

2. In what setting has praying this prayer been most meaningful to you?

3. In what setting has praying this prayer has seemed hurried, obligatory, rote, or simply the way to end a meeting?

4. Why do you pray this prayer?

5. Does it mean as much to you as you want it to mean?

~~~

The Foundation for Contemporary Theology provides the city of Houston, Texas, with outstanding speakers for periodic and regular weekend seminars, and John Dominic Crossan is one of my favorites. I've noticed that scholars like him and Marcus Borg, who focus on the study of the life and teachings of Jesus, have an engaging depth of joy and compassion.

Crossan's recent book, *The Greatest Prayer: Recovering the Revolutionary Message*, and his lectures during one seminar weekend provided one of the most profound experiences I have had with the Lord's Prayer, and I will never be able to pray it the same way. Crossan writes, "The Lord's Prayer is, for me, both a revolutionary manifesto and a hymn of hope."[43]

Take a minute to ponder that.

Manifesto? The dictionary definition of manifesto tells me that Crossan is saying something *huge.* A manifesto is a public declaration of intentions, objectives, or motives, as one issued by a government, a sovereign, or an organization.

The Lord's Prayer isn't something you pray on the run. It's not to be taken lightly, and I'm not sure we should toss it around casually without understanding that praying it identifies us with the followers of Jesus. When Jesus taught his disciples to pray this prayer, he knew that identification with him could threaten their lives.

Crossan continues, "It is *revolutionary* because it presumes and proclaims the radical vision of *justice* that is the core of Israel's biblical tradition. It is a *hymn* because it presumes and produces poetic techniques that are the core of Israel's biblical poetry."[44]

As I listened to Crossan unfold the ideas of distributive justice and fairness in his lecture, I began to come to terms with the height and depth and breadth of the prayer that I had prayed *for myself,*

The Lord's Prayer isn't something you pray on the run. It's not to be taken lightly . . .

and I was convicted of my selfishness and self-centeredness. I needed my mind opened and my narrow-mindedness exploded. Crossan asserts that "the entire biblical tradition flowed through every unit of this prayer."[45] Let's study the Lord's Prayer in Scripture.

What About You?
Read Matthew 6:9-13.

1. Have you ever felt that Jesus' prayer has been misused or trivialized in some way?

2. What purpose does this prayer serve for contemporary people?

3. Does this prayer mean the same thing to serious followers of Christ as it does to a crowd at a football game or at a civic meeting?

4. In what ways is this prayer meaningful or relevant to us today?

5. How do you feel about the simplicity of the petitions in this prayer?

6. What do you think of the fact that Jesus taught the disciples to pray for daily bread and that he taught them to pray for "us" and not just "me"?

7. What does praying "give us this day our daily bread" mean for those of us who have enough bread, meat, and jam to sustain us? Why would we need to pray that prayer?

8. What is the most important petition of this prayer?

9. Why does Jesus make such a big deal of forgiveness?

10. What kinds of temptations does his last petition cover?

11. What temptations popped into your mind? Do you think they are the same as the ones that concern Jesus? How seriously do you take those temptations?

12. What do you think Jesus means by "deliver us from the evil one"?

13. There are orders of monks and nuns whose mission is to pray this prayer for the world throughout the day. What effect do you think their prayers have?

For Your Eyes Only

14. Over this week, pray the petitions in this prayer one at a time, slowly and thoughtfully. How does this affect you?

Chapter 24

Meeting Jesus in the Lord's Prayer 2

Our Father.

I don't pray to *my* Father but to *our* Father.

From the first word of his prayer, Jesus establishes the model of praying for us. Indeed, we are privileged to address the Creator of the universe, the Source of all creation, and the Sovereign God as our *Abba*, but it is *our* Father—not just mine.

The second-person plural pronoun sets the tone for the Jesus way of praying. If you take time to meditate on that opening greeting to the Almighty, you may feel both close to God, as you would feel to a loving parent, and at the same time part of the family of God.

We use many images and metaphors for God, constrained by the limitation of language in speaking of what cannot be contained in words. I repeat often the words of a wise man who said, "I would not believe in a God I could define." Jesus, however, well schooled in all of the images of God he has learned in his religious training, chooses the tenderness of Abba—*Papa*. Addressing God in that way has always made me feel my childlikeness before a loving father. Using the word "father" inspires feelings of what it is like to be cared for, protected, provided for, and watched over, so I am comfortable calling God "Father."

But for others, that word is tattered with images of an earthly father who was absent, cruel, neglectful, or indifferent. When that is true for someone, there is an opportunity for deep reflection and inner healing, both in the process of praying with the wound and of talking through the memories and pain with someone who is able to listen in a redemptive way.

There is yet another important aspect of the image of God as Father. In using that image, and in using first-person plural pronouns throughout the prayer, Jesus is stating clearly that we are intimately interconnected with each other. John Dominic Crossan says that with this opening, Jesus reveals God as "Householder of the world house."[46]

For us there is one God, the Father, from whom are all things and for whom we exist, and one Lord, Jesus Christ, through whom are all things and through whom we exist. (1 Cor 8:6)

"Hey, Dad," the college student prayed. "How're ya doin' up there in heaven?"

I nearly fell out of my seat.

In attempting to bring Jesus down to a level we can understand, it's easy to walk over a line into easy familiarity. Casual familiarity can quickly become irreverence, but sometimes you don't know you've crossed a line until it's too late. That Jesus addressed his heavenly Father as *Abba* doesn't mean that we give up a sense of reverence in approaching the Holy One. Familiarity is not the same thing as intimacy.

The Lord's Prayer instantly offers a corrective to that tendency, as it immediately moves from the address, "Our Father," to an acknowledgment of God's holiness. To declare the name and character of God as holy is to differentiate God the Father from any earthly father.

What About You?

1. How do you usually address God in your prayers?

2. Does any experience you have had with an earthly father or father figure affect this prayer for you?

3. How comfortable are you with calling God "Father"?

4. What does it mean to you that God is holy?

5. Why is it important to remember and acknowledge the holiness of God?

6. What does Jesus mean with his first petition, "may your kingdom come on earth as it is in heaven"?

In the first lines of this greatest prayer, Jesus establishes an appropriate order. First, he acknowledges the nearness of God and the holiness of God, and then he states a desire for the rule of God—a rule of love—to be established on the earthly plane as it is in the heavenly or supernatural world. In a world where the Householder/God takes care of things in an orderly manner, there is justice.

In other words, this prayer begins with a request for harmony and integrity of God's purpose within the affairs of this earthly world. What is "above" (of God's kingdom) will be "below" in earthly affairs.

Are you shaking your head in dismay by now? How can things in this world even come close to being in harmony with heaven?

The great thing about living in a world with many challenges and problems is that we who attempt to follow Christ are given many opportunities to bring justice into the world, to love as Christ loved, to promote peace, and to remind each other that we're in this together. The Lord's Prayer is a constant reminder of that!

Return to Matthew's rendering of this prayer in Matthew 6:9-13. Imagine the vertical beam of a cross again, and see it grounded firmly in the earth.

See these words written vertically down the beam:

Our Father
who art in heaven
hallowed be your name.
Your kingdom come
your will be done
on earth
as it is in heaven.

Meditate on the vertical beam that connects heaven and earth, and let it remind you of the constant redemptive activity of God moving throughout creation. When you pray this prayer, you are agreeing with Jesus' prayer, joining him in praying for the Father's will and intention to be established on earth, and declaring your willingness to be a participant and partner in the redemptive process.

Now picture the horizontal beam attached to the vertical beam, making a cross. Picture the words "Our Father" written on the place where the beams connect. Imagine that across the beam is inscribed the petitions of Jesus—and, as we pray them, our petitions—for ourselves and others.

Give us this day our daily bread
Forgive us our trespasses as we forgive those who trespass against us
Lead us not into temptation and deliver us from evil

Meditate on those petitions, remembering that we ask for these things that are the qualities of God's kingdom not just for ourselves but for everyone.

Imagine that the words "For yours is the kingdom, the power, and the glory" are written above the petitions as a ringing affirmation of the truth.

The first part of this greatest prayer establishes our relationship with God as Father. The second part of the prayer moves outward from the heart centered in that intimate relationship and into concerns for oneself and for others.

During World War II, the great old cathedral in Coventry, England, was bombed and nearly completely destroyed. Devastated by the desecration of their holy space, the people of Coventry vowed to rebuild a cathedral, but they chose to leave the bombed shell of the old cathedral and build a new, modern one beside it.

Walking through the ruins of the old cathedral brought me to tears as I thought about the people who had built that first cathedral, the ones who had worshiped there, and the broken-hearted members who had surveyed the damage in the days after the bombing. In the ruins are statues and inscribed plaques that depict the power of forgiveness and reconciliation.

I walked slowly through those ruins, wanting to absorb the impact of what had happened to that cathedral and what resulted from its destruction. The new, modern cathedral stands a few steps across a sidewalk, and connecting the two structures—the old, bombed shell of what used to be and the fresh, contemporary structure—is a wooden beam that was once the cross over the altar in the former cathedral.

Notice that Matthew's version of the Lord's Prayer is followed by one of Jesus' piercing teachings on the power of forgiveness. Jesus must have wanted to emphasize that we must pray from a forgiving heart.

What About You?

1. In what areas are you out of harmony with the will of God?

2. Do you truly want the will of God? Or do you prefer your own will, no matter what?

3. Is Jesus speaking of physical bread—actual food—or the bread of life, spiritual sustenance? Why should we ask for it only one day at a time?

4. In what ways do you trespass in others' business? Who trespasses in your life, manipulating you or trying to control you?

5. Is this world God's "kingdom," whether we acknowledge and declare it or not?

Chapter 25

Meeting Jesus in the High Priestly Prayer

Jesus taught his disciples how to pray in other ways too. By his pattern of going away to commune with God, he modeled the life of prayer. Actions speak louder than words, even with Jesus.

But another of his prayers also teaches us how to pray. There is perhaps no more beautiful picture of Jesus than the one portrayed in what is called "the High Priestly Prayer," which he prayed near the end of his earthly mission.

In John 13, Jesus washes the feet of the disciples in the upper room, and in John 14, 15, and 16, he teaches the disciples some of his most important truths about the coming of the Holy Spirit, servanthood, and the power of love. It seems that the depth of Jesus' message deepens through these five chapters, and at the beginning of John 17, Jesus must have moved away from the disciples, for he began to pray for himself. The tone of this conversation with his Father is tender and poignant.

Clearly, Jesus is coming to terms with the fact that his earthly ministry will end soon, and because he had called these disciples "friends," he must have had a heavy heart at the thought of leaving them. Most likely, he felt the pain of unfinished business; he wondered if he had taught them enough to carry on his work and teach the mysteries and the gospel of good news that he had proclaimed with such fervor.

There are several important points about prayer in John 17. First, Jesus prays for himself. For those of us who were brought up to put ourselves last, this is a startling insight! Yet what Jesus does is crucial in the life of prayer. *He aligns himself with God, the Father, from the beginning of his prayer.*

Thomas Keating, my teacher who developed Centering Prayer, says that he does not offer petitions on behalf of others until he has first opened his mind and heart to the presence of God. How else, he asks, can you avoid imposing your will onto your petitions for another person?

Second, Jesus declares that he has completed the mission for which he was created. Jesus states from the beginning of this prayer that "the time has come." In other words, he knows that things are moving inevitably toward an omega point. There is a sense, as Jesus says to the Father, "glorify me," that he is acknowledging that he has finished his task and completed his assignment. After praying for himself, then, he reports to the Father in verses 6-10 what he has done before moving beyond himself to pray on behalf of his loved ones.

Third, in John 17:3, Jesus defines eternal life as *knowing God*. Eternal life is about intimacy with God! It is about becoming familiar with the ways of God by observing creation, spending time in silence with an open mind and heart, expecting to experience the presence of God, learning about God through the written word, and being willing to "walk and talk" with God in the communion of friendship.

It seems like a limited, earth-bound view of "eternal life" to interpret it in simple terms of length. Instead, consider that eternal life is knowing God. It's not knowing facts about God that keep God detached and impersonal. It's the type of knowledge that comes from deep intimacy, from time spent together, from being transparent, vulnerable, and trusting in the presence of God. Contemplatives and mystics experience the presence of God as a reality of their lives, and that communion with the Living God *is prayer*!

In John 17:5-10, notice Jesus' tenderness and care toward his disciples. Note, as well, what he says in verse 9b: "I am not praying for the world, but for those you have given me, for they are yours."

What About You?

1. What spiritual practices deepen your communion with God?

2. Is it for you to be open, trusting, vulnerable, and transparent in prayer? Why or why not?

3. In what ways do you "practice the presence of Christ"?

4. Is it hard for you to "be still and know" God's presence? Why or why not? (See Ps 46:10.)

5. In John 17, Jesus reveals the depths of his heart. What do you think about his being so open, vulnerable, and transparent? What kind of God does that reveal?

In the next few verses, Jesus petitions the Father on behalf of his disciples.

He prays for *unity* for the disciples with God (John 17:11). He says, "May they be one as we are one." Isn't it amazing to be created with the capacity for unity with the Father as Jesus has unity with the Father? What are the implications of such unity for your life?

Jesus prays that the disciples will have *the full measure of his joy within them* (John 17:13). Happiness is based on external things, but joy is a spiritual quality that comes from within. We do not manufacture joy; it is a fruit of the indwelling Spirit. (See Gal 5:22.) Sometimes we want the fruit of the Spirit, but we don't want to be bothered by the Spirit. Notice that joy flows from unity with God.

Jesus prays for *protection* for the disciples in verse 11, and he repeats the petition in verse 15. He doesn't ask that the disciples be removed from the world. He doesn't want them to live in a holy huddle, talking only with people who talk like they do, dress like they do, and vote like they do. In fact, Jesus instructed them to be salt and light in the world. This petition shows that the *unity* they have with the Father is protected and that the Father also guards the *joy* of that holy friendship.

Finally, Jesus prays that the disciples will be *useful for him,* that their lives and gifts will be set apart to help bring and sustain the rule and reign of God's kingdom (John 17:17). When I was growing up, being useful to God was a priority, but many of us tried to be useful without first aligning ourselves with the desires of God's heart.

What About You?

1. Try an experiment in praying Jesus' prayer in John 17. Over the next week, instead of offering your own prayer requests, petitions, and supplications to God, pray for yourself the petitions Jesus prayed for his disciples. Keep a journal and notice any shifts in your thinking.

2. Imagine that Jesus is sitting with you, praying for you. What would it be like to hear him praying specific petitions for you, asking God to give you these four things: unity with the Father, his joy made full, protection from anything that would come between you and God or destroy your joy, and usefulness that conforms with God's purpose for you?

3. When you pray for your loved ones, do you have in mind a list of what you want God to do for them? Do you believe that you know what is best for those who are nearest to you? Try praying the four requests mentioned in question 2 for your loved ones. How might this change your mind and heart?

4. When you pray for your enemies, how do you pray? Do you dare pray these four petitions for them?

One day as I walked in my neighborhood, I struggled with an issue related to someone I loved deeply who was in a difficult situation. I had no answers for that person, and I didn't even know how to pray for the person.

Paul's open and honest confession about his inability in prayer came to my mind: ". . . the Spirit helps us in our weakness. We do not know what we ought to pray for, but the Spirit himself intercedes for us with groans that words cannot express" (Rom 8:26). Suddenly, it occurred to me that the Spirit of Christ might be interceding for my loved one and me offering the petitions of John 17 to God on our behalf. From that time until now, I have been confident that as I pray these petitions for my loved ones, for myself, and even for those with whom I am estranged, I cooperate with the Spirit of Christ.

Of course, I often slip into my self-centered, selfish petitions, and sometimes I shake my fist at the heavens and demand that God do something my way right now. Then I have to confess and remember the words of the prophet Isaiah. God's ways are not my ways, and for that I am grateful.

My vision simply isn't broad or deep or long enough.

My understanding is not great enough, and I see, always, through a glass darkly.

My intentions are mixed and my motives are tainted by my own self-concern.

My heart is purer on some days than on others, and so it is wise for me to admit that and simply (and with great pain and difficulty, I might add) surrender the things I cannot change; the people for whom I am most deeply concerned, worried, and burdened; and my fondest dreams, my greatest disappointments, and my deepest longings to the hands and heart of God, whose name is Love.

If I am going to pray, "Thy will be done," I have to mean it. Or I have to tell the truth and say, "I'm saying this with my mouth, but in my heart you know I'm praying that my will is done."

It's tough to be honest with God.

It's even tougher not to be honest with God.

Chapter 26

Meeting Jesus and Abiding in Him

John 15 is my favorite chapter in the Bible, especially the image of abiding in Christ and his abiding in us, as branches are attached to a vine.

Imagine the place where the branch of the grapevine is connected to the vine. Envision the place where the life force of the vine rushes out into the branch, giving it the nourishment and energy it needs to produce fruit consistent with the nature of the vine.

That kind of intimacy with the Living Christ reminds me of some of the ways Christian mystics have expressed this phenomenon:

I live in the heart of Christ, who lives in my heart.
I look at God, who is looking at me.
I am searching for the One who has already found me.

Paul, whose experience of the Living Christ transformed him from the inside out, said it like this in Philippians 3:12: "I'm not saying that I have this all together, that I have it made. But I am well on my way, reaching out for Christ, who has so wondrously reached out for me."

In the middle of a restless night long ago, I prowled around in my husband's study, looking for something. Suddenly, for no known reason, a small paperback book fell out of the bookshelf and onto the floor. I reached down to pick it up and return it to the shelf, but when I saw the title, something in me knew that I had come to the end of my search.

I turned off the light in the study and went to the living room, where I began to read Andrew Murray's classic book/commentary on John 15, *Abide in Christ*.

That little book never made it back to my husband's shelf, and the truths contained within it formed the foundation for what was

. . . Christ in you, the hope of glory. (Col 1:27b)

It is to you who have heard and hearkened to the call, "Come unto me" that this new invitation comes, "Abide in me."
—Andrew Murray[47]

I pray that out of his glorious riches he may strengthen you with power through his Spirit in your inner being, so that Christ may dwell in your hearts through faith. (Eph 3:16)

to become a lifelong quest in the spiritual practices of the contemplative life and prayer. In John 15, I found what would nourish and feed me for the rest of my life.

The next week, over lunch, my husband's associate in the Baptist Student Union at Stephen F. Austin State University casually mentioned to me that she was going to lead a yearlong small group experience for some of the college students. "We are going to learn what it means to abide in Christ," she told me, and I felt a shiver run down my spine.

If we attune ourselves to God's movement, God often guides us through synchronicities, coincidences, and the amazing harmony between creation and daily life.

John 15 is an allegory that shows a picture of an individual's relationship with the Living Christ as the vine and the branches, tended in every way by the vinedresser, God, who knows when to prune and when to water, when to plant and when to harvest the fruit of the vine.

It is a beautiful yet everyday, ordinary image that connected with the people of Jesus' time, given their familiarity with vineyards and grapevines and the association with the image of Israel as the vine. Jesus had a way of using what was nearby and part of the everyday experience of his disciples to teach them about the transcendent and holy.

Through the years of reading and teaching this passage and teaching Centering Prayer, one of the many methods of silent prayer and other forms of contemplative praying, I have come to recognize that many of us live in fear or in anger instead of "living in Christ." People can live their whole lives in worry or resentment, guilt or shame, all the time proclaiming to have been "saved." It is possible to live in chaos and disorder, conflict and warfare, even while you proclaim yourself to be a "Christian."

I'm not in the position to determine who is and who isn't a true Christian. I do know, however, that the fruit—the evidence—of the presence of the Living Christ in a person is clearly stated in Galatians 5:22, and I know when I have detached myself from an intimate relationship with the Living Christ and am not dwelling/living/abiding in him.

Exploring the Scriptures
Read John 15 in more than one translation. Read it every day for a week and respond to these questions.

1. What is an *allegory*?

2. Why would Jesus use the image of a vine and branches to talk about his relationship with God? Why would he use that image to talk about our relationship with God/Jesus?

3. What does it means to "abide" in Christ? (Other translations use the terms "remain," "dwell," "live.")

4. How do we "remain" in Christ, practically? What is the result of "remaining" in Christ?

5. What is Jesus talking about when he refers to "the fruit" that is the result of abiding/remaining/living/dwelling in him?

6. What is the promise in verse 7? How do you feel about that promise?

7. What fruit is the result of this intimate relationship with Christ?

8. In terms of our lives today, what does the pruning Jesus talks about look like? How does pruning happen?

9. What is friendship with Jesus/the Living Christ like for us today?

10. How does this chapter connect with the idea of "the kingdom of God/heaven" and "the kingdom within"?

11. How does abiding in Christ connect with being a disciple of Christ?

12. What about love sets one apart from those whose primary motivating force is not love?

13. Paul wrote that we are to "pray without ceasing" in 1 Thessalonians 5:17. How does the practice of "abiding in Christ" support the practice of "praying without ceasing"? Are those terms synonymous?

For Your Eyes Only
14. How important is it for you to "remain in Christ"?

15. What do you do to keep the connection with the Living Christ alive and well?

Jesus invited his disciples to come to him with the promise of giving rest, and the secret of that rest is revealed in John 15. Andrew Murray said that "entire surrender to Jesus is the secret of perfect rest." He wrote that abiding in Christ has in it the conditions of discipleship without which there can be no thought of maintaining the rest that was bestowed on first coming to Christ. "The rest" is being in Christ, not something Christ gives apart from himself.

What About You?

1. Have you ever tried to give to others from an "empty well"? If so, when?

2. Have you ever tried to lead someone where you hadn't been? Explain.

3. Have you ever tried to teach someone something you didn't know? What was the outcome?

4. Have you ever tried to perform or produce like you think a Christian should without the experience of resting in Christ? If so, when?

I no longer call you slaves; I call you friends. (John 15:15)

Practicing the presence of Christ or abiding in Christ is the secret to an effective prayer life and to life itself. It is the way of connecting with the Source of life so that what you need can flow into your mind and heart from the invisible Source itself. It is the secret of the kind of love that is life giving and lasting; it is the secret of authentic discipleship. The practice of abiding in Christ is as necessary to an effective ministry of any kind as air is to water.

After you have read John 15, sit in silence with your eyes closed and imagine yourself as a branch attached to the vine. Imagine what it is like to have the life, love, power, and energy of the Living Christ flowing into you. Imagine that you have no barriers erected that might block or stop the flow of Christ's love into your mind and heart. Imagine that you hear the voice of Jesus saying to you the

words of John 15, especially these: "I no longer call you slaves; I call you friends."

In the cross on the previous page, note again that the words on the vertical beam related to one's relationship to God. The words on the horizontal beam refer to our human interaction.

Imagine a new way of being in the world. Imagine allowing the love of Christ to flow freely through you and out into the world you live in, manifested in acts of mercy and compassion, creativity and productivity, love, joy, and peace. Imagine.

Part Six

Meeting Jesus in the Eternal Now

Introduction

> One of the greatest needs of our age is for . . . a way through life that will lead us to a conscious awareness of God and of his intentions for us . . . .
>
> —John Sanford

"When the power of love overcomes the love of power, the world will know peace."

The interview on the talk show was background noise; I had only lukewarm interest in the guest. But when he spoke those words about power and love, I stopped what I was doing and grabbed a pen and paper.

Those words describe the kingdom of God.

Who knew that singer Jimi Hendrix could capture the concept of the kingdom of God for a contemporary culture? Is that what he intended?

> The kingdom of heaven is like . . . a treasure hidden in a field. (Matt 13:44)

When we citizens of the world think about the word "kingdom," we think of a specific span of land with boundaries that define the kingdom. In our understanding, that kingdom has a ruler with power over the kingdom and subjects who are to defer to the laws and rule of the ruler.

Jesus had a different idea when he talked about the kingdom of God or the kingdom of heaven, and teaching about that different kingdom formed a central portion of his mission.

Jesus was born into a time and a milieu—religious, political, and cultural—in which power and control ruled. Where power and control rule, people are desperate for love. Jesus embodied love, and when he said, "Follow me," he wanted people to follow him in learning how to love as he loved.

> Where love is lacking, power and control rush in.
>
> —Carl Jung

The kingdom of God, in Jesus' terms, is about *a way of being in the world*, a lifestyle that reflects the nature of God and the teachings of Jesus. It is about the rule and reign not of power but of love. It is a state of mind and a way of living that is informed by Jesus' greatest commandment: "Love the Lord your God with all

> The kingdom of heaven is like yeast . . . . (Matt 13:33)

your heart, mind and soul, and your neighbor as yourself" (Matt 22:37-38).

The kingdom of God is about the afterlife, but it is more than that. It is about this life, here and now. The present-tense reality of God's kingdom happens when anyone attempts to live according to the teachings of Jesus and under the guidance of the Living Christ.

Mark, the first of the four Gospels in the New Testament, introduced the idea of the kingdom of God, the *basileia*: ". . . Jesus went into Galilee, proclaiming the good news of God. 'The time has come,' he said. 'The Kingdom of God is near!'" (Mark 1:14-15). The "nearness" and "newness" of Jesus' proclamation carries urgency. "Come, follow me," he said, inviting his disciples into the project of communicating what the kingdom of God is all about.

Mark uses the term "kingdom of God" fourteen times in his Gospel, and Luke uses it thirty-two times. Matthew uses the term "kingdom of heaven" thirty-two times and "kingdom of God" five times, but there doesn't seem to be a distinction or difference between the two terms. Interestingly, the writer of John uses the term only twice, but it is thought that John's use of the term "eternal life" is synonymous with the term "kingdom of God." Eugene Peterson's phrase, "the Jesus way," also describes the type and quality of life that is characteristic of a follower of Jesus. The Beatitudes, recorded in Matthew 5, amplify the description of a follower of Jesus. Those who follow Jesus, attempting to live by his teachings and in surrender to his spirit, will be formed by his spirit.

Clearly, the kingdom of God that Jesus came to proclaim is a kingdom of love. Writer Scot McKnight says in his book *The Jesus Creed* that the prayer that accompanies this way of being in the world is the Lord's Prayer. "At the bottom," McKnight writes, "prayer is simple. It is the loving communication with God. All we need for prayer is an open heart."[48]

Thomas Keating, my teacher in Centering Prayer, says that we need an open mind and an open heart. I have learned through my experience in contemplative prayer that "practicing the presence of Christ" in everyday life is a powerful way to enter "the kingdom of heaven" or live "the Jesus way."

In order to lift water up from a well, it is necessary to have a rope long enough to reach the water. The teachings of Jesus are such a rope. They are the link that we can use to connect us with the depths of ourselves and so to God.

—John Sanford

The rediscovery of the personal and creative side of Christianity is more possible today than it has been for many centuries because of the uncovering of the unconscious . . . .

—John Sanford

The kingdom of heaven is like . . . a mustard seed . . . . Though it is the smallest of all plants, yet when it grows, it is the largest of garden plants . . . .
(Matt 13:31-32)

Chapter 27

Meeting Jesus in the Kingdom of God

Once again, I invite you to imagine the cross that appeared in chapter 14: the vertical beam placed firmly in the earth so that it is stable and still, with these words inscribed: "Seek first the kingdom of God." On the horizontal crossbeam are these words: "and all these things will be added to you."

Keep that cross in mind as you study the Scriptures.

Exploring the Scriptures
Read Matthew 6:33.
1. What did Jesus mean by the term "kingdom of God"? What does that term mean to us today?

Read Matthew 6:25-34.
2. What is the context of Jesus' statement in verse 33 about the kingdom of God? What comes before and what comes after?

3. List three behaviors that could be interpreted as "seeking the kingdom of God."

Read Matthew 13, in which Jesus compares "the kingdom of God" to several different things.
4. How would you describe the kingdom of God in your own words?

The kingdom of God is a spiritual reality, personally experienced by the individual, capable of psychological description.

—John Sanford

Read John 3:3.

5. What does Jesus say to Nicodemus about the kingdom?

6. What does being born again have to do with "seeing" the kingdom of God?

7. Why do you think Jesus taught the disciples to pray "your kingdom come" in the Lord's Prayer? What does it mean when you pray those words?

8. How would you describe the kingdom of God to a contemporary person?

Read Luke 9:23, 57-62.

9. How do these verses relate to "seeking first the kingdom of God"?

10. What is the difference between an earthly kingdom and the kingdom of God?

For Your Eyes Only

11. What do you want from God?

12. What do you think God wants for you?

13. What does it mean for you to "seek first the kingdom of God" in your daily life?

14. What does it cost you to follow Jesus?

I tell you the truth . . . no one who has left home or wife or brothers or parents or children for the sake of the kingdom of God will fail to receive many times as much in this age, and in the age to come, eternal life. (Luke 18:29-30)

When I try to wrap my mind around the concept of "the kingdom of God," it helps me to remember how easily I impose my limited, earth-bound understanding and definition of "kingdom rule" onto a spiritual reality. It also helps to remember that if I am to know anything about the kingdom of God, either on earth or in the afterlife, I should immerse myself in the teachings of Jesus to learn what Jesus thought and did. Finally, I need to remember that this kingdom of God is a spiritual reality, and it will be lived out in my daily life. What I experience on the inside will be manifested in outer-world behavior.

Jesus asked us to seek the kingdom—not seize it, capture it, purchase it, or earn it—and the act of seeking is an ongoing process. Indeed, the journey is the destination when it comes to seeking the kingdom of God.

In Matthew 7:7, Jesus said, "Ask and you shall receive; seek and you will find; knock and the door will be opened to you." The verb tense indicates that we are to keep on asking, keep on seeking, and keep on knocking, and the promise is that with that kind of quest, we will eventually walk into what we seek. In other words, for those who would love to be spoon-fed our spiritual strength and faith, we find what we are looking for by getting off the sidelines and joining the Spirit of God, who seems to love to move us toward what we seek.

To borrow a well-worn term, I have learned that the way truly is found by walking. I have learned that all who wander are not lost and that the goal or destination often changes on the way toward the goal. The point is to go on the journey.

We Americans are oriented for results. We want to be able to measure and graph what we're after. We want to be able to see a day's pay for a day's work, and we want rewards fast on our terms. We have been trained or programmed to work harder to achieve, accomplish, and acquire what we've decided is our goal, and when it comes to the pilgrimage of faith, it is sometimes hard to switch gears and allow ourselves to live in the paradox that says that we are both to seek and to wait on God. We are to knock on the doors of information, wisdom, and answers, but we are to allow ourselves to be guided toward something we may not be able to define.

In my Baptist tradition, we usually have the Lord's Supper served to us, and I have heard that is symbolic of God's coming to us and our serving each other. When I visit with my friends at Palmer Episcopal Church, we stand up, walk to the Communion rail, kneel, and receive the Eucharist. I like this observance both ways, but the act of standing up and walking to the altar always reminds me of the counsel of Jesus when he says that we are to seek the kingdom of God.

From my friends who are in recovery programs and in my own process of working the Twelve Steps, I have learned that the program is their first priority, and it is staggering and breathtaking to hear their witness to the absolute necessity of putting *first things first.*

Sometimes I wish that those of us whose character defects and addictions are not as life-threatening could have the same sense of urgency about overcoming our narcissism, materialism, control, and power issues as AA members do about keeping themselves sober and clean. It's easy to hate the substances that destroy lives, but we easily excuse, minimize, or trivialize the powers of selfishness and greed, hate and anger, fear and worry, envy and jealousy, resentment and bitterness—all of which can destroy relationship, devastate churches and organizations, and ruin the health of the one who holds those afflictive emotions to herself as tightly as an addict clings to a bottle or a needle.

First things first is a biblical principle. And isn't that what Jesus meant when he said, "Seek first the kingdom of God"?

> A person who once has seen the treasure of the kingdom of heaven will be willing to pay the price, for its value is above all other values, and a person who once enters into the new life of the kingdom of heaven will have in order his or her relationship to the material side of life.
>
> —John Sanford

To seek God first is to attune myself to God's presence and action at the beginning of the day.

To seek God first is to make time to orient myself to a right relationship with God throughout the day, to listen for guidance, to ask for direction, to be willing to surrender my will to God's will hour by hour, day by day.

To seek God first is to want the way of love more than the way of power and control.

To seek God first puts me in an inner dialogue and often an outer conflict with all the other gods that want to take first place in my daily calendar and in my affections and attention. You know those gods: family, work, play, success, money, position, achievement, power, education, pleasure, accomplishment, acquisition. These may seem like benign gods, I suppose, but they are usually behind the more overtly sinister ones: drugs, food, gambling, religion, work, other people, alcohol, shopping, chaos, conflict, the thrill.

To seek God first is to place God and our relationship as my top priority, knowing that what I am up against is my own self-will, run riot.

When I was a child and even a teenager, I seized the "ask, seek, and knock" Scripture with an egocentric delight. After all, Jesus made those promises in Matthew 7:8 that assure me of receiving what I ask for. How easy it is for us to take a spiritual truth and turn it into an ego-satisfying guarantee we've made up for ourselves.

The "all these things" that will be added to us when we choose to seek God's kingdom first are not the things of our selfishness and self-concern, but the spiritual realities that are the gifts and blessings of abiding in Christ, seeking first the kingdom, and loving the Lord our God with all our hearts, minds, and souls, and our neighbors as ourselves.

Over a lifetime, I've learned that my part of the covenant relationship with the Almighty is to seek God first, abide in and love God, and trust God with the results. It's my job to put God first in my affections and attention and then go on about my day, trusting that the one who loves me will give me what I need and, often, what I desire.

Taking our focus and obsession off what we have decided is God's will for us and trusting God with the processes is a huge challenge to those who love to plan, control, and be in charge. I've learned, however, that "the fruit of the Spirit" really is "love, joy, peace, patience, kindness, goodness, faithfulness, gentleness, and self control" (Gal 5:22). I've learned how often I want the fruit but don't want to be bothered by seeking first the rule of the Spirit within my inner life. I've learned that I can have everything in the outer world I could possibly want, but it is meaningless without the love of God within. I've learned that when I move, choose, act, and love from a center grounded in surrender to the Living Christ, which results from my seeking the kingdom of God first, everything in my life works better from the beginning of the day to the end.

Putting *first things first* works.

Chapter 28

Meeting Jesus Within

As if it were yesterday, I remember the night I first heard the words of Jesus recorded in Luke 17:21: "The kingdom of God is within you."

I was twenty-six years old and was sitting in a Yokefellow Spiritual Growth Group with a dozen other pilgrims on the path of learning what Jesus might have meant by that simple, life-changing truth.

Something resonated in me, as if the truth I heard and read in the Scriptures struck a chord of awakening. Though I had probably heard that verse countless times in the past, I was *hearing* it for the first time. And then again, *it was as if I had always known it.*

Learning what that truth means has been the journey of a lifetime for me. Indeed, the "inner kingdom" is the pearl of great price, the treasure hidden in the field, the place within where God is.

Naturally, if you should perform surgery on my heart, you wouldn't find "Jesus," though as a child I invited Jesus into my heart. If you were to do an autopsy of my body, you wouldn't find my soul, my unconscious, or my subconscious. And yet, when I speak of this inner reality, there is generally a sense of recognition in others.

It seems true that the reality of the inner life has been neglected in a culture that is more focused on outer-world accomplishments and external realities. In fact, some people within the culture either disdain the idea of an inner world or are embarrassed to talk about feelings, desires, inner conflicts, or inner warfare.

For many in Western culture, value is placed only on what can be seen or measured by the senses or by data—what can be manipulated, charted, bought, or sold.

Perhaps the impact of hearing those words was so strong because, intuitively, I knew about the inner kingdom but had been educated and had lived in a world that emphasized the outer world and minimized or discounted the inner world. Perhaps my reaction was one of relief because Jesus' words brought balance to a culture that was weighted toward the material, the tangible, and the measurable.

In that small group of seekers, we were assigned the task of "going within" to discover how the forces of anger, hate, guilt,

> The kingdom of God is within you. (Luke 17:21)

> The kingdom of God is a spiritual reality, personally experienced by the individual, capable of psychological description.
>
> —John Sanford

shame, feelings of inferiority and inadequacy, and the big demon, fear, were at work, fueling behavior that was self-destructive and counterproductive in our relationships. As we began awakening to our inner motivations and afflictive feelings, sharing them with each other, and praying for each other, I began to come at this truth from another direction. Indeed, when those afflictive emotions rule my inner life, what is within me is a kingdom of hell.

Several years later, I purchased a book at The Church of the Savior that has become one of the most important books of my life. Written by Jungian analyst and Episcopal priest John A. Sanford, *The Kingdom Within* (1987) has given me a new understanding of the teachings of Jesus, particularly about the kingdom of God and Jesus' parables. The understandings provided by John Sanford and the life-changing and life-giving process of depth analysis have made the life and teachings of Jesus move off the pages of my Bible and into my inner life.

I have always been a student of the Bible, and I have always been involved in a Christian church at an intimate, consistent level, but the understanding of the inner world and how I can have a relationship with the Living Christ in the "secret room" of this inner kingdom have changed my life. This inner relationship has healed and transformed me, empowered and liberated me, and for that I am profoundly grateful.

Here's even more good news: The process is ongoing. The journey continues. As I surrender my will to the care of God as I understand God, who for me is revealed by the man Jesus, I am being changed, healed, and transformed. As I continue to abide in Christ and ask him to abide in me, I am being empowered and liberated. Salvation is a process that begins with an event and then continues, carrying one on the road to becoming whole and healthy. And perhaps holy.

In his introduction, Sanford writes, "No treatment of the inner meaning of Jesus' sayings can be complete that does not take into account the reality of the unconscious, for only an appreciation of the realness of our inner life can return us to something like the New Testament view of human beings and the world."[49] As I write this, only three nights ago I sat in Dr. James Hollis's class at the Jung Center in Houston, Texas, and heard him lecture on the "discovery" of the unconscious by Sigmund Freud and Carl Jung. I listened intently as he described how part of the break between Jung and Freud was over Jung's belief in the spiritual dimension of the unconscious. Then Jim said, "Only ten percent of practitioners

> The reality of the inner world was known to the people of the New Testament. The demons and angels, principalities and powers, dreams and visions that throng the pages of the New Testament bear testimony to the conviction of the early Christians that conscious life was immersed in a sea of spiritual reality.
>
> —John Sanford

[meaning therapists, psychologists, psychiatrists] work with the unconscious."

Admittedly, it is big work to go into the depths of a person's unconscious and attempt to untangle the many factors that make humans do what we do. Jesus understood this. Notice how many times he said, "Fear not!" when he healed someone. Did he understand how the power of fear could sabotage even his healing? When he approached the crippled man at the pool of Bethesda, he asked, "Do you want to get well?" (John 5:1-15). Who wouldn't say, "Of course I want to get well! Are you crazy?"

Exploring the Scriptures
Read John 5:1-15
1. What do you think life was like for the invalid who had been lying by the pool at Bethesda for thirty-eight years?

2. What prompted Jesus to ask him if he wanted to get well?

3. What reasons might have kept the man stuck, lying forever by the pool?

4. Could the man's response to Jesus' question have been valid? Or was it an excuse?

5. If it is fear that makes us make excuses, what was the man's real fear?

6. Whatever his reason, Jesus confronted him with a new opportunity and a command to get up, pick up his mat, and walk. What do you suppose it was like for the invalid to hear that?

7. What was it in the man that made him respond to Jesus' command at once?

8. How is it possible that the Jews who were watching Jesus heal this man were more concerned with keeping the Sabbath law than the healing of the invalid?

9. When Jesus saw the man at the temple, he told him to "stop sinning" and stated that something worse might happen if he did. If sin is separation from God and "missing the mark" of who you are intended to be, what do you suppose the man's sin was?

For Your Eyes Only
10. What kinds of excuses do you use to keep yourself separate from that which might heal you or that which you know you should be doing?

11. You may not be an invalid physically. Are there other parts of your life where you are paralyzed either by fear, worry, guilt, or shame, or by feelings of insecurity or anger? What does that paralysis keep you from doing in your life?

12. If you heard Jesus saying to you, "Get up. Pick up your mat and walk," what might that mean for your life?

There are forces in all of us that crippled us from within. Paul knew this principle of human nature. He wrote, "For what I want to do, I do not do, but what I hate I do." And then he added, "What a wretched man I am!" (See Rom 7:14-20.)

However powerful these teachings are and however enormous their potential for change is, John Sanford has a warning for us: "At the same time, the sayings of Jesus must not be 'psychologized.' It would be dangerous to reduce what Jesus has said to anyone's psychological system and to equate the images of Jesus with the jargon of some particular psychological creed."[50] In other words, we shouldn't take Jung's system of thought (his hermeneutic) or anyone else's and place it over the holy Scriptures.

Sanford continues,

> The beauty of the teachings of Jesus is that they do not depend upon any system of thought, for Jesus did not express himself by means of jargon or concepts but by means of living images, figures and parables. In this way he succeeded in freeing his message from history and making it timeless and applicable to all ages. His teachings do not come from the world conceptualized and historically conditioned; they are drawn from the well of life itself.[51]

What I learned from that Yokefellow group, from the writings of John Sanford, and from a lengthy process of depth analysis and the teachings of Carl Jung opened doors of understanding in my mind. What I learned was communicated to me in contemporary language, and while the Scripture was already alive, the psychological truths that elucidated the teachings of Jesus made such sense to me that the more I learned, the deeper my understanding of Jesus' teachings became.

And I have much more to learn.

If you accept Jesus' idea that the kingdom of God is within, how do you connect with it? Here are my teachers' suggestions:

• Make a conscious effort to wake up, to become aware of what is going on within you and around you. Good communication training begins with an emphasis on *self-awareness* and consciousness.

• Pay attention to your thoughts, your reactions to outer-world events, your judgments, and your mental chatter. Especially notice what you criticize and judge in others, and ask yourself if you are judging in others what is actually in you. That is called *projection*, and Jesus knew about it. He's the one who said, "Judge not, or you too will be judged. For in the same way you judge others, you will be judged, and with the measure you use, it will be measured to you" (Matt 7:1-2).

• Become conscious of your behavior, your habits, and your routines.

• Pay attention to your feelings. What sets them off? Which afflictive feeling is most damaging to you?

• Make an inquiry into your desires and motivations. Ask yourself often, "What do I want?" and "Why am I doing this?"

• Wake up to your slips of the tongue, dreams, and physical symptoms. Make a habit of asking yourself, "What does this mean?"

These suggestions are intended to increase self-awareness, and self-awareness is a fine inhibitor of self-centeredness. The more you know yourself, the more energy you have to make good and loving choices. I've also been told that the more you know yourself, the more you know God, and the more you know God, the more you know yourself. My experience supports that 100 percent.

But what about the inner kingdom and practicing the presence of Christ, who dwells within? I learned that we do not "go within" to the inner kingdom alone. In a way, we are led there by the Spirit of God, and we are met there by the indwelling Spirit, and when we return our conscious awareness back to our outer-world responsibilities and tasks, that same Spirit is within us, guiding us, leading us, and directing us—if we allow it to happen.[52]

Although I have written in other places about how I experienced and witnessed in my parents the example of what it means to live in personal, dynamic love relationship with the Living Christ, I have also learned so much from these methods of praying:

• Practicing the presence of Christ as a moment-by-moment discipline.

• Centering Prayer as taught by Thomas Keating and some of his students.

• Using the imagination to enter into the Gospel stories and experience an encounter with Jesus as if you are in that story.

Thinking It Over

When I was a child, I learned a song that now astounds me with its simplicity and profundity: "Into my heart, into my heart— / Come into my heart, Lord Jesus. / Come in today. Come in to stay. / Come into my heart, Lord Jesus."

Even when I was a child, I knew that the literal Jesus didn't take up residence within my physical heart. With my child's mind and heart, I understood the metaphor.

As an adult, I have come to understand that my consciousness of the Living Christ as part of my inner landscape of characters is meaningful and helpful. When anxious or afraid, I turn to that kingdom within, asking for guidance from the Living Christ within. When lost or confused, I turn to that Living Christ within, and ask for clarity or direction. When lonely or in grief, I seek to connect with the Presence of the Comforter. When I am in need of healing, I turn to the Great Physician within, and when I am simply wanting to surrender to the Living Christ, I know that all I have to do is turn my attention to the "Christ in me," as Paul stated it.

It's interesting how it all works. I turn my attention to the inner kingdom and the presence of the Living Christ, asking for connection or asking for what I need, knowing all along that it is the presence of the Living Christ who starts the conversation.

I love that wisdom from many of the mystics: "I seek for God, who is seeking for me. / I rest in the heart of God, who rests in my heart. / I see the One who sees me."

1. What is your understanding of Jesus' term "the kingdom within"?

2. If your inner kingdom is ruled by all kinds of characters such as the Natural Child, the Adapted Child, the Free Child, the Inner Critic, the Nurturing Parent, the Indulgent Parent, the Judge and Jury, the Responsible Adult, the Wise Sage, etc., what place does the "Living Christ" have in your inner landscape?

3. What reaction do you have to the words from the child's song "Come into my heart, Lord Jesus"?

4. Would you prefer to stay focused on God's setting up a ruling kingdom like the ones we know about on earth, or do you prefer the idea of the kingdom within, a kingdom of love that is guided by the Living Christ? (Or does all of that give you a headache?)

Unless you change and become like little children, you will never enter the kingdom of heaven. (Matt 18:3)

I'm telling you, once and for all, that unless you return to square one and start over like children, you're not even going to get a look at the kingdom, let alone get in. Whoever becomes simple and elemental again, like this child, will rank high in God's kingdom. (Matt 18:3, The Message)

Chapter 29

Meeting Jesus as a Child

I have a lot of empathy for Nicodemus.

John tells about his dilemma in John 3. In the dark of night, the Jewish leader Nicodemus had an encounter with Jesus that can still teach us something about ourselves.

We can speculate about why Nicodemus went in the covering of night to ask Jesus what he could do to earn eternal life. He says that he had kept all the laws and lived as a righteous man, working hard to do good works and live an exemplary life, but for some reason something was missing.

Truthfully, many of us who have tried to be good enough and work hard enough understand Nicodemus's plight. There's just something about trying to adapt to outer-world authorities, rules and regulations, guidelines and standards that doesn't fill the hole in our souls.

Jesus' response to Nicodemus is strange, unless you understand Jesus' principle about following him. "You have to be born again," Jesus told Nicodemus, and of course, Nicodemus protested by challenging Jesus on the absurdity of returning to his mother's womb.

Again, to try to interpret the teachings of Jesus literally often trivializes what Jesus said. Instead of telling Nicodemus to return to his mother's womb, an obvious impossibility, Jesus was essentially saying the same thing Matthew records in 18:3: "You have to become like a little child if you're going to enter the kingdom of heaven."

This presents all of us with a dilemma. After all, we spend decades building an outer-world persona, the necessary ego that helps us get around in the world. We work hard earning a degree of proficiency or creating an image that makes people think we have it all together in our everyday lives. We work hard to build our defenses against the pain of life or to keep people from seeing our wounds and defects, our faults and our weak spots, and some of us—maybe most—work hard to act like adults. Then Jesus comes along and tells us that we have to be born again and become childlike in order to enter the kingdom of heaven.

What does he mean?

It is important to note that Jesus didn't say that we are to become childish, a state of being often associated with being self-centered, petulant, or demanding. Childish people expect other people to take care of them, and they whine when they don't get their way. Obviously, that isn't what Jesus means.

Instead, the childlikeness Jesus says is necessary for entering the kingdom of heaven is a state characterized by openness, vulnerability, trust, and wonder. To be born again indicates that we are to approach life with God with a sense of willingness to see God in a fresh way, to approach the spiritual life with a mind that is unencumbered by the ways of the past. (That doesn't mean that you discard the past altogether, but that you are not bridled or chained to the ways of the past.)

Once, when I related something my granddaughter had said when she was three—something spontaneous and so terribly honest that it took our breath away—my sister responded, "Why . . . when are we going to teach that child . . . to lie?"

Of course, we don't want our children to lie, but they still learn how to lie. And the greater the disapproval or chaos factor in their lives, the more they learn how to lie. My granddaughter Abby felt safe, and so she spoke freely, without fear of censure.

This doesn't mean that we can say anything we want to say without concern for others' feelings. It does mean that we are able to speak openly and honestly with God and in our inner lives, and the more honest we are with God and with ourselves, the more likely we are to be honest with each other.

There is another aspect to the childlikeness required for adults who want to enter the kingdom of heaven. John Sanford describes how the disciples had an "ego attitude" when they went to Jesus, represented by their concern about who was going to be the greatest in the kingdom of heaven. Clearly, the disciples were under the ego-driven impression that Jesus was going to set up an earthly kingdom where he would rule in the fashion of the political rulers of their day, and they would, by nearness to him, get to bask in the reflected glory of his kingship.

There are still some who want this kind of Messiah and are convinced that the day is coming when Jesus will set up a reign of power, control, and domination, and that if they are in the right place at the right time, they, too, can be part of his power group.

> The child is frequently used by Jesus to represent one who has entered the kingdom of heaven. . . . One reason for this is that little children have no mask; they are what they seem to be and express directly what they feel without hypocrisy.
>
> —John Sanford

But Jesus faced and triumphed over that temptation in the wilderness encounter with the Adversary.

For many, the little child within is a wounded child. For some, the little child we were was abandoned, neglected, or, sadly, abused. Some people grow up feeling cherished, beloved, and protected, and so that little child flourishes and thrives, secure in its parents' presence and affection.

The inner child in all of us is an important part of our inner landscape and has much to teach us.

Perhaps Nicodemus neglected the part of himself that was still open, curious, and spontaneous, and he became stuck being an adult, being in charge, taking care of responsibilities, being a big shot.

What About You?

1. Can you remember the last time you felt free?

2. When was the last time you engaged in some activity for the pure joy of it?

3. What last captivated your sense of wonder or awe?

4. When was the last time you let yourself look or feel foolish for the sake of a child?

5. When was the last time you expressed love and affection for someone spontaneously, freely and un-self-consciously?

> If we deny the child within, we become childish. We do not free ourselves form the child within by denying it, but fall victim to its negative qualities in the form of infantile, regressive or dependent attitudes.
>
> —John Sanford

> If we recognize and accept the legitimacy of the child-self, so that we become as a little child in the positive sense, then the child-self is expressed in our personality as freedom, creativity and the continual generation within us of new life.
>
> —John Sanford

6. When was the last time you let yourself cry when you were sad?

7. When was the last time you let yourself dance or sing without concern for what anyone would think?

8. When was the last time you let yourself wander through a day without concern for what time it was?

9. When was the last time you played at something you didn't have to win?

10. When was the first time you knew that you were the beloved child of God, no matter what?

11. When was the last time you learned something new that challenged everything you'd always believed was true?

12. When was the last time you laughed hard enough to feel like you'd had a workout?

When my first granddaughter was a toddler, she ran toward life with exuberance, often repeating, "Yes, Yes!" as she ran across the room, arms and heart wide open. This isn't the only poem my grandchildren have inspired, but this one seems to resonate with the idea of becoming childlike. It is dedicated to Abby Summer.

Yes!

Yes! Yes!
The yearling races toward the thing she wants—
a treat, a trip or a person—
pumping tiny legs and bobbing her head
in such gladsome affirmation
that sometimes
she trips on her own exuberance.
Yes! Yes!
she cries, picking herself up.
Her falls are only temporary annoyances
and necessary practice in
learning how to get up and go again
instead of signs
that she should stop her pursuit of
whatever she is "yessing."
I watch her and laugh—
and something forgotten stirs within me
for I am too long confined and restrained
by too many no's—
no's that have hardened my heart and imprisoned my soul,
They are good no's, most of them:
the no's of rules and rules, reason, logic and limitation,
convention and conformity—practicality and performance—
but the other no's—the no's born of defensiveness and denial,
uncertainty and fear and worry about what people might think
and what if I do the wrong thing . . . they are chains.
I watch this yearling and remember when I could
Yes! like she does,
reaching forward, stretching upward, running toward
that which I crave.
I wonder . . . is Yessing something I can still do?
Do I have what it takes after all this time to
say Yes to uncertainty?
Can I Yes toward that which I fear?
Can I say no only to those forces that build walls and silence the Yes?
Can I say Yes all the way through the pain to the joy?
Can I Yes! myself to freedom,
and when I trip on my own fear . . . can I get up like she does, and let
Yes!
take me home where I belong?
I think I'll try.
I'll start now—and practice saying Yes!
I speak the Holy Yes that
opens the door to all the other yeses . . .
I say Yes. I say Amen.
Yes! Let it be.

Chapter 30

Meeting Jesus in Your Heart

When I was pregnant with my second daughter, my three-year-old daughter Michelle came running to me one day, demanding to know if "it is Jesus in my heart and the baby in your tummy" or the other way around.

When you're three, it's hard to keep things straight.

When we speak of "inviting Jesus into our hearts" within the Christian community, what are we talking about? And how do people who are literal-minded, concrete thinkers interpret that?

Do people understand it as a metaphor to help us realize that a relationship with Christ is more than mental assent or verbal pronouncements?

If Jesus "lives in our hearts," what does that mean?

When I was Teaching Director for the Community Bible Study in San Angelo, Texas, I attended a training workshop in which the speaker posited an idea that was the basis for the workshop. "Stress," he said, "is caused by one thing, and it is this: you are not getting what you want, and you want life to change so that you can." I debated that in my mind, but in my gut I knew he was onto something true. Like any big truth, simplicity is the clue that what you're hearing is probably true.

The speaker also provided an antidote and a way out, and it was in this simple proverb: "Above all else, guard your heart, for it is the wellspring of life" (Prov 4:23). In other words, the wise composer of Proverbs tells us that we are to take personal responsibility for what is going on in our inner kingdom, for what is on the inside finds a way to come out, either through our words or behaviors.

In Hebrew thought, the "heart" of a person was the center of a person's life, where the emotions, the will, and the intellect came together. Perhaps a good analogy is that the "heart" is like an inner generator, motivating us from within. Jesus commented on this reality, but he also said hard and harsh words about it to the crowds and his disciples. In the riveting and disturbing discourse known as "The Woes Chapter" (Matthew 23), Jesus said, "Woe to you, teachers of the law and Pharisees, you hypocrites. You clean the outside of the cup and dish, but inside they are full of greed and self-indulgence" (Matt 23:25).

Above all else, guard your heart, for it is the wellspring of life. (Prov 4:23)

For out of the overflow of the heart, the mouth speaks. (Luke 6:45b)

You don't get wormy apples off a healthy tree, nor good apples off a diseased tree. The health of the apple tells the health of the tree. You must begin with your own life-giving lives. It's who you are, not what you say and do, that counts. Your true being brims over into true words and deeds. (Luke 6:45-46, The Message)

What is your reaction to these words? It's easy to excuse ourselves by saying that we're not teachers of the law or Pharisees, but we all fall into hypocrisy on occasion, pretending that we are something we know we aren't. We all go through times when the talk we talk doesn't match the walk we walk.

Jesus continues in verses 22 and 23, "You are like whitewashed tombs, which look beautiful on the outside but on the inside of full of dead men's bones and everything unclean." These are hard sayings. It's easy to pull away and say, "Not me!" This isn't baby Jesus in the manger or sweet Jesus, meek and mild. It isn't the pale Galilean or the dead body hanging on a cross. "In the same way," he said, "on the outside you appear to people as righteous but on the inside you are full of hypocrisy and wickedness" (v. 28).

An important principle I have learned in working a Twelve Step program and in the long process of depth analysis is that one of the most liberating, healing, empowering, and transforming actions I can take is to keep an ongoing moral inventory of my inner kingdom, the inside of the cup. This is the place where I know the unvarnished truth about myself and my motivations and am willing to own the truth, confess the truth, and be forgiven.

Jesus, the master psychologist, was on to something huge in the lives of human beings: to be whole, to be effective and productive, loving and serene, it is necessary to keep our internal accounts. Keeping one's own accounts, or guarding your heart with all diligence, is a discipline of responsibility. It is the sacred process of setting boundaries, accepting responsibility for one's own character defects and hurtful behavior, making confession and asking for forgiveness as part of one's spiritual disciplines. Keeping one's own accounts requires self-knowledge and consciousness, and both are vital keys in living the Jesus way.

~~~

Whenever I am teaching about the inner kingdom, I emphasize that the True Self is the part of us that is made in the image of God (see Gen 1:27). I make a big point that this part is the force that drives us toward growth, wholeness, fulfillment, and the place of living fully what poet Mary Oliver calls "your one wild and precious life."

When I lecture on being made in the image of God, I explain that we have the capacity to be creative, to communicate both with God and with each other, to love and be loved, and to make choices.

"Tell me, what is it you plan to do
with your one wild and precious life?"
—Mary Oliver,
"The Summer Day"

I communicate how important it is to see ourselves as made in the image of God, for the self-image and the God-concept are the two most important beliefs people have.

Our beliefs, after all, are the ideas that we "belove" (as stated by Marcus Borg). Our beliefs are lived out in behaviors. Our behaviors form our habits. And our habits shape and reveal our character. Jesus was indeed the master psychologist. He knew that if we wanted to take care of a problem, we had to go to the source, the heart, where the problems begin.

Inevitably, when I teach this concept, someone in the class or group asks a question that indicates his or her confusion about the term "True Self." Some think it points to their worst characteristics, the black hole in the heart, the character defect, the part that has to be hidden or, in Jesus' idea, polished on the outside to hide the filth on the inside. "I can't let anyone know my True Self," they say. "If they did see that part of me, they wouldn't like me!

Instead of being our worst characteristics, which—if we let them show—will make us look bad, the True Self is the part of us that is made in the image of God. It is the way we are intended to be, the soul's code. It is the natural part of us, which Oliver calls the "wild" part, meaning the pristine creation that we are. The True Self is the part of us that flows from the center outward. The false (or little, adapted, contrived) self is the ego self that is adapted to conform to the outer world. The True Self is the part of us that is connected with the Spirit of God within us.

The writer of Proverbs said it one way: Guard your heart. Jesus said, "Seek first the kingdom of God . . . ." People in recovery groups say, "Mind your own business," and "You can't change anyone but yourself."

Over a lifetime, I have come to understand that I am hard to change. It is easier to try to work over someone else. And when I do that, I have an obligation to myself to figure out if that method is actually working. I am led back over and over to the basic, simple truth that the only person I can change is myself, and when that is too hard, I am called to surrender my will and my life to the care of the one who is able to operate in the deep and hidden places and heal me from within.

Exploring the Scriptures

Wherever Jesus went, he was the catalyst for change. In every encounter with persons, he brought about the person's healing, transformation, liberation or empowerment, and sometimes, he did all of that in one person. For change to last, however, there has to be a change within, at the heart level.

Read Luke 8:40-48.
1. It was one thing for Jesus to heal this woman of her bleeding problem, but then, she had to go home and live as a healed person. What attitudes in her had to change in order for her to live fully into her new health with the people who knew her as an "untouchable"?

Read Luke 13:10-17.
2. Everyone could see that Jesus healed the woman in this event of her crippled back. What kinds of changes did that encounter with Jesus start, as this unnamed woman had to learn a new way of being in the world?

Read Luke 19:1-10
3. As a tax collector and as a wealthy man, Zacchaeus had a reputation in his community. He also was short enough that the writer of Luke made a point of his height, or lack of it. Jesus decided to go home with him and that decision of Jesus' began a process of change in Zacchaeus' heart. What had to change for Zacchaeus?

Read John 3:1-21
4. Apparently, Nicodemus had tried to change himself by following the rules of his religion. Jesus, though, introduced him to a different

kind of change, a radical transformation that began with something mysterious called a "new birth." What do you think happened in Nicodemus's inner life to change his heart?

Read John 8:1-11

5. How long do you think the woman in this account had lived under her old "rules" of life? Who do you think there was who was there for her, helping her trust the change Jesus had made in her perception of herself? Who was there to help her guard her heart?

6. Looking back at the five characters Jesus touched and changed, who do you imagine was there for them to support the new creation they became? What is the difference between "minding your own business" and supporting another person's growth process?

7. How hard do you think it was for each person to live from his /her new heart?

8. What temptations do you think each met to return to their old way of being in the world?

9. Do you suppose any one of these persons ever had another encounter with Jesus? If not, would that one encounter have been enough to sustain the change of heart in each?

10. What about today? Do you know anyone who has had an instant change of heart? Do you think that most people change their minds and change their hearts over time?

For Your Eyes Only

11. What about you? Do you feel that your relationship with the Living Christ has changed your heart? Have your changes only been about changing your behavior?

12. For lasting change to come, it must come from within one's own inner being. Who in your life supports that kind of change? Who is a stumbling block for you?

13. Who in your life needs your support, encouragement, love and compassion in order to change from within?

14. If you could look into the face of the human Jesus, what change of heart would you ask of him for you?

15. Do you believe—really believe—that a vital, personal, dynamic love relationship with the Living Christ/the Holy Spirit of Christ could change your heart? What evidence do you have, either way?

The Living Christ or the Divine Therapist, to use Thomas Keating's term, refers to the powerful reality that works from within to heal the wounds of a lifetime. The Living Christ, given my permission and sometimes in spite of my resistance, can do for me what I cannot do for myself. Sometimes, when I'm up against a big battle with my self-will run riot, all I can do is pray the short form of the first three of the Twelve Steps:

I can't.

He can.

I'm going to let him.

What About You?

1. What spiritual practices keep you "guarding your own heart"?

2. What afflictive emotions are your "specialty"? In what settings are you most likely to be overcome by an afflictive emotion (fear, guilt, shame, resentment, hate, anger, envy, jealousy, greed, etc.)?

3. In what ways does your walk not match your talk?

There is another part to the practice of "guarding your heart": focusing on the best part of you. Knowing one's personal strengths and gifts is a moral responsibility. We are responsible for the stewardship of our talents and abilities and for living from a place of inner love, joy, and peace, and so part of guarding one's heart is refining the spiritual practices that nurture a lifestyle of looking for the good and savoring the beauty and splendor of life.

Guarding our hearts means that we look for ways to carry out Jesus' great commandment to love God with all our hearts, minds, and souls, and our neighbors as ourselves. That is not a burden but a blessing, an opportunity that can bring delight into our lives.

Guarding our hearts means acknowledging what is wrong that needs to be righted, but it also means guarding our points of view. Paul wrote, "Finally, whatever is true, what is noble, whatever is right, whatever is pure, whatever is lovely, whatever is admirable or praiseworthy—think about such things" (Phil 4:8). Can you imagine the change in your daily life if you looked for those things instead of dwelling on what is wrong? Paul says that the result is that the God of peace will be with you.

Guarding our hearts also means trusting what Paul says in Romans 8:28: "God is at work in all things, attempting to bring about good." (In many translations, the verse starts with the subject as "all things," but I'm told that in the original language, it begins with God as the subject.) It is my job to be open and willing to look for where the Spirit of the Living God is at work, and then attune my will and actions to that activity. This requires awareness, consciousness, and alertness.

Guarding my heart—seeking first the kingdom of God—is good counsel.

It's such a simple principle, but it isn't easy.

The hard way, however, is the easy way.

And that is good news.

Sometimes when I am teaching, I am deeply challenged by the questions that come from all kinds of people with different motivations. Some people are curious, and others are profoundly cautious.

A young man approached me once and asked me about the goal for studying the life of Jesus, and I immediately responded, "I want you to fall in love with him so that you take his teachings and his Spirit into your heart so deeply that you will know forever how wide and how deep God's great love is for you."

You can guard the treasure of the Living Christ within your heart, attending to that presence by communing with him through prayer, but you can only start from where you are. If that starting place is caution or curiosity, the Living Christ will meet you there.

Chapter 31

Meeting Jesus as a Friend

I challenge you to find another world religion in which the central figure makes such a statement as the one Jesus made that his disciples are his friends (John 15:14-15). The central figure and founder of our faith as Christians showed us a radical God who, to use the Old Testament concept, "tabernacles" with us. The God Jesus came to reveal is involved with people in an intimate way, and Jesus called it "friendship."

I've written about friendship as a spiritual practice.[53] My life is richer and more meaningful because of the friends who have been my companions on the pilgrimage of faith. Intentionally and consciously, I work to stay connected with the people who have blessed my life in many different ways, so I respond positively to the idea of Jesus as friend.

I have to qualify that idea, however. I don't interpret this friendship/relationship with Jesus as a buddy kind of relationship. What I experience as friendship with the Living Christ is not some casual, let's-meet-for-pizza kind of deal. Instead, it is a holy friendship, and we are not exactly equals. Jesus is my elder brother, in a way, but not in the same way my sisters are siblings. He is God, after all. God Incarnate. And even with his friends, Jesus was Rabbi, Teacher. Jesus elevates friendship to an extraordinary plane.

Obviously, Jesus knew how to draw people to him. He drew the crowds, but the human Jesus was the kind of person who had a close circle of friends, such as the disciples. He was close to Mary and Martha and their brother Lazarus, and he must have had a close friendship with Mary Magdalene, as he trusted her to carry the message of his resurrection to the disciples. He had an inner circle of friends—Peter, James, and John—who were with him at the transfiguration and in the Garden of Gethsemane, and he allowed himself to be known fully in those moments.

Clearly, Jesus valued relationships. He was available to his friends. He spent time with them, eating with them and talking with them about important things. People wanted to have Jesus in their homes, and he was invited to wedding feasts in his hometown.

When I was a child, I loved hearing my grandmother sing "What a Friend We Have in Jesus" in her rich, alto voice. Though I hear the song rarely now, when I do it takes me back to my child-

You are my friends if you do what I command. I no longer call you servants. . . . Instead, I have called you friends. (John 15:14-15)

Surely, I am with you always, to the very end of the age. (Matt 28:20b)

They will call him Immanuel—which means "God with us." (Matt 1:23)

237

hood. Singing that song acquainted me from childhood on with the idea that the Living Christ was near and available to me *as a friend*. That's not a bad thing for a child to learn. In fact, that concept has been invaluable to me, and in my adulthood I have experienced what it means to be a friend of Jesus.

There are many dimensions to my relationship with the historical Jesus and the Living Christ that keep me curious about him and what he taught. My curiosity leads me to new levels of understanding of what my grandmother sang about and what I sing about when I sing about Jesus.

I cannot write or speak definitively and ultimately about what it means to be in a friendship with the Living Christ, but when I read John 13–17, I get some sense of what it might mean. In John 13, we see a glimpse of one of the most intimate and tender moments Jesus had with his friends, "the disciples." The event is filled with emotion, for the conflicts between Jesus and the authorities are increasing. John writes this poignant introduction to the event that took place in an upper room: "Having loved his own who were in the world, he now showed them the full extend of his love" (John 13:1b).

Read those words carefully and meditate on them.

What follows is the account of Jesus washing the disciples' feet, an act that was a revelation of what kind of Lord and Teacher he was. As the founder of our faith as Christians, Jesus' way of teaching was revolutionary. He was intimately involved with his followers/friends. He let himself be known by them; he was vulnerable and transparent. He modeled servant leadership. He loved them, personally and intimately.

After Jesus washed their feet, he asked the disciples if they knew what he had done for them. Of course, what he did was much more than ritual cleansing, and if we take that foot washing only in a literal sense, we miss the impact of what it means to be friends. Jesus was showing the disciples that friendship based on mutuality, humility, and reciprocity is the Jesus way. "Now that I, your Lord and Teacher, have washed your feet," he told them, "you also should wash one another's feet. I have set you an example that you should do as I have done for you" (John 13:14-15).

238

What About You?

1. How do you think it affected the disciples when Jesus washed their feet?

2. What do you think would be hard about having someone wash your feet?

3. In what other ways can we serve each other as friends?

4. What do you think about the idea of friendship as a spiritual practice?

5. Is it easier for you to be served or to serve? Explain.

In John 14, Jesus teaches the disciples about his new, mysterious, and indefinable relationship with them. "I will not leave you as orphans," he says. "I will come to you. Before long, the world will not see me anymore, but you will see me . . ." (John 14:18-19). Then Jesus describes the ongoing friendship. It is one in which, through the mystery of the Holy Spirit, the disciples will continue to experience his presence, his comfort, his guidance, and his teaching. He reminds them in John 14:28, "I am coming back to you," and in both John 14:1 and 27b, he says, "Do not let your hearts be troubled."

We are not to be troubled, Jesus says, because his presence is always going to be with us. This presence was promised in Isaiah 7:14 when the prophet said, "The virgin will be with child and will give birth to a son, and will call him Immanuel." It is the same presence promised to the children of Israel when God told Moses to tell the Pharaoh that "I am" sent you. "I Am" will be with you, and "I Am is with you."

How do we relate to the Almighty and to Jesus as friend? First, it is about attitude. This friendship is the most important relationship of a person's life. It is the one friendship that is constant. It is a friendship not of equals but of Lord and disciple, Teacher and student, in which there is nevertheless mutuality, respect, and reciprocity.

To begin, we have to accept that this kind of intimacy is possible and that it is the kind of friendship we want. Once we agree to it, my experience is that the Living Christ steps in to nourish and support that holy friendship in an infinite number of ways. We do our part to maintain the relationship/friendship through our spiritual practices. Just as Brother Lawrence imagined Jesus at work with him in the monastery kitchen, we can do our part to keep the friendship alive, dynamic, and personal through the power and wonder of the imagination. The Living Christ accompanies us as we go about our daily tasks, as companion, helper, guide, and friend. After all, he promised that he would.

People recovering from addiction tell amazing stories of the power of "acting as if," which means imagining what they want to be reality and then doing it consistently until they act themselves into a new way of being in the world.

This process really works.

For some, the idea of "being friends with Jesus" is difficult because it feels irreverent. On the other hand, others bring Jesus down to such a level that there is too much a sense of Jesus as a good buddy. If you think of friendship, however, as a sacred practice in which we meet more of God in each other and in ourselves because of our interactions, and if you think of the friendship with Jesus as another way of experiencing God, the relationship is lifted to another level.

After all, Jesus did say, "I no longer call you slaves; I call you friends" (John 15:15). To get an idea of what Jesus meant, it is helpful to reflect on how he interacted with his disciples and friends in the Gospel record.

Exploring the Scriptures

Read Luke 24:13-35.

1. Why didn't the disciples recognize Jesus on the Emmaus road? Why couldn't they see who he really was? What blinded them?

2. Why did Jesus ask them the questions he asked?

3. What do you think was going on in Jesus' mind when the disciples gave their account of what had happened in Jerusalem?

4. What do you think the disciples thought when Jesus gave them a history lesson?

5. Why do you think the disciples urged Jesus to stay with them?

6. Why were their eyes opened as he broke the bread? Why did this action allow them to see him for who he really was? What do you suppose they thought at that point?

7. What does it mean that "their hearts burned within them"?

What About You?

8. Have you ever experienced something similar to the encounter the disciples in John 24 had with Jesus, when you felt the presence of Christ joining you in your journey? What was that like?

9. Do you believe that the Presence of Christ is with you always?

10. How has that Presence comforted you? guided you? taught you? corrected you?

11. How do you remind yourself to be aware of the Presence of Christ with you? How does Jesus remind you that he is with you?

Part Seven

Meeting Jesus in the Big Events

Introduction

> Think of yourselves the way Christ Jesus thought of himself. He had equal status with God but didn't think so much of himself that he had to cling to the advantages of that status no matter what. Not at all. When the time came, he set aside the privileges of deity and took on the status of a slave, became human! Having become human, he stayed human. It was an incredibly humbling process. He didn't claim special privileges. Instead, he lived a self-less, obedient life and then died a selfless, obedient death—and the worst kind of death at that—a crucifixion. Because of that obedience, God lifted him high and honored him far beyond anyone or anything, ever, so that all created beings in heaven and on earth—even those long ago dead and buried—will bow in worship before this Jesus Christ, and call out in praise that he is the Master of all, to the glorious honor of God the Father. (Phil 2:5-11, *The Message*)

The soaring hymn to the Living Christ in Philippians 2:5-11 is called the "kenosis hymn." *Kenosis* is the Greek word for the doctrine that states that Christ willingly relinquished his divine attributes to take on the experience of being human. Within the Christian community we talk and have often argued about the "Incarnation," which is another doctrine that states that Jesus assumed human form as the person Jesus, and that he was both fully human and fully divine.

It takes an open mind to contain this paradox and understand both the human Jesus and the Living Christ as God. It appears to me that Jesus himself struggled with this tension, and we will see some of that in the big events of Jesus' life.

Tomes have been written about each of these events, the purpose of this book is simply to give an overview. That overview will necessitate leaving out parts of the Jesus story. Curiosity about any of those parts of Jesus' human/divine experience can lead you down interesting and exciting pathways of discovery and meaning. I hope you will take those journeys.

Chapter 32

Meeting Jesus in the Nativity

Mary, the Mother of Jesus

I love the season of Advent, and I love Christmas.

There is something about this season of waiting and expectancy that expands my mind and heart, and with that, hope is born again.

When I was growing up, we did not observe Advent in my religious culture, but my family has adopted the practice of observing the four weeks of Advent since our children were young. Nothing has deepened my joy in the Christmas season like this deeply spiritual and religious practice.

I love the Mystery that infuses the story of Jesus' birth with grace, and I am comfortable with the fact that I don't have to understand how it all happened in order to experience the wonder of the Incarnation. God, as I understand God, can do whatever God chooses and is not obligated to explain it to me. My heart understands what I cannot understand with my rational and logical mind.

So it is that every year, I willingly enter this time of Mystery and am graced by the experience of the beautiful story of the birth of Jesus. I am fascinated by the life of Mary, the young girl who was willing to risk her reputation and her life to participate with God, working through her, to birth the Christ Child. I often wonder about what her life was like, asking questions like these:

• What did God look for in a woman who would bear the Christ Child?

• What kind of person would be able to stand the burden of giving birth to Jesus?

• Did Mary have a choice?

• What were the risks for Mary?

• Did she understand what was happening?

• Mary said," Be it done to me according to your will," which was her statement of surrender that gave God permission to work in and through her. What would God have done if Mary had said "no"?

• Mary's song (Luke 1:46-55) indicates her understanding of God's doing a new thing. What is that new thing?

By her surrender, Mary showed us a model of discipleship that Jesus would also reveal to us. With her "yes" to God's invitation, she

Behold! I am . . . making all things new. (Rev 21:5)

If Mary had been full of reason instead of grace, there would have been no room for the Christchild.
—Madeleine L'Engle

245

because a participant—at great cost to herself—in God's redeeming action in history; through her cooperation with the Spirit of God, she was an instrument of God's grace. Perhaps we can say that she was the embodiment of grace. Indeed, she was full of grace, and her son was the instrument of the grace that leads us back to God.

In pondering the life of Mary, I have come to understand that for God to work in or through any of us, we have to have certain qualities: openness, strength, availability, resilience, willingness, pliability, cooperation, attentiveness, awareness, alertness.

Exploring the Scriptures
Read Luke 1:26-56.
1. Who is the initiator in this story?

2. Read Genesis 1:1. Is this the same initiator? How do you know?

3. If you were the Great Initiator, what kind of woman would you desire to take part in your next big creative act?

4. What do you think the words "You are highly favored" meant, from God's point of view? How do you think Mary heard those words?

5. What kind of response do you think a young Jewish girl might have had to the words, "The Lord is with you"? In other words, why do you think she was "greatly troubled"?

6. What did Mary do that caused her to have "found favor" with God? Or do you think it was more a matter of who she was than what she had done?

7. Read Genesis 1:2. Is this the same Spirit, hovering over the void, that hovered over Mary? How do you know?

8. Luke 1:37 is a strong statement. Do you believe it?

9. What does Luke tell us in verses 38-45 that illustrate Mary's humility?

10. As you read Mary's song in verses 46-55, what do you learn about her?

For Your Eyes Only
11. How did the birth of Jesus change Mary's life?

12. In practical, everyday terminology, what would it mean for "the Living Christ" to be born in you?

13. It has been said that Mary was Jesus' first disciple. What do you think that means?

14. How can humility and power work together for good?

15. When has God asked you to participate with him in some act of grace?

Joseph, the Husband of Mary

In the gift shop of the great Cathedral in Chartres, France, I found a small hand-carved piece of the Holy Family and brought it home with me. It called to me, in a way, from the first visit I made to that gift shop during my twelve days in Chartres in 2011, and I tried to resist buying it. Each day, the woman in the gift shop would smile at me and say, "Today?" and I would shake my head and leave without it. Finally, though, I knew the piece had to come home with me.

What I love about it is that the three figures—Mary, Joseph, and the Infant—are carved from one piece, and Joseph, standing over his family, has his robe outstretched, covering them with his own outer garment. The symbolism of his posture moves me deeply. Joseph is one of my favorite men in the entire Bible. By his life and his obedience to God, he shows us another aspect of discipleship.

The Scripture says that he was a righteous man, and that means he kept the Jewish law and he attended to his relationship with God. Joseph did three things that make me admire him. First, Joseph listened to his dreams. Obviously, he was open and receptive to God. Read Matthew 1:18 through Matthew 2. God spoke to Joseph through dreams five times.

Second, I love Joseph because he was willing to put listening to God's guidance above following the religious law in order to protect and provide for Mary and her child. Joseph was willing to follow

God even if it put him at odds with the laws and legalism of his religious work, his culture, and perhaps even his family. A man who does the right thing, regardless of what other people say about him, is a man of moral courage. In this case, it seems that Joseph was also a man with a deep love for the young woman to whom he was betrothed, a young woman who was vulnerable and who had a serious problem.

Finally, I love Joseph because he was decisive, bold, and action-oriented. He was courageous enough to bear criticism and was protective of his family.

Exploring the Scriptures

Read Matthew 1:1-16 and Luke 3:23-38.

1. How are these genealogies alike? How are they different? Why do you think the writers included them?

2. Why do you think Mark and John didn't include a genealogy?

Read these references to the life of Joseph: Matthew 1:18-25; 2:13-23; John 1:45.

3. From these Scriptures, what do you know about the man Joseph?

4. Matthew 1:19 says that Joseph was "a righteous man." What do you think God chose him instead of someone for whom the laws were not important?

5. How many times was Joseph given an important dream?

6. What made Joseph willing to listen to his dreams and follow them?

7. How do you think it affected Joseph to break the laws of his religious culture?

8. How is Joseph's willingness to break the laws evidence of his righteousness?

9. How is Joseph's participation in this important drama evidence that God was "doing a new thing"?

10. How do you think Joseph felt about parenting Jesus?

11. How do you suppose Joseph responded to questions from his family, his friends, or his rabbi about his willingness to participate in this new thing?

12. In what ways do you think Joseph protected the young Jesus?

13. What qualities did Joseph have to develop in order to do what was asked of him? Did he have a choice?

For Your Eyes Only
14. Do you think God has ever spoken to you through a dream?

15. Do you pay attention to your dreams, or do you discount them?

16. Do you ever tell anyone about your dreams? If so, who?

17. Have you ever made a decision based on a dream?

18. Why is it remarkable that Matthew, who was writing to the Jews, included Joseph's dreams in his account of the birth of Jesus?

The Birth of Jesus

During the Advent season, I pray that my own heart will be a worthy Bethlehem, a safe and receptive birthplace for yet another coming of the Christ Child into my inner life. I focus on what might impede my experience of the presence of the Living Christ, born in me again and again, and I confess it, asking God to remove it. I wait expectantly, thinking of how Mary waited for the birth of her child, and I pray for special grace during the season of waiting.

I also ponder the idea that God works in "the fullness of time" (Gal 4:4). It's a good reminder that I am not in control of how or when God works, but I can rest in the confidence that God acts when the necessary aspects of a situation come together.

I know that I cannot manufacture spiritual experiences or force God to act on my timetable or calendar. But when I faithfully follow my spiritual practices, I become more available to the breakthroughs of grace when God does choose to move or speak or reveal God's self to me in an extraordinary way.

Exploring the Scriptures

Read the account of Jesus' birth and early days in Luke 2:1-40.

1. Given Mary's condition, why do you think she and Joseph took the trip to Bethlehem?

2. Why do you think the angels appeared to common shepherds? What is meaningful about this?

3. How did the shepherds know to go to Bethlehem?

4. Why do you think people would believe the report that mere shepherds gave?

5. Scripture says that Mary "treasured up all these things and pondered them in her heart" (v. 19). What do you think it means to "ponder" something "in your heart"?

6. Compare Luke's account to Jesus' birth to Matthew's account in Matthew 1:18–2:23. How are they alike? How are they different?

7. Why do you think Matthew included the account of the magi's visit to the Christ Child but not the shepherds'? Why do you think Luke included the shepherds' visit, but not the magi's?

8. Mark, who wrote his Gospel first, does not mention the birth of Jesus. John begins his Gospel by setting the "birth" of Jesus in cosmic context in John 1:1-18, called "The Prologue." What does John's approach add to the significance of Jesus' birth? Why do you suppose Mark did not include a birth narrative?

9. The event described in Luke 2:21-38 is especially tender and powerful, describing the fulfillment of the coming of the Christ Child to an old man and an old woman. Seen symbolically, what is the meaning of this event?

For Your Eyes Only
10. Consider praying this prayer: "God, make my heart a worthy Bethlehem into which your son can be born." What does this prayer mean?

11. What crowds your heart so that Christ, symbolically, cannot be born? Is there not enough room in the inn of your life for the Christ Child?

12. Why do you think we observe Advent and Christmas year after year? What is the point?

13. What is the difference between a religious observance and a popular celebration?

14. How can a follower of Christ participate with integrity in both the observance and the celebration?

A Prayer at Christmas

Come, Holy Infant
    be born in us anew
Come, sweet Christchild
    restore our childlike wonder and wisdom
Come, Good Shepherd
    lead us into the places we dare not go alone
Come, Great Physician
    heal our wounds—our self-inflicted injuries and those we have inflicted
on others—Make us whole and healthy
Come, Redeemer
    and buy us back from the lesser gods
    Set us free into joy—give us life and love and laughter
Come, Prince of Peace
    and turn us from war—Re-form us as your Peace-makers
Come, Light of the world
    into our shadows and dark places where we love to hide—
    Give us courage to let our own light sparkle and shine
Come, Living Water
    and quench our thirst with that which satisfies
Come, Bread of Life
    nourish us with that which makes us strong and bold
Come, Beloved
    and make us lovers of you, of each other, of the world
Come, Emmanuel

dwell in our hearts—be with us always and in all ways

Come, Holy Mystery

shatter our small ideas of you; break open the boxes in which we have confined you—take away our certainty of anything but your great love for us

Come, Lord Jesus

be born in us again and again and again.

Chapter 33

Meeting Jesus at His Baptism

It must have been interesting to be the cousin of Jesus. I've wondered what it was like for someone as strong and forceful as John the Baptist to be assigned the task of preparing the way for Jesus.

What was it like for John when Jesus asked him to baptize him? And why did Jesus need to be baptized?

What precipitated Jesus' going to John for baptism? Why on that day? What components came together for Jesus "in the fullness of time" (Gal 4:4) to propel him out into his public ministry?

Exploring the Scriptures

Read the story of the baptism of Jesus in Matthew 3:13-17; Mark 1:9-11; Luke 3:21-22; and John 1:31-34.

1. How are these accounts alike? How are they different?

2. What do you think it was like for John to baptize his cousin Jesus?

3. Do you think John knew that Jesus was coming to him to be baptized before the actual event? Do you suppose they had discussed this possibility?

4. What purpose did Jesus' baptism serve?

This is my servant, whom I uphold, my chosen one, in whom I delight; I will put my Spirit on him and he will bring justice to the nation. (Isa 42:1)

5. Who do you think heard the blessing of God for his beloved Son besides Jesus?

6. What do you think it was like for Jesus to hear the words, "This is my beloved Son, in whom I am well pleased"?

I've always been fascinated by the blessing Jesus heard when John brought him up out of the baptismal waters. Part of a coronation formula recorded in Isaiah, the words were an obvious expression of God's pleasure that Jesus himself heard, whether audibly or in the secret room of his inner life. Those words carried both an affirmation from God and the sense of being blessed or empowered for the work Jesus was given to do.

My father baptized me when I was nine years old. As I reflect back on that experience through a lifetime of other kinds of experiences, I remember that some of the church ladies—well intentioned, I'm sure—had made comments to my father about how the preacher's daughter was already nine years old and hadn't yet been baptized. They indicated that the fact that I had not "walked the aisle" didn't look good to the other church members.

That didn't sit well with my dad, and that it did not sit well endeared him to me. His own conversion at twenty-eight and his subsequent baptism in Tucumcari, New Mexico, had been a dramatic, Damascus-road experience similar to the one the Apostle Paul had. My father didn't think something as sacred as his daughter's conversion should become a topic of either gossip or pressure for me to "make a decision" just to placate church members.

I'm not sure how I feel about childhood evangelism now. It seems that the demands of following Jesus are made for adults. I do know that my preference is for believer's baptism, but I know for sure that in my childlike way, I gave as much as I knew of myself to as much as I knew of God, and I have never doubted that my childhood decision was authentic. Whatever that means and whatever the terms are for the afterlife, I will have to leave up to God and God's grace.

At nine, I didn't have a sordid past to confess or leave behind. I didn't have a lot of vices to give up, and I certainly didn't have a riveting story about awful things I had done that had gotten me into trouble with the law, my parents, or any other authority. Indeed, I had a most narrow and limited understanding of what it meant to give my heart to Jesus. I wanted to go to heaven and stay out of hell in the afterlife. In spite of the fact that my dad didn't want me to make my decision to be baptized to please or placate anyone, including himself, I had picked up from my Baptist culture that doing so was the thing for a child to do, and, in fact, I was a bit delayed in making that decision.

I wanted to please my parents, and I didn't want to cause them problems with the church members. If that was my motivation at the time, I believe that God understood and has somehow, in spite of my immaturity and innocence and even ignorance, still worked in my life.

Looking back on the experience, the most treasured part of my baptism were the words my father said when he baptized me. "I baptize you, my daughter," he said as he lowered me into the water, "and I raise you to eternal life, my sister in Christ."

I've never felt the need to be baptized again, but I have experienced countless turning points in my life when I came upon yet another thing I needed to surrender to God. And I have experienced the truth Paul wrote about when he said that we have to "work out our salvation with fear and trembling" (Phil 2:12).

I've experienced a lot of fear and trembling, a lot of surrender, and many new beginnings on my pilgrimage of faith. My salvation journey began when I invited Jesus into my heart, and the process of becoming whole continues. I think it will be a journey all the way.

What About You?

1. If you have been baptized, what do you remember most about your baptism? If you were baptized as an infant, what were you told about this event?

2. What did your baptism mean to you or to your family at the time? What does it mean to you now?

3. Who was present at your baptism?

4. How was life different for you or your family after your baptism?

5. If you have not been baptized, how do you feel about this observance? Do you think it is an important symbol?

Whatever the reason for Jesus' baptism, its meaning can be different for all of us. I do know that the image of a new beginning provided by a ritual such as baptism can be powerful, both for the person being baptized and for those who witness the baptism.

And lead us not into temptation, but deliver us from the
evil one. (Matt 6:13)

Keep us safe from ourselves
and the devil. (Matt 6:13,
The Message)

Chapter 34

Meeting Jesus in the Wilderness

Looking back over my "mountaintop" experiences, I know that I am never more vulnerable to the onset of a desert or wilderness experience than I am when I return from a meaningful spiritual retreat.

Early on, when I would return home and life seemed "off" for me, either in the outer world or in my attitude, it felt as if I were being punished for having such a meaningful and rich time. Eventually, I learned that this idea reflected misguided thinking, but I did learn to prepare for the return home.

We might think that Jesus could have been spared his time of testing in the wilderness. After all, he had a huge job ahead, and besides, he had just received a beautiful blessing from his Father at his baptism. Surely he was ready for his ministry. I can understand why Jesus chose to be baptized, but why he had to be tested is a puzzle to me unless I understand and accept that Jesus had the experience of being human.

The record of this experience appears in all three Synoptic Gospels, so it was certainly a significant experience in Jesus' life. Perhaps we can say that it must have been necessary for him to have this time of wrestling with the force that opposes.

That Jesus revealed to others the details of this time of wrestling and struggling shows once again his vulnerability and transparency. He talked about what happened to him in his wilderness experience, giving the disciples insight into his struggle to understand the kind of Messiah he would be. And his wilderness encounter with the evil one is also instructive to those of us who attempt to follow Jesus now. Doing time in the desert or the wilderness seems to be a requirement on the spiritual journey.

Exploring the Scriptures

Read the story of the temptation of Jesus in Matthew 4:1-11; Mark 1:12-13; Luke 4:1-13.

1. Why do you think the Spirit of God led Jesus from his baptism into this terrible encounter with the devil?

2. Do you think the "devil" was an actual being that Jesus could see, hear, and touch? Or was it an internal voice within Jesus' mind?

3. What purpose did each temptation serve in Jesus' life?

4. Which temptation do you think caused Jesus the most struggle?

5. Why do you think the Gospel writers included this event in their account of Jesus' life?

6. How is this event helpful for those of us who read it today?

7. How do you think the Gospel writers knew about this private experience Jesus had when he was alone with the devil?

8. What keeps you (tempts you/seduces you) from being the person God created you to be? Are you able to be vulnerable and transparent about your struggles?

9. Is it helpful to you to know that Jesus had to struggle with "the adversary"?

10. Why is spiritual struggle important?

That all three writers of the Synoptic Gospels—Matthew, Mark, and Luke—begin their account of this experience by writing that Jesus was *led by the Spirit* into the wilderness fascinates me. Why would the Spirit of God do that? Couldn't God have spared Jesus the wrestling match with what Matthew calls "the tempter"?

Along my spiritual journey, I have learned this important truth: becoming who you are and discovering and doing what you were intended to do is no easy task. That it was such a struggle for Jesus leads me to give great respect to the process of defining and refining one's life purpose.

Even Jesus was confronted with the opportunity to take an easy way out, to placate outer-world values, and satisfy and gratify certain egocentric needs! The tempter pushed Jesus in three ways:

1. He offered him the challenge of turning stones into bread, thereby meeting an immediate, physical need.

2. He tempted Jesus with the seductive drug of doing the spectacular and sensational.

3. The Scriptures say that the tempter "led" Jesus to a high mountain and tried to get him to yield to the drive for power.

That Jesus even followed the tempter could trouble me, but it doesn't, and here is why: I've learned that sometimes we have to explore and examine what is not us in order to find out what is true, authentic, real. Jesus' struggle with these three temptations gives me both comfort and information. Reading this account, I can see how I, too, am tempted to take the easy way out, fall victim to the need to be entertained, and seek to have power over others.

Jesus not only resisted the tempter's offers but also rebuked him with strong words, and each time he did that, I am convinced that Jesus' sense of what kind of Messiah he would be became stronger. It is important for all of us, on the journey toward becoming who we really are, to face down the alternatives. It makes us stronger, clearer, and more committed to be able to say, "No, I am not that. I am this."

Sometimes we don't know what we really believe and who we really are until we are confronted with the opposite of what we believe and the opposite of what we are.

It seems to me that the Body of Christ, the church, has had to confront the same temptations from the culture and often, sadly, from within, throughout the history of Christianity. It is easy for the church to forget its real mission and succumb to the temptations of meeting immediate needs, gratifying people's desires to be entertained and thrilled, and giving in to the ever-addictive buzz of power over others.

When I read this account, I linger over the last line of it, when the Scriptures say that the devil left Jesus, and the angels came and attended him. When I finally wrestle through a hard place in my life and commit to the challenge of living my authentic purpose, I am always amazed at the breakthroughs of grace. And sometimes God works through human agents who act like angels.

Luke adds something else to this story in Luke 4:14-29. The Spirit led Jesus out of the wilderness and back to Nazareth and to his synagogue, where he read from the scroll, as was his custom. Jesus read words from the prophet Isaiah that essentially gave Jesus' mission statement. Fresh from his wilderness experience in which he formulated a clear idea of his mission, Jesus read the words that would define what he was to do.

Eugene Peterson renders the mission statement from Luke 4:18-19 in this way:

God's Spirit is on me;
he's chosen me to preach the Message of good news to the poor,

Sent me to announce pardon to prisoners and
recovery of sight to the blind,
To set the burdened and battered free,
to announce, "This is God's year to act!"

Throughout this book, I have said that in Jesus' encounter with human beings, he did these things: he healed, transformed, liberated, and empowered people. Do you think that my statement is consistent with what Jesus said he was going to do and what he actually did? Do you think that he was talking about people who were literally poor, imprisoned, blind, burdened, and battered, or was he speaking more broadly? Did he mean that he would address both people with those literal needs *and* people who are imprisoned by chains of their own making, people who are spiritually blind, wounded, broken, and bereft?

I think he did.

What About You?

1. Do you ever experience yourself as "poor"? Are you spiritually poor? Relationally impoverished?

2. In what ways are you blinded by prejudice, bias, fear, shame, or guilt? Does anger or hate ever blind you?

3. What kinds of things have battered you in life? What emotional wounds have you endured?

4. Today, if you could meet Jesus, would you want him to heal, transform, liberate, or empower you? How would that look? How would you be different?

5. Have you written your personal mission statement? What is your purpose in life? Why are you here?

6. What is the benefit of writing a mission statement?

One of my most meaningful experiences began at a retreat at the Church of the Savior in Washington, DC, in which we were asked to write a statement of our calling. We were all expected to do the exercise, and because I didn't want to be different or noncompliant, I stumbled around and wrote what I thought might be my calling. I'm not sure I even meant it at the time, but I didn't want to embarrass myself by being the only one there who didn't do the assignment.

Stating my calling to a small group of witnesses and hearing their affirmation of my calling changed my life forever.

Mysteriously, living out my calling is healing, transforming, liberating, and empowering.

If you haven't written your mission statement or calling, why not try it?

Chapter 35

Meeting Jesus in the Transfiguration

His splendor was like the sunrise; rays flashed from his hand, where his power was hidden. (Hab 3:4)

The LORD bless you and keep you; the LORD make his face shine on you and be gracious to you; the LORD turn his face toward you and give you peace. (Num 6:24-26)

I am the light of the world. (John 8:12)

Let your light shine before men, that they may see your good works and praise your Father in heaven. (Matt 5:16)

My daughter Amy reported that her eight-year-old son, Lucas, asked if God was a boy or a girl. Lucas's six-year-old brother, Sam, responded with authority, "Lucas, God isn't a boy or a girl. God is a bright shining light!"

Of course, that comment sparked an interesting discussion in the family.

Apparently, Sam was pleased with himself, but a few minutes later he punctured his own inflation. "I guess I'm the better Christian," he responded, "since I know more about God.

Some of us never move past that six-year-old pride, do we? And some of us will fight to the death and involve others in our wars to prove who knows more about God! What is cute in a six-year-old becomes something else in an adult.

And yet God continually shows up in ways we'd never imagined, breaking his own rules sometimes and certainly breaking down the walls in which we have encased him with our doctrines, philosophies, and images about who God is.

The story of Moses and his ongoing dialogue with the Holy One has fascinated me since I was a small child. As a child, I loved the story of how he was found in the reeds along the bank of the Nile River by Pharaoh's daughter. As an adult, I have found meaning in his struggle to follow the Lord of Israel and help God liberate the people from the bondage of the wicked pharaoh. Particularly, I am drawn to the idea that God kept assuring Moses of God's continuing Presence and also guided the wandering pilgrims with a pillar of cloud by day and a pillar of fire by night. Sometimes I would give anything for such visible guidance from God!

In Exodus 33, as Moses argues with God about God's guidance and how the people will recognize that Presence, Moses demands, "Show me your glory" (v. 18). We cannot demand that God show up and be revealed on our schedule. We do not determine when a spiritual experience happens, but we can be available to that holy moment, that thin place when the separation between ourselves and God makes it possible for us to experience God's presence.

Who among us isn't a bit like Moses, wanting some assurance of God's presence? Sometimes we experience God's presence in the moment, but many times we sense it only in retrospect.

The mystic John of the Cross said, "If you wish to be sure of the road you tread on, close your eyes and walk in the dark." I yearn for the light of knowledge, a light on my path, the Light of Christ, and yet I am more often asked to walk in the dark and into what John of the Cross calls "the cloud of unknowing." Perhaps being willing to walk without light and wait something out in the long, dark night of the soul is a prerequisite to an experience of "seeing" God.

I've often wondered what made Peter, James, and John fortunate enough to witness the transfiguration of Jesus. The account of what is called the transfiguration of Jesus seems like an otherworldly story about Jesus' divinity, stuck in the first century when Jesus took his inner circle of Peter, James, and John on a hike up a mountain. I've always wondered if Jesus knew before they began the climb that something unusual would occur at the top.

Exploring the Scriptures

Read Matthew 17:1-13; Mark 9:2-13; Luke 9:28-36.

1. Note what comes immediately before and immediately after the transfiguration event in all three Gospels. In other words, where each the Gospel writer place this event in his account of Jesus' ministry?

2. What do you think motivated Jesus to take these three men—Peter, James, and John—up the mountain?

3. Do you think the same Spirit that affirmed Jesus at his baptism and then led him into the wilderness also led Jesus and his friends up to the high mountain?

And the LORD said, "I will cause all my goodness to pass in front of you, and I will proclaim my name, the LORD, in your presence. I will have mercy on whom I will have mercy and I will have compassion on whom I will have compassion. But," he said, "you cannot see my face, for no one may see me and live." Then the LORD said, "There is a place near me where you may stand on a rock. When my glory passes by, I will put you in a cleft in the rock and cover you with my hand until I have passed by. Then I will remove my hand and you will see my back; but my face must not be seen." (Exod 33:19-23)

4. What is the symbolism of the "high mountain"?

5. What do you imagine the four men talked about as they gathered on the mountain?

6. What do you suppose this experience was like for Jesus?

7. Do you think Jesus caused this event, or was it the work of the Father/Holy Spirit within him?

8. What do you suppose this experience was like for the three disciples?

9. Why do you think Peter wanted to put up three shelters for them?

10. What is the meaning of the appearance of Moses and Elijah? Why was it those two men rather than someone else, like Abraham and Isaiah?

11. If you had been at this event, what would you have wanted to tell others about it?

12. What purpose do you think this event had for the three disciples who witnessed it?

13. What purpose do you think this event had in their lives after the crucifixion?

14. Do you think that the disciples ever doubted that the experience was "real"?

15. What is the meaning of this event for us today?

16. Is there any meaning in this event for the church today?

For Your Eyes Only
17. When was the first time you had a "mountaintop" experience? Who was there? What happened afterward?

18. When was the most recent time you had such an experience? How has it affected your life since that time?

This experience in the life of Jesus made him vulnerable and transparent, allowing his three friends to see the full splendor of who he was.

It takes a lot of courage to let someone see you cry or witness your behavior in a time of weakness or vulnerability, but for many people, it also takes courage to reveal strengths and giftedness. Some people, in fact, spend their whole lives with their "light" hidden under the bushel Jesus cautioned us against. "Let your light shine!" Jesus told others, and that light is the inner light of the presence of Christ, the light of one's uniqueness, the light of one's beauty and giftedness (Matt 5:16).

Some are afraid that someone will think they are showing off. Some are afraid that someone else will be jealous, and others are also afraid that someone will criticize or exploit their light.

On the mountaintop, however, Jesus chose to let the full splendor of who he was shine, and, appropriately, the three friends were dazzled. Peter wanted to build tabernacles and stay on the mountain with Jesus. Aren't we all like Peter? We want to seize a holy moment and capture it in a building to keep it for ourselves, just like a six-year-old. But those experiences are portable, and they need to be taken back down into the valleys and highways of our lives to bless others and light their way.

We are not blessed just so that we can have a holy high. We are blessed to bless others. We do not experience the presence of the Living God to puff up our egos. Instead, we are granted epiphanies, mountaintop experiences, and the movement of the Holy Spirit within our lives so that we can be equipped to be a light in the world wherever God has placed us.

I want to see Jesus, but I love this world, too, and so between now and the hereafter, which I cannot define or describe, I will be content to bask in the moments when I sense the presence of God and experience the reality of love in my brothers and sisters in Christ, in the family of humankind, and in the beauty of nature. I will experience those moments for which the only appropriate response is to drop to my knees and say, "Thank you!"

Sometimes we experience rare moments of breakthrough grace, and sometimes it seems that Jesus really is walking with us. Those times are wonderful gifts. Always, though, we "see though a glass darkly," as Paul wrote in 1 Corinthians 13. Whatever experience we might have of the Living Christ is only a fragment of what is possible.

My grandson Sam wasn't wrong about the nature of God. In fact, he probably picked up his understanding of God from hearing this Scripture read in Sunday school or church: "God is light; in him there is no darkness at all. If we claim to have fellowship with him yet walk in the darkness, we lie and do not live by the truth. But if we walk in the light, as he is in the light, we have fellowship with one another" (1 John 1:5b-7a).

No one has ever seen God; but if we love one another, God lives in us and his love is perfected in us. (1 John 4:12)

Walk while you have the light . . . . Put your trust in the light while you have it, so that you may become sons of the light. (John 12:35-36a)

Chapter 36

Meeting Jesus in Gethsemane

When you are about to leave someone, you often say important things that you want them to remember.

It is fortunate when family members get to say what they most need to say to a loved one before that loved one dies. We call it "saying our goodbyes," and it is hard to do.

Jesus seems to have carried a heavy weight of sorrow and dread in his heart as he approached the time when he knew he had to leave his disciples. John 13–17 gives us a sense of how much he wanted to make sure the disciples understood the essence of his life and ministry. Those chapters are filled with many important truths Jesus wanted to leave behind; they are also filled with deep sorrow.

Exploring the Scriptures
Read John 13:1-17.
1. How did the human Jesus know that it was time for him to leave this world and go to the Father?

2. Why do you think it was so important to him to show the disciples "the full extent of his love" (John 13:1)? What does this say about Jesus' nature and his mission?

3. John 13:3 contains a powerful statement about what God the Father invested in Jesus, as well as Jesus' awareness of that power. What did Jesus do with that power?

Your kingdom come, your will be done on earth as it is in heaven. (Matt 6:10)

My Father, if it is possible, may this cup be taken from me. Yet not as I will, but as you will. (Matt 26:39b)

Into your hands I commend my soul; I offer it to you with all the love of my heart, for you are my Father and I so need to give myself, to surrender myself without reserve and with boundless confidence.

—Charles de Foucauld, from "The Prayer of Abandonment"

4. What else could Jesus have done with the power God gave him?

5. What does it reveal about Simon Peter that he resisted when Jesus wanted to wash his feet?

6. What do you think the mood was among the disciples as Jesus washed their feet?

7. Some people take this event literally and become "foot-washing believers." If you take it symbolically, what are the interpretations and applications of this teaching in our lives today?

For Your Eyes Only
8. How would you have responded if you were in the room and Jesus washed your feet?

9. Is it harder for you to wash the feet of another person (either literally or symbolically) or to have yours washed?

10. What do you think is the central meaning of this incident for us today?

Exploring the Scriptures
Read John 13:18-30.
11. Why do you think Jesus mentioned his coming betrayal and identified the one who would betray him?

12. After the tender gathering of the disciples in the upper room, everything changed for them and for Jesus. John 13:30 ends with these poignant words: "And it was night." Does John mean that the day had come to an end, or is there more to his words? What could that phrase mean symbolically?

Read the other accounts of the upper room dinner: Matthew 26:17-39; Mark 14:12-21; and Luke 22:7-20.
13. What are the differences in these accounts? What are the similarities?

For Your Eyes Only
14. If it is true that there is a "Judas" in each of us, in what ways does the "Judas" in you betray Christ?

Exploring the Scriptures
Read John 13:31-38.
15. What is the distinguishing mark of a follower of Christ, according to Jesus?

16. How do you suppose Peter felt when Jesus predicted his denial of him?

For Your Eyes Only
For Your Eyes Only
17. How can people tell that you are a follower of Jesus?

What follows in this poignant story is hard to believe, given all that Jesus had said to his disciples, all that he had done for them, and all that he had done for others in their presence.

Jesus took the disciples with him to a place called Gethsemane, or "Old Press Park," a garden filled with gnarled olive trees. As he went deeper into the garden, he had his inner circle with him—Peter, James, and John, the same three who witnessed the transfiguration on the mountain. He asked for their support, and their response is astonishing.

Read about it, and be astonished with me at the unfolding events when Jesus asked for support. You can find this part of the story in Matthew 26:36-46, Mark 14:32-42 and Luke 22:40-46.

Exploring the Scriptures
Read Matthew 26:36-46; Mark 14:32-42; Luke 22:40-48.
1. Why do you think it was so important for Jesus to draw apart for solitary prayer?

2. What does it mean to you to read that Jesus was sorrowful and troubled "to the point of death"? Wasn't he fulfilling his purpose? Hadn't he anticipated this moment?

3. What do you think Jesus meant for the disciples to do when he asked them to "keep watch with me"?

4. In Matthew 26:39, we read of another struggle Jesus had as he wrestled with his mission and ministry. Why, after his time with the devil in the wilderness, did he have to face yet another intense struggle?

5. How do you view Jesus' vulnerability in sharing his struggles?

6. What must it have felt like to Jesus to return to the disciples, his closest friends, and see that they were sleeping during his time of desperate need?

7. What made Jesus think that the disciples could actually keep watch with him? Why did he give them a second chance?

8. Why do you think Jesus prayed the same request three times? (Matthew 26:39b, 42b, 44)

9. Why do you think Jesus didn't awaken the disciples the second time?

10. How does it make you feel to know that even Jesus wrestled with surrender?

For Your Eyes Only

11. When you are in a deep spiritual struggle, do you want to be alone, or do you want someone with you?

12. Who do you want to be with you when you are at a difficult crossroads experience in your life?

13. What is the hardest thing you have ever had to accept in your life? Did acceptance get any easier after you surrendered your will and your life, as well as the situation, to God?

Someone said that the human Jesus had to die in order for the Risen Christ to be born. How does that resonate with you?

For me, surrender often feels like defeat, and my ego would have me feel that way. Through depth analysis, I have learned that every triumph of the True Self/God within feels like defeat for my frail ego, which is the central organ of consciousness or, as I prefer to say, who I think I am and the person I present myself to be.

An ego, in the language of depth analysis, is not the same as egocentricity. Having an ego doesn't mean being egotistical; everyone has and needs to have an ego, for the ego helps us get around in the world, get to work on time, know and say and do what is appropriate for a situation, and keep things stable, predictable, and

277

familiar. Ego keeps the status quo and makes us anxious when anything threatens that comforting condition.

Jesus had his mission in full bloom. He was training his disciples, and people were catching on to what it meant to live in the kingdom of God, as a kingdom person united with the Creator. He wanted to finish his mission. He didn't want to leave his friends, and he, as the human Jesus, did not want to endure physical suffering. And so he wrestled with God and even asked that the cup of suffering be taken from him.

The significant aspect of this wrestling, however, is Jesus' overriding willingness to surrender to the will of God, who was at work in him, attempting to bring about good. Just as the ego experiences defeat when the True Self/God-within triumphs, the True Self/God-within is also relentless and ruthless in accomplishing a purpose.

Countless times in my life when I have been hard-pressed against the thing that I cannot change, praying for God to rescue me or work so that I don't have to go through it, I have returned to Jesus in Gethsemane for encouragement. Over and over, I have returned to this scene, remembering my visit there and what it was like to stand in that eerie place in Jerusalem, a place where I could almost feel the earth and the trees screaming the horrors of the wrestling match Jesus had with his Father.

That Jesus struggled so mightily against the inevitabilities of his life and that we can read of those struggles brings me to my knees in thanksgiving. Who couldn't love a Savior who is willing to let you see him struggle?

The most troubling part of the Gethsemane account, though, is that the disciples couldn't stay awake. I know what it is like to need someone to sit with me in my sorrow and terror and yet be left on my own. It is an awful feeling. I also know what it is like to need to struggle and pour out my grief and have someone say, "I can stand this. I will hear this as many times as you need to say it."

I wish Jesus' friends had come through for him on that dark night, but the truth is that it takes a stout and tender heart and steady nerves to be with another person who is in the depths of agony. For their sake, I wish Peter, James, and John had been able to stay awake and pray for Jesus while he did the hard work of wrestling with God, but the hard truth is that sometimes a person has to walk through the lonesome, lonely, and terrifying valleys of life alone, without the comfort of a friend's presence.

The angels didn't come to Jesus at the end of his solitary struggle in Gethsemane like they did in the wilderness struggle. Perhaps the difference is that the wilderness struggle was with the Adversary, and this struggle was with the will of God. Perhaps there comes a time for all of us when it is necessary to go it alone.

Chapter 37

Meeting Jesus at Golgotha

Little in life seems more painful than a friend's betrayal.

Putting myself in the middle of the events that happened after Jesus left the garden of Gethsemane, I am deeply affected by how it must have felt to be treated with such brutality by the soldiers and authorities—but mostly to be betrayed by those whom he had taken into his inner circle.

The events that follow Jesus' acceptance of the inevitability of the human events and his surrender to his Father's will are recorded in the following passages. The order of the events is not the same in all the Gospels; I have followed the order in John.

The Last Events of Jesus' Earthly Life

Jesus' arrest	Matthew 26:47-56; Mark 14:43-50; Luke 22:47-53; John 18:1-11
Jesus taken to Caiaphas/Annas	Matthew 26:57; John 18:12-14, 24
Peter's first denial	Matthew 26:69-70; Mark 14:66-68; Luke 22:55-57; John 18:15-18
Jesus questioned by	Matthew 26:59-68; Mark 14:55-65; Luke 22:63-71; John 18:19-24
Peter's second and third denials	Matthew 26:71-75; Mark 14:69-72; Luke 22:58-62; John 18:25-27
Jesus before Pilate	Matthew 27:11-18, 20-23; Mark 15:2-15; Luke 23:2-3, 18-25; John 18:28-40
Jesus sentenced	Matthew 27:27-31; Mark 15:16-20; John 19:1-16
Jesus crucified	Matthew 27:33-44; Mark 15:22-32; Luke 23:33-43; John 19:16b-27
Death and burial of Jesus	Matthew 27:48-50, 57-61; Mark 15:36, 37, 42-47; Luke 23:46, 50-56; John 19:28-41

If there is anywhere on earth a lover of God who is always kept safe, I know nothing of it, for it was not shown to me. But this was shown: that in falling and rising again we are always kept in that same precious love.

—Julian of Norwich

Father, into your hands I commit my spirit. (Luke 23:46)

What About You?

1. Of the various people in these significant moments, which one intrigues you the most? Explain your response.

2. What does each event in history mean to you now?

3. Do these events make any difference in your everyday life? Explain.

4. Was Peter's denial a necessary part of his becoming who he was intended to be? Explain your response.

5. How do you think a young girl could cause such a fervent follower of Jesus to fold and deny even having known him?

6. Matthew's account of Pilate's part in this story includes a message from Pilate's wife about a dream she had (see Matt 27:19). John's account states that Pilate tried to set Jesus free. Ultimately, he gave in too. What made him fold?

7. Do you suppose Pilate ever realized what he had done and who Jesus really was?

8. How do the accounts of Pilate's sentencing of Jesus and Peter's denial of Jesus affect you? What meaning do these incidents have for you?

For Your Eyes Only

9. What is most disturbing to you about the events leading up to the crucifixion of Jesus?

10. Of these people—Peter, Mary the mother of Jesus, Barabbas, the soldier who mocked Jesus, Pilate, or the ones who nailed Jesus to the cross—who would you have least liked to be? What was the sorrow of each?

In 1632, the bubonic plague ravaged the village of Oberammergau, Germany. Desperate for relief and help, the town's residents made a vow that if God would spare them, they would produce a play every ten years depicting the life and death of Jesus.

So it was that the Passion Play was performed in this tiny Bavarian village for the first time in 1634. It has been performed every ten years since then, except for 1770 and 1940. The 1920 performance season was delayed until 1922 because of World War I. The seven-hour play, interrupted by a break for a meal in a local restaurant, is performed for five months and involves more than 2,000 performers from the small village. People come from all over the world to see the reenactment of the events surrounding the crucifixion of Jesus.

I have been twice to this Passion Play, and as I walked up to the enormous amphitheater the first time, my sister said, "There will be a moment that grabs you, and you will always remember it. It's different for every person, but something that you see and hear today will haunt you the rest of your life."

My sister was right, and for me the moment was when Mary the mother of Jesus held her son's lifeless body in her arms and wept, "*Mein sohn! Mein sohn.*"

In addition to that moment, one of my most meaningful encounters with the story happened recently when I attended the Palm Sunday service at Palmer Episcopal Church in Houston with my children and grandchildren and heard the events of what we call Passion Week read aloud from the pulpit. There was no drama, no spectacle, no thrill. It was simply the reading of the Scriptures, and the story came alive to me as never before.

Perhaps there are particular moments of each scene in this terrible drama that stand out for you, as there are for me. Below, I have chosen three moments that I find deeply meaningful. I encourage you to choose the ones that are meaningful to you and meditate on them. Then ask yourself these questions:

1. What captivates me about this particular moment in the story?
2. What in this moment connects with something in my own life?
3. Is the story asking me to change a certain attitude or behavior?

It's hard for me to choose only three moments of Jesus' last days, for I have lived with this story my whole life in such a way that at different times, different parts have stood out for me. But the first moment that grips me every time I read it is *when Jesus cries out, "My God, my God, why have you forsaken me?" from the cross.*

I can hardly bear to think about the human Jesus hanging naked and exposed on a criminal's cross. It is painful for me to consider the unfairness of this treatment of the Rabbi Jesus, whose entire work was intended to heal and transform, liberate and empower human beings. I want to rail against the awfulness of it all, and then when I read the words that indicate that even Jesus felt the absence of God, I have to stop and ponder that for a long time. Every year, I have to rethink the idea that Jesus, whom I call the Son of God and the second person of the Trinity, experienced the abandonment of God the Father.

It is easy for me to tell myself that God could not abandon God. I try to remind myself that Jesus' crying out to God with a wrenching question/accusation is evidence that God did not abandon the Son. Am I playing mind games? I don't know if I am or not, but I do know this: I have had intellectual doubt about the reality of God, but there have also been terrible, hard, terrifying moments in my life when I did not feel the presence of God and when I felt alone, lonely, abandoned, and afraid. In those moments, Jesus' terrible time on the cross comes to me, and, in the most inexplicable way, I am comforted by the moment when Jesus, too, felt abandoned.

I cannot explain it. I just know that entrusting my pain and agony to a Savior who is a wounded healer makes a difference to me. The writer of Hebrews said,

> Now that we know what we have—Jesus, this great High Priest with ready access to God—let's not let it slip through our fingers. We don't have a priest who is out of touch with our reality. He's been through weakness and testing, experienced it all— all but the sin. So let's walk right up to him and get what he is so ready to give. Take the mercy, accept the help. (Heb 4:14-16, *The Message*)

These verses mean so much to me because, at a terribly painful moment in my life, I wailed out my pain to Sister Mary Dennison, ending by demanding an answer to how I could continue to write my book *ChristHeart* and teach Bible studies when I had such difficult, unsolvable problems.

"How can you write about the suffering Jesus if you haven't also suffered?" my beloved spiritual director asked me.

Indeed, I wish life were easier, but it's not. When I pray, I know I'm not praying to a distant, uninvolved God who can't relate to suffering.

The second moment is *when Jesus said from the cross, "Forgive them, Father, for they don't know what they are doing."* This is a tragic comment about human beings. Who among us hasn't had a moment when someone has said, "What were you *thinking*?" In utter confusion and disbelief, we've had to say, "I wasn't thinking! I just did it."

We are people of reflexive action, often catapulting ourselves down the roads of conflict and devastation because we don't realize that what we're doing is wrong or stupid or sinful. If we are honest, we can all relate to doing or saying the wrong things when trying to get through a day, a hard situation, a crisis, or simply life itself.

I'll never forget sitting in a courtroom for jury selection, hearing the lawyer present a task for those of us who were in the selection process. "You are going to have to decide if this woman did this heinous deed out of negligence, ignorance, or willful intent." Any way you look at it, the result of the woman's *unconsciousness*, either of what she did or of the results of what she did, had wreaked loss, sorrow, trauma, and ongoing difficulty in her life and the lives of her loved ones.

I've heard it said that the only real sin is unconsciousness, and though that makes some people nervous, it is an idea worth pondering. I'll admit that it's easier to focus on a list of sins that we can measure and count, behaviors or attitudes that are easily identified and catalogued. I confess as well that I am attached to my list of sins, which includes the things I think are the worst based on my upbringing, my culture, my biases, and my prejudices.

But Jesus penetrates to the heart of an important truth that catches just about everyone in its profundity. Being unconscious—being asleep at the wheel of your life, being tuned out and unaware—causes a person to do things that hurt other people. When unconscious, we can act wrongly and dangerously and then shrug it off and say, "Who, me? I didn't do anything!" or "I didn't know any better." When unconscious, we can be indifferent to the results of the words we say, the harm we do, and the consequences of the behaviors we repeat. When unconscious, we can act as if we don't have any accountability to the supremacy of God.

The people who condemned Jesus to death, the ones who nailed him to the cross, and the ones who cast lots for his clothing didn't have a clue what they were doing. Jesus knew that, and still he asked his Father to forgive them. In his agony, he still acted on behalf of those who were oblivious to the significance of the moment.

In response to the disciples' concern about who might sit at his right and left hands, Jesus asked, "Can you drink this cup?" (Matt 10:38). It seems to me that he was asking, "Can you bear the light of consciousness? Can you stand to be as awake and aware as I am? Can you hold up under the weight of feeling the pain of the world and suffering the conflicts that come with being conscious?"

> When unconscious, we can be indifferent to the results of the words we say, the harm we do, and the consequences of the behaviors we repeat.

The third moment is part of the second: *when Jesus said, "Father, forgive them."* If you look back on everything Jesus said about the issue of forgiveness, it will bring you to your knees.

"I am afraid of unforgiveness more than just about anything else" was the daunting opening to a speech given by Miriam Burke at a retreat at Laity Lodge Retreat Center in the Hill Country of Texas.

Is there any bigger struggle than the one we face with the offenses others have committed against us? Is there anything worse than the guilt we can't shake, no matter how many times we ask for forgiveness? What can damage our souls and our relationships more than not being able to reconcile with a brother, a sister, a spouse, a parent, or a child?

What can we do when an act is *unforgivable*?

When I look at the cross event and imagine what it must have been like for Jesus in those last few moments of his earthly life, I am struck by what he did. Jesus, the victim of wrongly motivated people, handed the problem to his Father. He asked God to do the hard work of forgiveness.

Sometimes I'm up against things that are so painful for me that I can't, in my own humanity, forgive. But I want to forgive, not only because it is one of the most serious teachings of Jesus but also because I know from experience that what Miriam Burke taught is true. Unforgiveness is a dangerous thing; it will make us sick, and it will reap a bitter crop, sometimes contaminating relationships for generations.

So the Rabbi Jesus shows us from the cross what we can do. In our own pain and agony, we can surrender to the hands of the Almighty our pain over being hurt and even the forgiveness of the ones who have harmed us.

"You do it for me," I have prayed in the long, dark night of the soul. "I can't do it yet, though I am willing."

Chapter 38

Meeting Jesus, the Resurrected Christ

Often, when I am teaching or sitting with someone in the sacred space that is called spiritual direction, I refer to the resurrection of Jesus. It is never in the context of debating whether the resurrection actually happened, but it is in the context of giving encouragement in the face of what seems hopeless. I've learned that any encouragement I give and any hope I want to engender has to come from a place of authenticity.

Some people respond to shallow or sentimental bromides that give momentary relief, but when people are really hurting, most of them don't want simplistic answers to complex problems. When it comes to reading and following the Scriptures, I acknowledge and embrace the fact that good teachers and examples of deep faith have taught me to live with Mystery and tolerate not having to prove what cannot be proven with logic or reason. Wise and faithful people have shown me by their lives and words that it is possible to discern the difference between fact and truth and accept the anxiety of living with paradox, irony, ambivalence, and ambiguity.

When it comes to the miracles of Jesus and the resurrection, I have no problem believing that they happened as the Scriptures reveal they did, and whether that is because I was taught them as believable and actual or because I have chosen belief as an adult doesn't matter to me. Understanding those things is a matter of accepting the Mystery of the unseen God.

I would love to know exactly what happened within the human Jesus in those three days between the cross and the resurrection, but for now, I'm content to accept what Paul wrote in Romans and declare that I can continue to live with hope and faith and trust because I am not a life-death person, but a life-death-life celebrant of the power of the Spirit of God, who raised Jesus from the dead.

I believe in the resurrection of Jesus because I heard the accounts of it from the time I was a child, and because for my entire life I have experienced the thrill of worshiping with a community of faith on the Sunday in which we celebrate the resurrection. For my entire life, I have sung the hymns of Easter, and I have pro-

Praise be to the God and Father of our Lord Jesus Christ. In his great mercy, he has given us new birth into a living hope through the resurrection of Jesus Christ from the dead. (1 Peter 1:3)

All shall be well, and all shall be well and all manner of things shall be well.
—Julian of Norwich

And if the Spirit of him who raised Jesus from the dead is living in you, he who raised Christ from the dead will also give life to your mortal bodies, through his Spirit, who lives in you. (Rom 8:11)

Always be prepared to give an answer to everyone who asks you to give the reason for the hope that is within you. (1 Peter 3:15)

claimed with my fellow sisters and brothers in Christ, "He is risen! He is risen, indeed!"

Is it a leap of faith? Of course it is, but I'd rather take a leap of faith than sit in my despair. And here's the other side of this stance of faith: if I should find out that it's all a story made up by someone, my faith will not be shattered or shaken.

This isn't some masochistic practice. I'm not into beating myself up repeatedly for the same things. Because I am a follower of Christ, I have taken the surrender of my wrongs seriously so that I am free to celebrate the joy and wonder of resurrection on what I still call Easter Sunday.

I believe in the resurrection because I have made that story a part of my spiritual practice, year after year. I have kneaded the wonder and mystery of that event into my life, making the power of resurrection real to me.

I believe in the resurrection because I have experienced reconciliation between people who were once estranged and lost to each other. I have seen forgiveness at work.

I believe in the resurrection because I have experienced the healing of deep, old, and painful wounds.

I believe in the resurrection because I have seen new life come back to the earth in the springtime and at the dawn of a new day, not once but countless times.

I believe in the resurrection because I have watched the fire of love warm the hearts of cold-hearted people.

I believe in the resurrection because I have seen people endure impossible hardships over long years, and in those years become lovelier, wiser, and more compassionate.

I believe in the resurrection because I have seen beauty come out of the broken shards of destruction and devastation.

I believe in the resurrection because I have seen practical atheists come to a vibrant faith.

I believe in the resurrection because I have seen impossible situations work out in ways that can only be called miraculous.

I believe in the resurrection because I have seen hopelessly addicted people become sober, mean people become gentle, hate become social action for good, and despair become courage, all within the warmth of a loving and faithful group of people known as the Body of Christ.

I believe in the resurrection because I have known what it is like to dread the next day, fear getting out of bed, tremble with grief, and shake with terror, and then be changed from the inside out to

Belief is a wise wager. Granted that faith cannot be proved, what harm will come to you if you gamble on its truth and it proves false? If you gain, you gain all; if you lose, you lose nothing. Wager, then, without hesitation, that He exists.
—Blaise Pascal, French mathematician and philosopher

It is the heart which perceives God and not the reason. That is what faith is: God perceived by the heart, not by the reason.
—Blaise Pascal

I've had lots of experience learning that things I once believed were not as I had believed them, but the real truth is that when I sing an old hymn, I know that the Spirit of Christ is not bound by my intellectual constructs, my mental constraints, or my dogma, doctrine, or definitions.

> He lives, He lives
> Christ Jesus lives today.
> He walks with me, he talks with me
> Along the narrow way.
> He lives, He lives, Salvation to impart.
> You ask me how I know he lives.
> He lives within my heart.
>   —Alfred Henry Ackley (words and music)

The child in me believes in the resurrection and the Living Christ, and the student, the adult, the doubter, and the believer in me all believe in the resurrection.

Exploring the Scriptures
Read about Jesus' resurrection in Matthew 28:1-15; Mark 16:1-8; Luke 24:1-12; and John 20:1-18.
1. How are these accounts alike?

2. How are they different?

I believe in the resurrection because year after year I have taken the forty days of the Lenten season seriously and have made it a time to do a fearless and searching moral inventory of my life. I have walked through Holy Week over and over. I have sat in the darkness following a Maundy Thursday service. I have let myself feel the weight of my brokenness and the wrongs I have done to myself and others, and I have made an intentional attempt to surrender those to the Living Christ.

be a person who looks forward to the day, to face my fears with courage, to cry out my tears and come to gladness, and to find the boldness to live the one wild and precious life I've been given.

I know personally what it is like when the Spirit of the God who raised Jesus from the dead lives in me and begins to do the work of the Divine Therapist in the deep, unconscious, and shadowy crooks and crannies of my inner world, healing the emotional wounds of a lifetime.

What About You?

1. If pressed you to answer for the hope that is in you, what would you say?

2. What do you believe about the resurrection of Jesus? Is that belief an inherited belief or a chosen belief?

3. How does the resurrection of Jesus affect your personal life today?

4. How would you like for the resurrection of Jesus to affect your life today?

5. What meaning does the resurrection have for individuals today—realistically?

6. Is the Easter story about something more than living forever after death? What about living in the world now?

Few scenes in the Gospel narrative touch me as deeply as the moment when Jesus appeared to Mary Magdalene outside the tomb where he had been buried.

Exploring the Scriptures
Read John 20:11-18 (see vv. 1-10 for background).
1. How do you explain the fact that Mary Magdalene was the first person to whom the Risen Christ appeared?

2. Do you think it was a coincidence that Mary Magdalene was there when Jesus came from the tomb?

3. This was Jesus' first post-resurrection appearance, made to Mary Magdalene. What do you think qualified her to be the one who was granted this special experience?

4. Why do you think Jesus told Mary not to cling to him?

5. What made Jesus know he could trust Mary to deliver the message to the disciples that she had seen him?

6. How do you think the disciples felt about the fact that it was Mary Magdalene who brought them the news of Jesus' resurrection, telling them, "I have seen the Lord"?

Here in this story of Mary Magdalene is another reason I believe in the resurrection of Jesus.

Mary Magdalene was cast to the dustbin of Christendom when in the sixth century, Pope Gregory, trying to make sense of the Mary's in Luke's Gospel, decided that the seven demons Jesus had cast out of Mary Magdalene must have related to her sexual immorality. Historian Jane Schaberg, author of *The Resurrection of Mary Magdalene*, calls this the "harlotization of Mary Magdalene," and Mary had to live with that label for centuries.

It must be noted that when Jesus cast demons out of the crazed man who lived among the tombs, the one called "the demoniac," it was not automatically assumed that his demons had to do with sexual issues.

In 1969, 1,378 years after Pope Gregory conflated the Mary's, the Catholic Church finally declared that Mary Magdalene was not a prostitute, and recent scholarship has supported the idea that in fact, Mary Magdalene was one of Jesus' most ardent disciples who helped teach others after Jesus' ascension.

There is good news in this story, even after nearly 1,400 years of wrong done to the memory and person of Mary Magdalene. Even when it seems that those who play loose with truth are winning and that evil is more powerful than good, I hold to what my father used to call "resurrection power." Mary is proof that the labels we wear can finally be removed and that the resurrection power of grace is at work in the world.

I am not about life and death. I live my life in hope not because things will always work out my way or be easy or because I have faith and sing my resurrection songs.

I live in hope because I choose to be a life-death-life person.

I live in hope because the Living Christ lives. He lives within my heart.

Chapter 39

Meeting Jesus after the Resurrection

The post-resurrection appearances of Jesus give one's imagination a workout, and if your curiosity works overtime as mine does, you can get caught up in asking of questions about why things happened as they did, how Jesus was able to appear as he did, and how he chose the people to whom he appeared.

I have explored these happenings many times, and each time I do, I have more questions.

Exploring the Scriptures

Read John 20:1-9.

1. What do you think the disciples thought when they heard from Mary Magdalene that the tomb where Jesus had been buried was empty?

2. What do you think they felt?

3. What did they say to each other about this unusual happening?

Read John 20:10-18.

4. Why didn't he appear first to someone with personal or political power?

Then their eyes were opened and they recognized him, and he disappeared from their sight. (Luke 24:31)

5. Imagine what it would have been like if Jesus had first appeared to one of these people: Pilate; Peter, James, or John; his mother Mary; people in the synagogue or temple.

6. What do you think the disciples thought when Mary Magdalene said, "I have seen the Lord"?

7. We cannot "see" Jesus with our eyes today, so what is the meaning of this powerful phrase for us?

8. To what kind of person might the resurrected Jesus appear today?

Now let's delve more deeply into the actual historical appearances as recorded in Scripture. The chart lists the post-resurrection appearances of Jesus. After reading each reference, use the questions to move the truths of the appearances into your everyday life.

The Post-resurrection Appearances of Jesus

Matthew 28:16-20
Mark 16:12-20
Luke 24:13-35
Luke 24:36-49
John 20:19-23
John 20:24-31
John 21

Exploring the Scriptures

Read the references for Jesus' post-resurrection appearances. Imagine yourself in each event, and answer the following questions.

1. In each instance, who was there when Jesus appeared?

2. In each instance, what did Jesus do or say?

3. What instructions did Jesus give to those to whom he appeared?

4. Which of these appearances do you think was the most dramatic?

5. What do you think was Jesus' intention in making these appearances?

6. How were the lives of these people changed by the post-resurrection appearances?

Peter

Thomas

The two disciples on the Emmaus road

Mary Magdalene

7. What basic message did Jesus give each of the following?
Peter

Thomas

The disciples on the Emmaus road

Mary Magdalene

Without the resurrection of Jesus, does his life make sense or matter to us today?

The first time I heard that question, I rushed almost reflexively to respond that the resurrection mattered and that of course it matters to us today, but then the questioner asked me, "Why does it matter to you?"

He didn't ask if it mattered to the world. He didn't ask if it mattered to my parents, whose faith I borrowed until I could form my own faith. Nor did he ask if it mattered in the grand scheme of history. *He asked if it mattered to me.*

How would you answer that question today?

What About You?

1. Does the resurrection of Jesus relate more to your life now or to the afterlife?

2. Which one of the post-resurrection events would you have most wanted to experience?

3. Of all the people who experienced an encounter with the Risen Christ, with whom would you most like to talk? Who would you have liked to be?

4. How do you think Jesus chose the people to whom he would appear?

5. What purpose did each appearance serve?

6. Is it possible to have "an Emmaus Road experience"?

7. For what reason would you want to experience the Living Christ?

8. In what ways do you make yourself available, with an open mind and an open heart, to an encounter with the Living Christ?

I am especially fond of Thomas, the disciple who said that he wouldn't believe Jesus was alive unless he could touch the wounds in his hands. Thomas's encounter, recorded in John 20:24-29 resonates with me. I relate to Thomas, and I like him because he was open and honest about his doubts. I like him because he wasn't afraid of his questions, and neither am I. I have learned, in fact, that I am more comfortable with other seekers who have honest questions and doubts than I am with people who are certain.

I am certain that God loves me, and I am comfortable with Mystery, but I get nervous when someone acts as if he has the corner on truth. I am nervous as well when people are shamed for asking hard questions or when they are given pat answers to serious questions.

A bumper sticker caught my attention the other day: "All who wander are not lost" (the words are attributed to J. R. R. Tolkien). Indeed.

I've learned that an opening and questioning spirit and mind keeps us curious, and people who are curious keep on learning. I think that must be why Jesus said in Matthew that we are not to get only a few insights or make a few steps on the journey and then sit down in self-satisfaction. Instead, we are to "keeping on asking, keep on seeking, and keep on knocking" (Matt 7:7).

Once we stop asking and only answer, we stop growing. Once we stop seeking and sit down where we are, we begin to harden into rigidity. Once we stop knocking on the doors of Mystery, we get stuck in an arrested spiritual developmental stage, often assuming that we have arrived.

It's one thing to be a seeker and another to be a cynic or a skeptic, and the difference is in the intention. Thomas needed to be met at the point of his need, and Jesus did that. Thomas didn't have Jesus on trial so that nothing Jesus could do would satisfy his questioning. Instead, when Jesus appeared to Thomas, the true nature of Thomas's questioning was revealed by his instant recognition of the

Risen Christ. Thomas touched the hands of Jesus and said, "My Lord and my God." It was a tender but powerful moment.

My life experience supports the belief that God accommodates himself to meet us at the point of our honest and authentic need.

If I were Simon Peter after the crucifixion, I would have been in the fetal position, wrapped up in a blanket in the back of my house, shaking and trembling with guilt and shame. I would have hated to go back home, especially if I might risk the ridicule of my wife and mother-in-law. Did they interrogate Peter about why he followed the itinerant rabbi in the first place, or were their questions about why he didn't stand by Jesus? Did they think that Jesus' healing of Peter's mother-in-law was real, or did they question if he was, after all, a fake? Did they shame Peter for running from a young servant girl, or did they understand his terror?

Whatever happened to Peter in those agonizing hours between the time he betrayed Jesus, brought to his duplicity by a young girl, and the moment Jesus appeared to the disciples in the early hours at the Sea of Tiberias, it must have been huge for Peter to look Jesus in the eyes and bear his questions.

I am fascinated by the fact that Jesus didn't say, "Why did you lie about me, Peter?" or "Why couldn't you hold it together?" Instead, Jesus went straight to the heart of things and asked, "Do you love me?" That question cascades down through the centuries and lands in our lives, time after time.

Apart from all the doctrine, dogma, ritual, and rules, and beyond our flaws and failures, the Living Christ must want to know from each of us, "Do you love me?"

How we answer that question determines everything about our lives with Jesus.

When it comes to Jesus, in the end, it's all about love.

Chapter 40

Meeting Jesus as You Go

If you had discovered something that changed your life, would you keep it to yourself? What if you had the cure for cancer, for Parkinson's, for ALS—would you keep it a secret?

The four books of the Bible that contain the record of the life and teachings of Jesus are called "Gospels" for a reason. Gospel is *good news,* and when you enter fully into the story of Jesus, you see that his life embodied the good news that his words proclaimed.

My hard confession is that every time I have heard such questions asked in a sermon, I have felt guilty. I have felt guilty, you see, because I've never been able to be the kind of evangelist my particular religious group has tried to get me to be. It's not that I'm a contrarian; it's just that I've never been able to do what I'm supposed to do in spreading the gospel of Jesus!

My other confession is that every time I heard the "Great Commission" read in church, I felt terrified that God might call me to go to the outermost parts of the world as a missionary, and what I wanted to do more than anything was get married and have my own family.

I was so thankful when I learned that I didn't have to be a missionary in a far-off place but could actually serve God right where I was.

For many years, I have worked through the Twelve Steps of Alcoholics Anonymous as an aid in helping me overcome codependency. In these years, I have learned much from the people I call "black belt recovering people." I have been impressed with how seriously those who are in the programs of recovery from all kinds of addictions take their responsibility to newcomers whom they sponsor. I've noticed how eagerly recovering people sponsor new people in the program, and I've been inspired by the joy they seem to get in being a sponsor to someone else.

It isn't a burden to someone to sponsor a new person in the program; instead, it is both a privilege and a way to stay sober. Sharing

Having had a spiritual awakening . . . we tried to carry this message and practice it in all our affairs. (Twelfth Step of A.A., adapted)

We no longer believe just because of what you said; now we have heard for ourselves, and we know that this man really is the Savior of the world. (John 4:42)

the good news of recovery and the steps is necessary, in fact, to staying sober.

Neither, however, is the way of spreading the good news of recovery a hit-and-run event. Instead, taking on a sponsor means that you take that person on for "as long as it takes," and you are willing to be available to that person around the clock. The kind of evangelism that fits my temperament and my beliefs is that of building a relationship with someone and then sharing the good news as we go through life together. That, I believe, is the way Jesus must have been as he took his little band of disciples and spent hour after hour with them, answering their questions, and showing them how to let go of their old way of life (to recover from it) and take on the new way of Jesus.

Jesus wanted his work to continue after his ascension, but he also knew an important principle of life. If you want to keep something, you have to give it away. I have learned that the best way for me to learn something is to teach it. If you want to stay on the path of spiritual awakening and spiritual growth, the best way to do that is to help someone who is just a step or two behind you.

I must confess, though, that when I was growing up in a Baptist church, I heard two messages. I heard the message of salvation, and I heard the call to go out into the highways and hedges of the world and bring in others so that they, too, could be saved.

The problem with my hearing that as a young child was that, while I knew that I should be sharing the good news of Jesus with others, I didn't have enough knowledge or ability to do it with integrity or authority, and so I always felt guilty because I wasn't "witnessing."

The other problem for me is that I am an introvert, and the ways of evangelism of my religious culture were almost impossible for me to do. I simply couldn't buttonhole a stranger, hand him a tract, and be on my way. I couldn't knock on doors, asking people personal questions about their faith, and I wasn't willing to witness to waitresses, seatmates on an airplane, or even my next-door neighbor!

My religious culture has sent brand-new Christians and ill-equipped though well-intentioned people out into a complex society to tell the good news before we have anything to tell. My culture has also supported and promoted, encouraged and rewarded preachers whose message is not gospel, good news, but is scary, terrifying, bad news, ill-informed opinion, and prejudiced vitriol.

That is not the gospel of Jesus Christ.

Jesus' model of spreading the good news was multi-faceted. He did preach to the crowds, but his primary mode of passing along the secrets of the kingdom of God was done one on one or one on some, as with the small group of disciples. He seemed to know that when you are dealing with the big truths of the kingdom, you have to mentor people, walking alongside them as they learn, usually slowly, to let go of their old way of being in the world and begin to incorporate their new way, the Jesus way, into their minds and hearts and then into their daily lives.

Matthew's account of Jesus' giving what is called the "Great Commission" takes place during one of Jesus' post-resurrection appearances.

Exploring the Scriptures
Read the "Great Commission" in Matthew 28:19-20.

1. What was the setting for Jesus' giving this "commission" to the disciples (see Matt 28:11-18)?

2. Is there any significance to the fact that Jesus gave this commission to the disciples and not to the multitudes? If so, what is that significance?

3. Jesus gave the disciples a multi-step task. What is the order in which they were to do the steps?

4. What is the significance of Matthew 28:20b?

5. How is Jesus "with us always"?

6. How does this promise Jesus gives the disciples correlate with John 15?

7. How does this promise correlate with Matthew 6:33?

8. What happens if you practice only the "Great Commission" without awareness of, concern for, or obedience to the other imperatives?

9. How would following the Great Commission "work" if you didn't follow Matthew 22:37-39?

10. Why do you think The Great Commission is the only commandment of Jesus' that some people know or teach?

11. If you were designing a discipleship-training program for your church or for a group of people who wanted to know and understand who Jesus was and what he did, what would your program include?

12. How does giving money to missions organizations help carry out the Great Commission?

13. In what ways do you carry out the Great Commission?

14. Do you feel responsible for helping carry it out, or do you leave that to missionaries or religious professionals?

As I come to the end of this book, I recall the times when I have told people what I do—teaching Bible studies, leading retreats, acting as a spiritual director, and writing books. Sometimes people want to know more, but sometimes it is as if an invisible curtain goes down over their eyes.

Particularly, as I have been writing this book, people have inquired about what I'm working on now, and when I've told them I'm writing a "Jesus book," the responses have been interesting.

Some are curious, but many are cautious. Some have even asked me why I am doing this. "Aren't there enough books about Jesus out there?" people ask.

Some are over eager, as if I am going to join the ranks of their religious/political organization or initiative and finally write about the real truth.

Now and then, though, someone is authentically interested in what yet another book about Jesus might be and what I might do with the gospel.

I wrote this book for other people who are curious and cautious. I hoped to give an overview of the life and teachings of Jesus for the people I know who are working to reconcile what is happening within the churches and what Jesus taught. Most of all, I know now that I wrote this book as part of my Twelve Step work. I wrote it because I needed to share the good news—from my own life and not a tract—about what it has meant to me to practice the presence of Christ and attempt to integrate the truths and guidance of Jesus into my personal relationships, my difficulties and heartaches, my writing and teaching, and the challenges I face.

To keep my own faith alive, I need to tell the good news I have learned that indeed Jesus saves, but not as I understood the process as a child. Instead, my declaration is that Jesus saves as I allow the Living Christ to come to me as Divine Therapist, working deep within my inner life to heal the wounds of a lifetime.

Jesus saves when I grapple with his big commandment and attempt to love God with all my mind, heart, and soul, and my neighbor as myself. He saves when I try to figure out what that means, especially when the needs of my neighbor are so enormous and my own needs have been unmet for so long.

Jesus saves when I take his teaching on forgiveness seriously, working hard to understand the difference between forgiving and simply overlooking what I don't have the courage to confront.

Jesus is the answer because he calls me out of my childishness and narcissism, my self-centeredness and selfishness, my biases and prejudices, my fears and hesitations, asking me to get beyond myself and my fears of not having enough, not being good enough, not working hard enough, and not being acceptable enough and simply love myself so that I can love others as he has loved me.

Jesus is the answer because over and over I am reminded, as I attempt to follow him, that he is the one who said he came as a human being because God so loved the world that he gave Jesus to us, and as I read those words, I am pushed out of my small circle of who's in and who's out and am compelled to make the circle wider and wider, including the whole world.

Over and over, I am reminded of the song I learned as a child:

Jesus loves the little children,
all the children of the world.
Red and yellow, black and white,
They are precious in his sight.
Jesus loves the little children of the world.

Jesus saves me, and Jesus is the answer as I attempt to follow his example of love. When I am unable to do that, some old hymn always comes back to me, reminding me that no matter how I flail and falter in following this challenge, the love of God is always bigger than my failures.

Indeed, in some mysterious way I cannot prove and feel no need to defend, Jesus is the "love that will not let me go."

This is a matter not of my rational mind but of my heart, which does, in fact, have its own reasons, some of which are hidden to my conscious mind.

I'm thankful for a religion and spiritual practices based on learning how to love and be loved instead of being right.

Who is this Jesus person?

As I conclude this book, I realize how much of his teachings I left out. I am acutely aware that there is so much more to learn about him. There's more to know, understand, and experience, and there's more asking, seeking, and knocking ahead.

There's more life to live with this mysterious, inexplicable relationship with *the Living Christ.*

If I could have captured it all in this one book, it wouldn't be the Mystery that it is.

Right before my precious friend Elizabeth Pool died, her family members gathered around her bed, singing to her, telling her they loved her, sharing stories about her, and reading Scriptures to her.

Elizabeth had traveled all over the world with her husband and family. She read widely and kept up with current events. She was smart and wise and funny, and she had a heart that was open and tender.

She was elegant and sophisticated and could find her away around in any part of the world and with all kinds of people, *and* her faith was grounded in beliefs of her Christian faith.

As Elizabeth was transitioning into the next life, family members tended to her with the same kind of love she had given to them.

Whenever there was a lull in the room, her husband and sweetheart of sixty-six years would begin singing this simple child's song, and her family would join in: "Oh, how I love Jesus; oh, how I love Jesus; oh, how I love Jesus because he first loved me."

That simple child's song echoes a great truth recorded in 1 John 4:19: We love because he first loved us . . . and he has given us this command: Whoever loves God must also love his brother and his sister."

Love.

It's the Jesus way.

And we must all be about our Father's business, don't you think?

I close this book with a prayer for myself and for all of us—the curious, the cautious, and the committed.

May all of us on this pilgrimage path
come to see the Living Christ more clearly,
follow him more nearly,
and love him and each other more dearly.
(based on a prayer by Richard of Chichester, 1197–1253)

Notes

1. Marcus Borg, *Meeting Jesus Again for the First Time: The Historical Jesus and the Heart of Contemporary Faith* (San Francisco: HarperSanFrancisco, 1994) 1.

2. Geza Vermes, *The Changing Faces of Jesus* (New York: Viking Compass, 2001).

3. John Killinger, *The Changing Shape of Our Salvation* (New York: Crossroad, 2007).

4. Thomas Keating, *Reawakenings* (New York: Crossroad, 1992).

5. Elton Trueblood, *While It Is Day* (New York: Harper & Row, 1974).

6. Marcus Borg, *Speaking Christian* (New York: HarperCollins, 2011).

7. Erich Fromm, *The Art of Loving* (1956; repr., New York: Perennial, 2000).

8. Scot McKnight, *The Jesus Creed: Loving God, Loving Others* (Brewster MA: Paraclete Press, 2004).

9. For deeper exploration into any of these passages, you might find either of my books on Jesus helpful: *ChristHeart* or *Becoming Fire*.

10. Borg, *Meeting Jesus Again*, 16.

11. Ibid.

12. David Dark, *The Sacredness of Questioning Everything* (Grand Rapids MI: Zondervan, 2009).

13. Ibid., 13.

14. Rainer Maria Rilke, *Letters to a Young Poet* (1984; repr., Cambridge MA: Harvard University Press, 2011.)

15. Two of my books, *Becoming Fire* and *Christheart,* provide daily exercises for using these encounters with Jesus as a way of entering more deeply into prayer and making the stories personal to you. See *Becoming Fire* (Macon GA: Smyth & Helwys Publishing, 1998) 129–36; and *ChristHeart* (Macon GA: Smyth & Helwys Publishing, 1999) 171–78.

16. *Becoming Fire (BF)*, pp. 72–80; *ChristHeart (CH)*, pp. 137–44.

17. *BF*, pp. 193–200; *CH*, pp. 229–36.

18. *BF*, pp. 49–56; *CH*, pp. 163–70.

19. *BF*, pp. 90–96; *CH*, pp. 103–10.

20. *BF*, pp. 113–20; *CH*, pp. 153–60.

21. *CH*, pp. 87–94.

22. *BF*, pp. 250–56; *CH*, pp. 206–12.

23. *CH*, pp. 273–80.

24. Burney, cited in Peter Rhea Jones, *Studying the Parables of Jesus* (Macon GA: Smyth & Helwys Publishing, 1999).

25. John Dominic Crossan, *In Parables: The Challenge of the Historical Jesus* (Sonoma CA: Polebridge Press, 1992) 22.

26. Susan E. Colón (Baylor professor) *Victorian Parables* (London; New York: Continuum International Publishing Group, 2012) 7.

27. John Claypool, *Stories Jesus Still Tells: The Parables* (Cambridge MA: Cowley Publications, 2000).

28. For a beautiful meditation on this story, see Henri Nouwen's *The Return of the Prodigal Son: A Story of Homecoming* (New York: Continuum, 1995). Other books that highlight Jesus' parables are John D. Crossan's *In Parables: The Challenge of the Historical Jesus* and *The Power of Parable*, John Claypool's *Stories Jesus Still Tells*, William Barclay's *The Parables of Jesus*, Robert Capon's three books *Parables of the Kingdom*, *Parables of Judgment*, and *Parables of Grace*, Richard Q. Ford's *The Parables of Jesus: Recovering the Art of Listening*, Peter Rhea Jones's *Studying the Parables of Jesus*, and Lloyd John Ogilvie's *Autobiography of God*.

29. Eugene Peterson, *Christ Plays in Ten Thousand Places: A Conversation in Spiritual Theology* (Grand Rapids MI: W. B. Eerdmans, 2005) 4.

30. Henri Nouwen, *Jesus: A Gospel* (Maryknoll NY: Orbis Books, 2001) 39.

31. Borg, *Meeting Jesus Again*, 31.

32. Henri Nouwen, *The Road to Daybreak: A Spiritual Journey* (New York: Doubleday, 1988) 222.

33. F. F. Bruce, *The Hard Sayings of Jesus* (Downers Grove IL: InterVarsity Press, 1983).

34. C. S. Lewis, *Miracles: A Preliminary Study* (1947; repr., San Francisco: HarperSanFransciso, 2001).

35. For more on the account of Jesus in the temple at age twelve, see my book *ChristHeart* (pp. 3–10). You can also find more on Jesus' baptism (11–18) and temptation (19–26).

36. To enter into this story through imaginative prayer, see my books, *Becoming Fire* (pp. 17–24) and *ChristHeart* (45–52).

37. Many of these stories are included in my books, *Becoming Fire* and *ChristHeart*. To go deeper into these stories, refer to the table of contents in each book.

38. Samuel Becket, *The Unnamable*, trans. Becket (New York: Grove Press, 1958).

39. To go deeper into this story, see my earlier books: pp. 129–36 in *ChristHeart* and pp. 25–32 in *Becoming Fire*.

40. Thomas Merton, *Thoughts in Solitude* (1958; repr., Boston: Random House, 1993) 29–30.

41. John A. Sanford, *The Kingdom Within: The Inner Meaning of Jesus' Sayings* (San Francisco: Harper & Row, 1987).

42. John Dominic Crossan, *The Greatest Prayer: Rediscovering the Revolutionary Message of the Lord's Prayer* (New York: HarperOne, 2010).

43. Ibid., 4–5.

44. Ibid., 2.

45. Ibid., 8.

46. Ibid., 40.

47. Andrew Murray, *Abide in Christ* (1895; repr., Nashville: Lifeway Press, 2007).

48. McKnight, *The Jesus Creed.*

49. Sanford, *The Kingdom Within,* 11.

50. Ibid.

51. Ibid.

52. One of the best books in my library for accessing the inner kingdom is *Inner Work: Using Dreams and Active Imagination for Personal Growth* by Robert Johnson (San Francisco: Harper & Row, 1986). A classic book that informed the beginning of my journey in understanding the inner landscape is *Our Many Selves* by Elizabeth O'Connor (New York: Harper & Row, 1971).

53. Jeanie Miley, *Dance Lessons: Moving to the Beat of God's Heart* (Macon GA: Smyth & Helwys Publishing) 2012.

26020625R00181

Made in the USA
Charleston, SC
20 January 2014